THERAPEUTIC CONSULTATIONS
IN CHILD PSYCHIATRY

RUTH AT THE MOMENT OF BECOMING A DEPRIVED CHILD

THERAPEUTIC CONSULTATIONS
IN
CHILD
PSYCHIATRY

D. W. Winnicott

BasicBooks
A Division of HarperCollins*Publishers*

Library of Congress Cataloging-in-Publication Data
Winnicott, D. W. (Donald Woods), 1896–1971.
    Therapeutic consultations in child psychiatry/D.W.
Winnicott.
        p.   cm.
    Reprint. Originally published: New York: Basic Books,
© 1971.
    Includes bibliographical references.
    Includes index.
    ISBN 0–465–08511–3
    1. Child psychiatry—Case studies.   2. Child analysis—
Case studies.   I. Title.
    [DNLM:1. Child Psychiatry.   2. Psychoanalysis—in
infancy & childhood.   3. Psychoanalytic Therapy—in
infancy & childhood.
WS350 W776t 1971a]
RJ499.W49   1990
618.92'89—dc20
DNLM/DLC
for Library of Congress   90–899
                                                            CIP

Contents

PART ONE

Introduction   *page*   1

1 'Iiro' *aet* 9 years 9 months   12

2 'Robin' *aet* 5 years   28

3 'Eliza' *aet* 7½ years   42

4 'Bob' *aet* 6 years   64

5 'Robert' *aet* 9 years   89

6 'Rosemary' *aet* 10 years   105

7 'Alfred' *aet* 10 years   110

PART TWO

Introduction   127

8 'Charles' *aet* 9 years   129

9 'Ashton' *aet* 12 years   147

10 'Albert' *aet* 7 years 9 months   161

11 'Hesta' *aet* 16 years   176

12 'Milton' *aet* 8 years   194

PART THREE

Introduction   216

13 'Ada' *aet* 8 years   220

14 'Cecil' *aet* 21 months at first consultation   240

15 'Mark' *aet* 12 years   270

16 'Peter' *aet* 13 years   296

17 'Ruth' *aet* 8 years   315

18 'Mrs X' *aet* 30 years   332

19 'Lily' *aet* 5 years   342

20 'Jason' *aet* 8 years 9 months   344

21 'George' *aet* 13 years   380

Bibliographical Note, by M. Masud R. Khan   397

Index   399

Acknowledgments

I wish to express my thanks to Mrs. Joyce Coles for a great deal of work carefully done in the preparation of this book, including the Index, for which she is largely responsible.

Masud Khan has given generously of his time, advice and constructive criticism, so that I feel that but for him this book would not have appeared.

The publishers have been most co-operative in the matter of reproduction of drawings which, as they were not drawn for show, have often given rise to severe difficulties in regard to presentation. The trouble here is that I myself prefer the original state of children's drawings to the better pictures that can be obtained by skilful touching up.

Some of the cases in this book have been presented before as lectures or as published papers, and I am most grateful for permission to include them. Details of previous publication are as follows:

Case III: *Voices* (Spring 1968), a journal published by the American Academy of Psychotherapists; also *Handbook of the Psychotherapy of Children,* edited by Dr. G. Bierman (Ernst Reinhardt, Munich, 1969). Case IV: *International Journal of Psycho-Analysis,* Volume 46. Case VI: *St Mary's Hospital Gazette,* Jan./Feb. 1962, under the title 'A Child Psychiatry Interview'. Case VII: *A Crianca Portuguesa,* Ano. XXI, 1962–63 (Lisbon). Case IX: *Foundations of Child Psychiatry,* edited by Emanuel Miller (Pergamon Press, 1968). Case XII: *The World Biennial of Psychiatry and Psychotherapy* (Basic Books, 1970). Case XIII: *Crime, Law and Corrections,* edited by Ralph Slovenko (Charles C. Thomas, 1966), under the title 'A Psychoanalytic View of the Antisocial Tendency'. Case XIV: *British Journal of Medical Psychology* (1963), Volume 36, Number 1, under the title 'Regression as Therapy'. Case XV: *Modern Perspectives in Child Psychiatry,* edited by John G. Howells (Oliver & Boyd, 1965). Case XVII: published in shortened version as 'Becoming Deprived as a Fact: A Psychotherapeutic Consultation', *Journal of Child Psychotherapy* (December 1966), Volume I, Number 4; also delivered as a lecture, 'Principles of Direct Therapy in Child Psychiatry', at the invitation of the Judge Baker Guidance Center, April 1967, the Fiftieth Anniversary of their Founding.

Part One

INTRODUCTION

THIS book concerns the application of psycho-analysis to child
psychiatry. To my surprise I find that my experience over three
or four decades of the analysis of children and adults has led me
to a specific area in which psycho-analysis can be applied in the
practice of child psychiatry, thus making sense of psycho-analysis
in economic terms. It is obviously not useful or practicable to
prescribe a psycho-analytic treatment of every child, and the
psycho-analyst often has found himself or herself in difficulties
when attempting to put what has been learned to good use in
child psychiatry practice. I have found that by full exploitation of
the first interview I am able to meet the challenge of a proportion of child psychiatry cases and I wish to give examples for the
guidance of those who are doing similar work and for students
who wish to make a study in this field.

The technique for this work can hardly be called a technique.
No two cases are alike, and there is a much more free interchange
between the therapist and the patient than there is in a straight
psycho-analytic treatment. This is not to decry the importance of
the long analysis in which the work is done on the day-by-day
emergence into the clinical material of unconscious elements in
the transference, elements in process of becoming conscious because of the continuity of the work. Psycho-analysis remains for
me the basis of this work, and if I were asked by a student I would
always say that the training for this work (which is not psycho-
analysis) is the training in psycho-analysis. I do believe, however,
that selection is the most important part of the psycho-analytic
training. It is not easy to turn a badly selected candidate into a
good analyst, and no doubt the main part of the selection is
always self-selection. The student's own analysis extends this
matter of self-selection. One would rather have a really suitable
person for doing this sort of work than an ill person made less ill
by the analysis that is part of the psycho-analytic training. Of

1

course it can be said that if one has been ill oneself one has greater sympathy with ill people, and that to be convinced of the value of reaching to the unconscious is to have experienced it. But somehow, it would always have been better if we had not been ill and in need of treatment.

If only we knew how to select properly we should know how to choose those who are suitable for doing the work that I describe in this book even when psycho-analytic training is not available. For instance, one can say at once that there must be evident a capacity to identify with the patient without loss of personal identity; there must be a capacity in the therapist to contain the conflicts of the patient, that is to say, to contain them and to wait for their resolution in the patient instead of anxiously looking around for a cure; there must be an absence of the tendency to retaliate under provocation. Also, any system of thought which provides an easy solution is of itself a contra-indication since the patient does not want anything but the resolution of internal conflicts, along with the manipulation of external obstructions of a practical nature which may be operative in the causation or the maintenance of the patient's illness. Needless to say the therapist must have professional reliability as something that happens easily; it is possible for a serious person to maintain a professional standard even when undergoing very severe personal strains in the private life and in the personal growth process which, we hope, never stops.

An extended list of desirable qualities of this kind would leave a big proportion of people who could come forward with an urge to do professional work either in psychiatry or in social work, and for me these things are even more important than the very important training in psycho-analysis. An experience of long deep-going personal analytic treatment is as near as possible essential.

If I am right, then the type of work that I am describing in this book has an importance that psycho-analysis does not have in meeting *social need and pressure* on clinics.

It must be emphasised at the start that this technique is extremely flexible; it would not be possible for anyone to know what to do by studying one case. Twenty cases might give a good idea, but the fact remains that no two cases are alike. A further difficulty in contributing to the understanding of this work is that there is no way of teaching by talking about the cases. It is necessary to demand of the students a careful and detailed reading and study and enjoyment of total cases.

Naturally the basis of this part of the demand that I am making on the student is the accuracy and honesty of the reporting and it is well known that it is difficult to report accurately. Neither tape-recording nor the video tape can provide the solution to this problem. When I wish to report a case I take notes of everything that happens throughout the interview, including the things I myself do and say, and although this imposes a severe task on myself this is counterbalanced by the reward that comes from the reconstruction of almost a whole interview from the notes taken, often illegible after two or three days. I have enjoyed making this effort to write a full account of case-work because, as is well known, a great deal of an interview, and especially its rich detail, gets lost 'as a dream dies at the opening day'.

A certain amount of over-simplification must appear in these cases that I am presenting here because of the fact that in nearly all of them I have employed an exchange of drawings. My technique in these reported cases usually takes the form of what could be called the Squiggle Game. There is nothing original of course about the squiggle game and it would not be right for somebody to learn how to use the squiggle game and then to feel equipped to do what I call a therapeutic consultation. The squiggle game is simply one way of getting into contact with a child. What happens in the game and in the whole interview depends on the use made of the child's experience, including the material that presents itself. In order to use the mutual experience one must have in one's bones a theory of the emotional development of the child and of the relationship of the child to the environmental factors. In my cases described here an artificial link is made between the squiggle game and the psychotherapeutic consultation, and this arises out of the fact that from the drawings of the child and of the child and myself one can find one way of making the case come alive. It is almost as if the child, through the drawings, is alongside me, and to some extent taking part in describing the case, so that the reports of what the child and the therapist said tend to ring true. There is also a practical significance of the squiggle or drawing material in that there can be a gain from taking the parents into one's confidence and letting them know what their child was like in the special circumstances of the thera-peutic consultation. This is more real for them than if I report

3

what the child said. They recognise the types of drawing that adorn the nursery wall or that the child brings home from school, but often they are amazed when they see the drawings in sequence, drawings which display personality qualities and perceptive abilities which may not have been evident in the home setting. In several of the cases given here this aspect of the matter will come up for discussion, and naturally it is not always good to give parents this insight (that can be so useful). Parents might perhaps abuse the confidence that the therapist has placed in them, and so undo the work that depends on a kind of intimacy between child and therapist.

My conception of the special place of the therapeutic consultation and the exploitation of the first interview (or reduplicated first interviews) arose gradually in the course of time in my clinic and private practice. There was a point, however, which could be said to have been of special significance, in the mid-twenties when I was a practising paediatrician, seeing many patients in my hospital practice and giving the opportunity for as many of the children as possible to communicate with me and to draw pictures and to tell me their dreams. I was struck by the frequency with which *the children had dreamed of me the night before attending*. This dream of the doctor that they were going to see obviously reflected their own imaginative equipment in regard to doctors and dentists and other people who are supposed to be helpful. They also reflected to a varying degree the attitude of the parents and the preparation for the visit that had been made. Nevertheless here I was, as I discovered to my amusement, *fitting in with a preconceived notion*. The children who had dreamed in this way were able to tell me that it was of me that they had dreamed. In language which I use now but which I had no equipment for using at that time I found myself in the rôle of subjective object. What I now feel is that in this rôle of subjective object, which rarely outlasts the first or first few interviews, the doctor has a great opportunity for being in touch with the child.

There must be a relationship between this state of affairs and that which obtains in a much less useful way in hypnosis. I have used this in the theory that I have built up in the course of time in explanation of the very great confidence which children can often show in myself (as in others doing similar work) on these special occasions, special occasions that have a quality that has made me use the word sacred. Either this sacred moment is used or it is wasted. If it is wasted the child's belief in being understood is shattered. If on the other hand it is used, then the child's belief in being helped is strengthened. There will be those cases in which deep work is done in the special circumstances of the first interview (or interviews) and the resulting changes in the child can be made use of by parents and those who are responsible in the immediate social setting, so that whereas a child was caught up in a knot in regard to the emotional development, the interview has resulted in a loosening of the knot and a forward movement in the developmental process.

In a proportion of cases, however, the work done in this kind of an interview is simply a prelude to a longer or more intensive psychotherapy, but it can easily happen that a child is only ready for this *after* experiencing the understanding which belongs to this kind of interview. The child may of course feel to have been more understood than in fact he or she was understood, but the effect will have been to have given to the child some hope of being understood and perhaps even helped.

One of the difficulties arising out of this kind of interview is that, when it is successful in terms of understanding, the child may easily expect to go straight on from there into an intensive therapy, with the kind of dependence on the psychiatrist or social worker which makes frequent sessions over a period of time essential. This is not what usually happens.

There is a category of case in which this kind of psychotherapeutic interview is to be avoided. I would not say that with very ill children it is not possible to do useful work. What I would say is that if the child goes away from the therapeutic consultation *and returns to an abnormal family or social situation* then there is no environmental provision of the kind that is needed and that I take for granted. I rely on an 'average expectable environment' to meet and to make use of the changes that have taken place in the boy or girl in the interview, changes which indicate a loosening of the knot in the developmental process.

In fact, the main difficulty in assessing cases for this kind of work is a difficulty of assessing the child's immediate environment. Where there is a powerful continuing adverse external factor or an absence of consistent personal care, then one would avoid this kind of procedure and would feel inclined either to explore what could be done by 'management', or else to institute a therapy which would give the child the opportunity for a

5

personal relationship of the kind that is generally known as transference.

If the reader should *enjoy* reading the details of a series of these cases it is likely that there will emerge in the reader a feeling that I as the psychiatrist am the constant factor and that nothing else can be predicted. I myself come out in these case descriptions as a human being not exactly like any other human being, so that in no case would the same result have been attained if any other psychiatrist had been in my place. The only companion that I have in exploring the unknown territory of the new case is the theory that I carry around with me and that has become part of me and that I do not even have to think about in a deliberate way. This is the theory of the emotional development of the individual which includes for me the total history of the individual child's relationship to the child's specific environment. It cannot be avoided that changes in this theoretical basis for my work do occur in the course of time and on account of experience. One could compare my position with that of a 'cellist who first slogs away at *technique* and then actually becomes able to play *music*, taking the technique for granted. I am aware of doing this work more easily and with more success than I was able to do it thirty years ago and my wish is to communicate with those who are still slogging away at technique, at the same time giving them the hope that will one day come from playing music. There is but little satisfaction to be gained from giving a virtuoso performance from a written score.

The test of these case descriptions will hang on the word enjoyment. If they are a labour to read then I have been too clever; I have been engaged in displaying a technique and not in playing music. I am of course aware that this actually does take place from time to time in the case descriptions.

The Cases Selected

As can be imagined, the difficulty is to know where to start. I choose to start with the case of Iiro, a Finnish boy who could not speak English, and I could not speak Finnish. We had an interpreter, Miss Helka Asikainen, who cleverly caught the ball and threw it to the other as we used the few words in the game; in this case the drawings had special importance because of the language barrier. But I choose this case not because of the language difficulty, which both he and I soon forgot all about; I choose it because there was no need for me to have seen this boy. It was simply that I was visiting the hospital and the staff wished me to talk about a case that they all knew. Iiro was in the orthopaedic ward and I gave him an interview in order to be able to describe a method of communicating with a child. It will be seen that the case incidentally illustrates the axiom that if opportunity is given in the proper and professional way for a child or for an adult, then in the limited setting of the professional contact the client will bring and display (though at first in a tentative way) the current problem or the emotional conflict or the pattern of strain which obtains at this moment of the client's life. I think that this is true if one simply listens to the story of the person sitting next to one on a bus journey; if there is any kind of privacy the story will begin to evolve. It may be just a long tale of rheumatism or of injustice at the office, but already the material is there for a therapeutic consultation. The reason why it leads nowhere is simply that you yourself at the time are not giving yourself deliberately and in a professional way to the task of using the material presented, and for this reason the material offered in the bus becomes diffuse and boring. In the therapeutic consultation the material becomes specific and acutely interesting since the client soon begins to feel that understanding may perhaps be available and that communication at a deep level may become possible. Obviously it would be irresponsible to turn neighbours on a bus journey into clients who would inevitably become dependent, needing further opportunities or else suffering a sense of loss at the bus stop. But with children brought in child psychiatry the professional situation is exploited, and work is done, as these case-histories show; and also there are ways and means of keeping in touch, and here again emphasis is put on the need that I feel for *sensitive* parent figures who can be informed and who can help make judgements in regard to further procedure.

In some of the cases reported there are dramatic changes following one or two therapeutic consultations. These have to be taken not only as evidence of the work done but also as evidence of the parents' attitude. Undoubtedly the best cases for this kind of work are those in which there is already parental confidence in myself. It would seem to me that this is a state of affairs that can be expected; that is to say that in general people are willing to believe in the doctor they have chosen to consult, often after a great deal of discussion and after the overcoming of natural

7

doubts. If in fact things go well, or a child does make some changes, this immediately puts the consultant in the position of someone that the parents believe in, and a benign circle is set up which operates favourably in terms of the child's symptomatology. In assessing results it is necessary, however, to make allowance for the fact that parents would naturally rather believe in the consultant than find that their effort has been wasted. They are therefore, some of them, liable to report favourably if they possibly can do so. The parents' report, which is the report which has to be used in many cases, is highly suspect as an objective account and in the assessment of results, and this must be always remembered. I am not so naïve as to take what the parents tell me as a final assessment. I wish to emphasise, however, that my aim in presenting these consultations is not to give a series illustrating symptomatic cure. I am rather aiming to report examples of *communication with children*. There seems to me to be a need to report work done with children. This need arises partly out of the fact that there is a tendency at the present time for workers to concentrate on group situations and, although there is much value to be gained from group work the value of work with the actual patient as an individual can only too easily get lost by group workers. In a group situation, surely, the aim is to detect which member of the group is at the moment in trouble, and it certainly may not be the member who is presenting the symptoms which bring the case to the notice of the psychiatrist or the social worker who is the ill member of the family or social group.

In some of the cases presented in this series it will be seen that the child's symptomatology reflects illness in one or both of the parents or in the social situation, and that it is this which needs attention. Nevertheless it may be the child who best puts us in touch with the principal defect in the environment. The series as a whole does, however, according to my claim, show that in many cases the child who is brought by parents who are concerned about their child's condition is in fact the ill member of the group, and it is the child then who needs primary attention. Every child or grown-up has a problem, and it is this problem as it is causing tensions at the moment that will appear in the consultation material. When several problems appear at once in a first interview then this is evidence of a need for work of a more prolonged kind so that the various problems may be sorted out and be dealt with separately, and perhaps in various ways.

It is almost necessary to warn the reader against being excited when there is a symptomatic result because this is not the main object which I have in mind when I am presenting these cases. In some of the cases there will be no clear-cut result and in other cases there may even be a bad result. Certainly it would not be considered a failure of the method if the work led on to some other form of management or treatment; indeed alternative methods must always be held in readiness.

Perhaps my main hope is that this work described in considerable detail may prove to be good teaching material. It happens that in many of these cases the whole of what happened can be described, something which is never true of an analysis or even of a once-a-week therapy. The student therefore is in a position to argue about anything that appears in the material because the student knows as much as the teacher does about the material that is there for examination and discussion. It would be from my point of view a satisfactory outcome if the material could be used for criticism and I would much prefer this to the alternative whereby what I have described here might simply be imitated. As I have already stated, the work cannot be copied because the therapist is involved in every case as a person, and therefore no two interviews could be alike as they would be carried through by two psychiatrists.

I wish to draw attention to one other thing about these psychotherapeutic interviews. It will be noted that interpretation of the unconscious is not the main feature. Often an important interpretation is made which alters the whole course of the interview, and there is nothing more difficult than to account for the way one finds oneself making no interpretation over a long period of time, or throughout the whole interview, and then at some point using the material for an interpretation of the unconscious. It would seem almost as if one has to tolerate the existence of two contrary trends in oneself. For me, there is some easing of the problem here in that when I make an interpretation, if the child disagrees or seems to fail to respond, I am immediately willing to withdraw what I have said. Often in these accounts I have made an interpretation and I have been wrong and the child has been able to correct me. Sometimes of course there is a resistance which implies that I have made the right interpretation and that the right interpretation is denied. But an interpretation that does not work always means that I have made the interpretation at the

9

wrong moment or in the wrong way, and I withdraw it unconditionally. Although the interpretation may be correct I have been wrong in verbalising this material in this way at this particular moment. Dogmatic interpretation leaves the child with only two alternatives, an *acceptance* of what I have said as propaganda or a *rejection* of the interpretation and of me and of the whole set-up. I think and hope that children in this relationship with me feel that they have the right to reject what I say or the way I take something. Actually I do claim that it is a fact that these interviews are dominated by the child and not by me. The work is easy to do for one, two, or perhaps three sessions; but, as the reader will be only too well aware, if the interviews become oft-repeated all the problems of the transference and of resistance begin to appear and the treatment must now be dealt with along ordinary psychoanalytic lines. One thing that will be noticeable to the reader is that I never (I hope) make interpretations for my own benefit. I have no need to prove to myself some part of the theory that I use by hearing myself verbalise the material of this case. I have done all the interpreting that I want to do for my own benefit. I have nothing whatever to gain from converting someone to a point of view. Long psycho-analytic treatments have had an effect on me and I have found that interpretations that seemed right ten years ago and that the patient accepted because of awe turned out in the end to be collusive defences. A very crude example could be given. One might have a slight propagandist tendency to think of all snakes as penis symbols, and of course they can be. Nevertheless if one has to get to early material and the roots of what a penis can mean to a child one has to see that the child's drawing of a snake can be a drawing of the self, the self not yet using arms and fingers and legs and toes. One can see how many times patients have failed to convey a sense of self because a therapist has interpreted a snake as a penis symbol. Far from being a part-object, a snake in a dream or phobia can be a *first whole object*. This example gives a clue which a student can use in reading these case-histories and no doubt there will be many examples in my attempt to give honest reports in which I have made just exactly this kind of mistake. I give this as an indication of the way in which the material of these cases may be used in the student–teacher situation.

The backbone of all the work described here is the theory that has grown up with me of the emotional development of the individual. This is inherently complex and it would not be appropriate for me to attempt to restate what I understand of the theory which I use in all the work that I do. There is a vast literature on this subject and the student who wishes to follow the development of my own thought may find what is needed in the other books that I have written and which I have listed for this purpose.

Finally, I hope it will be recognised that in presenting these cases I am not trying to prove anything. The criticism that I have failed to prove my case would not be appropriate as I have no case. I would add that it would always be better if the student could gather the material for himself or herself from personal contact with children instead of from reading my descriptions, but this is not always possible, especially for a student. At the lowest assessment this kind of attempt at honest reporting may have lessons for the student, whether social worker, teacher or psychiatrist, who tries to grow on the experiences offered by work done in the field of dynamic psychology.

CASE I 'Iiro' *aet* 9 years 9 months

During a visit to Lastenlinna[1] (Children's Castle)–the Children's Hospital at Kuopio in Finland–I was invited to describe a case to a gathering of the staff. This heterogeneous group included the doctors, the matron, several of the nurses, the psychologist, the social worker, and some visitors; and it seemed to be better on this occasion that I should describe to them a case that they already knew, rather than give a case of my own. For this reason a child was chosen from the orthopaedic ward and I interviewed him without there being any urgent presenting problem that would ordinarily involve a child psychiatrist.

I learned that there had been certain symptoms of a vague kind, including messing and headaches and abdominal pains, but the boy was in hospital on account of syndactyly, a congenital condition for which he had had almost continuous attention from infancy. He was well known in the orthopaedic department and was generally liked. The outcome of this interview could not in any way be predicted. Iiro could speak only Finnish, a language of which I had no knowledge. We used Miss Helka Asikainen as interpreter, she having some knowledge of the case and having been involved as a social worker with the mother. Miss Asikainen proved to be an excellent interpreter in that she became quickly forgotten by both Iiro and myself, and it could be said that she did not influence the course of events. Indeed, there was not much talking, and therefore the part she played was minimal. Iiro and I and the interpreter sat down to a small table where there were two pencils and some paper already laid out, and quickly we were involved in the squiggle game which I briefly explained.

> I said: 'I shut my eyes and go like this on the paper and you turn it into something, and then it is your turn and you do the same thing and I turn it into something.'

> (1) I made a squiggle which turned out to be of the closed variety. He quickly said: 'It's a duck's foot.'

[1] Under the auspices of World Health Organisation.

This came as a complete surprise to me and it was clear immediately that he wished to communicate with me on the subject of his disability. I made no observation but, wishing to test the situation, I did

    (2) a drawing with the webbed foot of a duck delineated.

I wanted to make sure that we were talking about the same thing.

He now chose to draw and he produced
(3) his own version of the webbed foot of a duck.

I knew now that we were firmly entrenched on the subject of webbed feet and that I could lean back and wait for this to turn into a communication about his disability.

(4) Next I did an open squiggle which he immediately turned into a duck swimming in the lake.

I now felt that Iiro had communicated to me a positive feeling about ducks and about swimming and about lakes. Incidentally, Finland is composed of lakes and islands and all children in Finland are involved in swimming and boating and fishing.

(5) He now did this squiggle and he turned it into a horn.

We had gone off the subject of ducks and began to talk about music and the way his brother plays the cornet. He said: 'I can play the piano a little'—but such was his disability that I could only assume that he was referring to the idea of picking out a tune with a deformed finger. He said he was fond of music and would like to play the flute.

Here I made my first reference to the material. Using the fact that I could see that Iiro was a healthy and happy boy and that he had a sense of humour I said that it would be difficult for a duck to play the flute, and he was amused.

It will be observed that I did not go on to explain to him that he was representing his own disability in terms of ducks. This would have been clumsy because it was extremely unlikely that he knew what he was doing or that he had any conscious intention of using a duck to represent his own disability. I think in

15

fact that he was not able to acknowledge and to cope with the idea of his syndactyly.

(6) I made a squiggle and he quickly turned it into a dog.

He was pleased with this and it can be seen that some strength from my squiggle came into his drawing of the dog. This could be used as an illustration of ego support. It can be seen that ego support while necessary could also be too much alive and active.

(7) He made a squiggle which I turned into a question mark. This was evidently not what he had in mind as he said: 'It could have been a hair.'

It will be agreed that it was part of a natural process that I should not know that he had in mind a hair. He would be disturbed if he thought that I had magical knowledge of his intention.

(8) His squiggle which I made into a rather awkward-looking swan.

I suppose I was vaguely continuing the duck theme, although at the time I was engaged in playing the game that we were both enjoying, and I do not remember thinking this out.

> We were now free to talk a little about things and I said: 'Can you swim?' The way he said 'Yes' showed that he takes pleasure in swimming.

(9) My squiggle which he said was a shoe. He said it did not need anything doing to it.

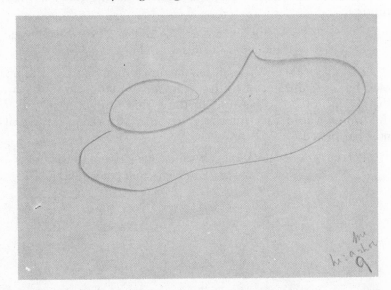

(10) I made a squiggle which I can see now was rather deliberately shaped so that he could have made it into a
hand.

I cannot say whether this was right or wrong but I felt like
doing it.

Iiro turned it into a flower by adding a line. What he said
was: 'If I join this and this with a line it is a flower.'

As I look at this now I can see his unwillingness to look at his
own hands. I did not of course make any remark and I am glad
that I did not do so because anything that I might have said at
this point would have interfered with the surprising thing that
now happened.

(11) He now did a squiggle which was more of the nature of a
deliberate drawing, although done very quickly. There

could be an influence here from the shape that I gave my squiggle (No. 10). The squiggle looked like a drawing of a deformed hand. This was an important moment because when I asked him what he was thinking of he said: 'It just happened.' And *he had surprised himself*.

It could be said that he was now near to looking at his own hand and that this was a reaction to the denial that shows in No. 10 where he made what could have been a hand into a flower. I allowed things to rest a little at this stage, being confident that we were communicating significantly.

I asked him about dreams and he said: 'I sleep with my eyes closed so I don't see anything.' After a while he said: 'My dreams are mostly nice. I have not had a nasty dream for a long time.' I felt that we had finished with the dream theme and I waited.

19

(12) He now did this, and I said to him: 'It is like your left hand, isn't it!'

In fact the angle was almost exactly the same as the angle between two prominent fingers of his left hand which of course were on the table three or four inches away from the drawing, holding down the paper.

He said: 'Oh yes, a bit.'

So now he had become objective about his hands and I am not sure that he had ever talked objectively about his condition before with anyone. He told me he had had a lot of operations and would have a lot more. He said that his feet were the same, and I saw now that the shoe that he saw in my squiggle had relevance (No. 9).

He said: 'I have only four toes; I used to have six.'

I now said: 'It is rather like the duck, isn't it!'

I began to feel round now for anything that he might want to say about orthopaedic surgeons. Actually, although I did not know it at the time, the surgeon had made the observation that he felt that Iiro was 'almost too compliant'.

At this point an idea was beginning to formulate itself in my mind and I may have started to talk about it by saying:

20

'The surgeons are trying to alter what you were like when you were born.'

He said he would like to be able to play the flute and he told me about future operations.

For me, with his hands on the table in front of me, I was only too aware of the absolute impossibility of his ever being able to play the flute.

While nothing much was going on I asked him: 'What would you like to be when you grow up?'

And he started, as children often do, by saying: 'I don't know,' and then he said: 'I will be like daddy, a building contractor.' Another idea he referred to was to be like the man who teaches handicrafts at school.

I could see that we were continuing with this difficult idea that he would like to be able to do the very things that his condition would make difficult or impossible.

I asked him whether it ever made him cross to be operated on and he quickly replied: 'I am never cross.' He added: 'It is my own choice; I choose to be operated on; it is better for work to have two fingers than it was when I had four all joined together.'

I felt that he had now not only looked at his hands but had looked at the handicap, and had made a significant verbalisation of his problem. I think it was this that (without conscious intention) he was reaching out for in the professional contact which I was providing for him.

(13) We now returned to the squiggle game and he turned mine into a hilt of a sword. He followed with

(14) a drawing that he wanted to do, and he called it an eel. I can see on looking back that this could have been the sword belonging to the hilt. It was eel season in Finland at the time, and I played about with his idea that he had drawn an eel. I said: 'Shall we put it back in the lake or cook it and eat it?' And he quickly said: 'We will let it go back and swim in the lake because it is so small.'

He had now identified himself with the eel and I felt confident that he was referring to his own primitive state, a kind of fantasy of pre-birth, and this joined up with the idea that I had already formulated in my mind.

I said to him therefore: 'If we think of you as small, you would like to swim in the lake or swim on the lake like the duck. You are telling me that you are fond of yourself with your webbed hands and feet and that you need people to love you that way as you were when you were born. Growing up, you begin to want to play the piano and the flute and to do handicrafts, and so you agree to be operated on, but the first thing is to be loved as you are and as you were born.'

He seems to have responded to this remark of mine by

saying: 'Mother has the same thing that I have got'—a fact which I had not known. In other words, in dealing with this condition in himself he had to deal with it also in terms of his mother.

(15) Here I made a complex squiggle. He quickly saw in it lights and lampshades. In his home his mother had just bought a big lampshade just like that. His mother was therefore still in his mind. I made various alternative suggestions about this squiggle as a test, but he rejected all of them.

(16) He now took a piece of paper and deliberately drew. This was a very accurate copy of the deformity of his left hand which was holding down the page. He was surprised and exclaimed: 'It's the same again!'

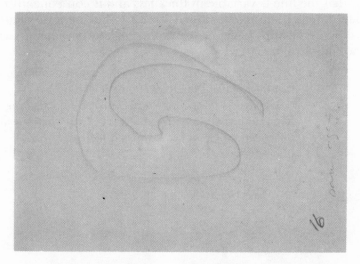

Somewhere about here, by way of relief from the tenseness of the central theme, we talked about his family and his home. He said positive things about his home and about the place of his father in it and gave me very much the idea of his home as a going concern with the possibility of new babies arriving.

> At some point I asked if he was a happy sort of chap and he answered by generalising: 'One knows if one is sad.'
>
> We returned to the squiggle game.

(17) Here was his squiggle and I made it into feet and shoes.

It will be noted that in making this squiggle he had adopted my technique of holding the pencil near the horizontal position so that the line is variable in thickness and is consequently more interesting. I suppose I turned it into a shoe because of an unwillingness on my part to risk introducing any new theme so near the end of an interview.

> (18) We now came to the last squiggle, which was mine. I deliberately made it complex, doing it with my eyes shut, and I challenged him, saying: 'I bet you can't do anything with that.' He turned it round and quickly saw what he wanted, putting in an eye and the webbed feet, and again he said: 'It's a duck.'

We had come at the end therefore to a restatement of his love of himself, which indicates that he has felt loved. The need is emphasised, however, for him to be loved in the state in which he was born, that is to say, before orthopaedic surgery and the whole process of altering and mending had started.

(19) Finally, at my request, he wrote his name and age (not reproduced here) on the back of No. 18.

Interview with the Mother

Unexpectedly I found myself in the position of being needed by the mother. She was in the hospital and she knew that her son was being interviewed, and now she wanted to see me. I had no knowledge of why this should be, but I felt that she had a right to know what kind of a man this visitor from England might be who had spent an hour with her son. Once again the interview had to be conducted through the interpreter Miss Asikainen, who had in fact already seen the mother on several occasions as social worker. (In fact Miss Asikainen is a psychologist, but there is a shortage of staff in the hospital and the rôles of the various workers are not clearly delineated.) Once again it can be said that the translation quickly became forgotten by both of us. I personally do not remember the translating, and I feel that I had a direct confrontation with the mother.

There is no need here for a description of the session with the mother, which lasted nearly an hour. For most of the time the

25

mother was simply going over the ground that she had already gone over with the social worker. Suddenly something happened which was quite unexpected and which threw light on the whole case and confirmed the idea that I had formulated in my mind during my interview with Iiro. The mother burst into tears and was obviously very moved. She then unburdened herself of something which she said she had not told the social worker, something which she had probably never really dealt with in the conscious and verbalising part of the mind.

In short, what she said was this: 'I know that everyone has guilt feelings about sex. For me it has been different. All my life I have felt free sexually and in marriage sexual experience has been a fulfilment. Instead of feeling guilty about sex what I have always felt is that my condition of fingers and toes will be handed down to one of my children. In this way I would be punished. Since marriage, with each pregnancy I have become increasingly anxious about the baby that was to be born, anxious in terms of the inherited disability. I knew I must not have babies because of this disability. Each time when the baby is born and the baby is normal I feel immense relief. With Iiro, however, I had no relief because there he was with fingers and toes like mine and I had been punished. When I saw him I hated him. I completely repudiated him, and for a length of time (perhaps only twenty minutes or perhaps longer) I knew that I could never see him again. He had to be taken away from me. Then it came over me that I might get his fingers and toes mended by persistently using the orthopaedic surgeon. I immediately decided to persist in getting Iiro's fingers and toes mended although this seemed impossible, and from that moment I found my love of him returning and I think I have loved him more than the others. From his point of view, therefore, it could be said that he gained something. Nevertheless I have been obsessed with this drive to use the orthopaedic surgeon.'

She seemed to be altered by having verbalised this which must have been near consciousness often in her mind, but which she had never before had the chance or the courage to talk about. It occurred to me immediately that she was telling me exactly the same thing that Iiro had been telling me in the way he used the therapeutic consultation. He may have gained something from this mother's special love of him, but he had to pay for it by being caught up in an obsessive drive which indeed the orthopaedic surgeon had noticed, and the staff of the hospital had wondered why it was that this mother and this child were so persistent while so many parents and children have to be persuaded to do what ought to be done surgically.

It could be said that there was some result to the work that I did in interviewing the child and the mother. Incidentally, it gave me clear material for description to the staff group that were waiting for me about a child that they already knew. More important, it was reported to me afterwards that following this work a more realistic attitude had been adopted towards the mending of Iiro's hands and feet. The limitations had become more easily accepted and this provided a general easing up of tension. It is perhaps of interest also that the fact of this interview with this boy was not lost sight of by him. It is unlikely that he remembers what I am like or that he could talk about the interview and the drawings. Nevertheless he has continued to keep in touch with me by letter duly translated by Miss Asikainen and he sends me photographs of himself with his dog or himself fishing with his friend on a lake. It is five years now since this interview took place.

CASE II 'Robin' *aet* 5 years

In this case there again presented no psychiatric problem, so that my work consisted in providing a setting in which the child could present himself in terms of his immediate strivings and conflicts. There is no doubt but that although one gets paid for this work there is great pleasure to be derived from meeting in this professional way a child who is well within the meaning of the word normal.

There are other children in this family, all teenagers. In the management of this case it worked out that I saw Robin's mother first and also that I saw her after my interview with him. In the second interview I was able to let her know what had happened between me and Robin. This was a case in which I think the step forward in Robin's development would have taken place spontaneously. It was not absolutely necessary for him to get help from outside the family, as his parents were capable of dealing with the situation themselves. They, however, felt that they wanted help, and it seems likely that the interview I had with Robin facilitated the work which these parents and the whole family were already doing, with the help of the school.

The trouble was that Robin was just beginning to go to school and he was showing signs of school refusal. This was a boy with a rich family life and for him going to school certainly marked an important stage. Incidentally, being the youngest and presumably the last in the family, the problem of Robin's conflict about school was to some extent overlaid by his mother's personal conflict. Here might be the last of her children. When he should go to school she would never recapture the feeling of having a family with all the dependence that this involves. On the other hand, the mother is a woman of immense energy and with specific interests, and the end of this decade of maternal preoccupation could mean for her a release so that she could return to the special skill for which she has been trained. In this particular case these matters would have resolved themselves naturally, but the fact remains that Robin had this symptom about starting school and along with this were certain regressive claims on the mother's attention which reminded her of the experiences of Robin's infancy when he could count on her meeting his needs.

It was interesting to me to have the chance to interview this boy and to find out how he would present himself and his personal problem in the course of the interview. There was no difficulty about his coming to my room with me and leaving his mother in the waiting-room. I was not sure, however, about his being able at five years to play my game of squiggles. It will be observed that a great deal in this interview depends on me and the way I acted. Nevertheless in the end it is the boy's own display of himself and his immediate problem which wins. It was quite clear that Robin and I did communicate with each other in the forty minutes that we spent together and it is likely that if I had been more strict in my technique and not contributed from my end there would have been a premature or artificial termination of the interview with nothing accomplished.

I started then, without great confidence, making a squiggle.

(1) Of this he could make nothing.

(2) He responded with this. I made it into a spider.

 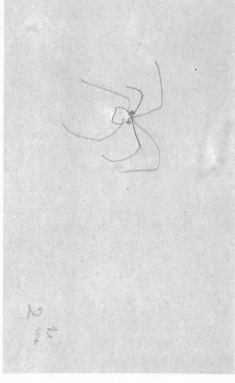

(3) Mine again. He started by putting curly hair on the top of this and I noted that he himself had tousled hair. He added eyebrows and eyes and something to do with legs and he said it was a fish.

I now felt hopeful. Here was a primitive drawing that was personal to him and which pleased him and he had started to play in a creative way. I noted that he was one of those children who do not hold the sheet of paper with the other hand when drawing. Probably I held it for him, because otherwise the drawing goes haywire and nothing is accomplished. I take this as a very small sign of dependence and it is something that may quite well disappear as a symptom during the course of an interview. After confidence has been gained the child may begin to hold his own paper with his free hand. I wait for these changes, and note them.

(4) He now made a squiggle which I made into a snake. This was not entirely my idea as I consulted him as I went along. Nevertheless the idea of the snake originated from me rather than from him.

(5) My squiggle. This I felt was a good squiggle. It could have been made into almost anything and it had some kind of value of its own as squiggles can have. He could make nothing of it. After a while he said:

'Of course it's a jar already'—so I said: 'Well, you have made it into something by giving it a name!'

This is an example of a found object, just as walking along a beach anyone may find a stone or a piece of the root of seaweed and it seems to be already a sculpture and it finds its place on the mantelpiece.

(6) His squiggle and I turned it into a face.

I realised that in doing this I was doing something that he could not do in terms of deliberate drawing, but I took the risk, and it could be said that its realism was not something that he wished to imitate.

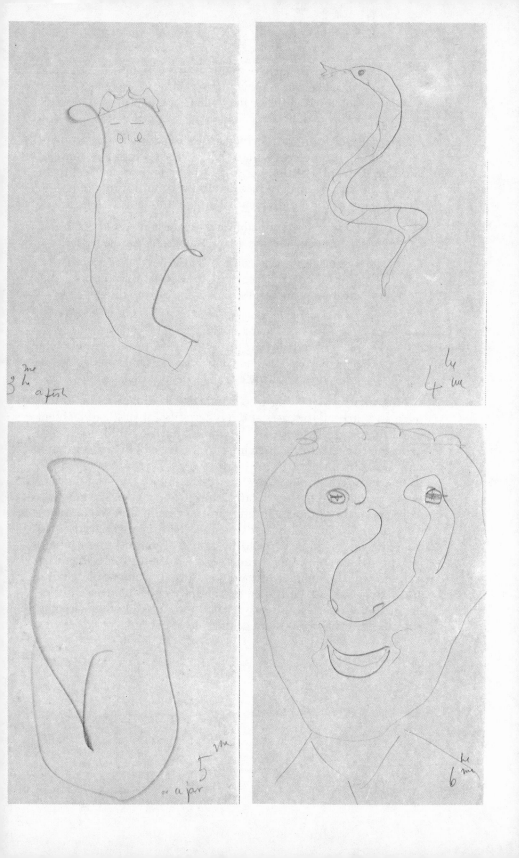

(7) My next squiggle he most surprisingly turned into a pig. This, like No. 3, was a personal drawing, a pig that no-one but he would have made that way, and the tail gave me evidence of his sense of humour.

This sense of humour is evidence of a freedom, the opposite of a rigidity of the defences that characterises illness. A sense of humour is the ally of the therapist, who gets from it a feeling of confidence and a sense of having elbow-room for manœuvring. It is evidence of the child's creative imagination and of happiness.

He was now thoroughly in the game and he said: 'Is it your go or mine? It is fun, isn't it!' It was his turn so he did

(8) a squiggle which I turned into a duck after consultation with him. Here I began to make tentative enquiries about dreams but at the same time going on with the game.

(9) I did a squiggle which he could not use. It will be observed that I have a definite intention in these interviews to get to real dream material; that is to say, to dreams dreamed and remembered. Dream contrasts with fantasying, which is unproductive, shapeless, and to some extent, manipulated.

This matter of getting into contact with dream material will recur in nearly all the cases and it is a matter for subtle judgement when the therapist feels that the material arising in the drawings or in the conversation is reaching to the level of dream, so that it may be appropriate to put the question: 'Do you ever dream?' In fact most children have a dream or some dreams that interest them, perhaps recurring dreams, and if one gives them any help in regard to the understanding of one dream they tend to produce more dreams. This is obviously something that parents cannot give, and I think it could be said that parents ought not to interpret their children's dreams. The reason for this is that, as is well known, the manifest dream contains an element of defence, and defences must be respected. If one begins to deal with the defences then one has already turned into a psychotherapist and automatically has moved out of the rôle of parent.

7 _me_
a pig.

8 _he_
_me_
a duck

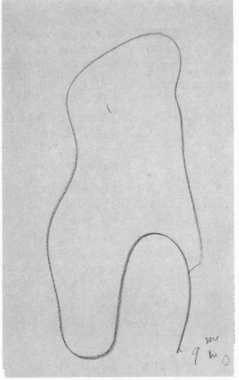

9 _me_
_he_
0

Robin volunteered that he dreams about dogs and elephants and kangaroos. In his case dreams were simply evidence of things being alive and lively, so we left the subject.

At this point I asked him if he was cross about coming to see me, as I knew that his mother had brought him up from the country, and he enjoys himself there. He emphatically denied that he was cross about this and he made a squiggle

(10) which he himself turned into a snake. We can see in this a perseveration of the idea in No. 4, which of course I have to remember was my idea. This drawing, however, was quite different from his point of view because it was all his own. He had made deliberate use of his own squiggle.

(11) I now made a squiggle which he again turned into a snake. This time he took a lot of trouble over detail and he enjoyed the way in which this particular snake had a new quality which could be described as symbolical of an erection. It was reaching upwards in a very obvious way.

(12) Next was his squiggle which I turned into a lump of earth. I could not think of anything else to turn it into. I said to him: 'Do you think it might be faeces?' (I asked him while I was working what they called faeces in his family, and he told me.)

But he said it was earth. Perhaps I had in my mind a need to portray something which was as far as possible away from the concept of erection, so that I would not be emphasising the quality which might have been a chance phenomenon in the last drawing. Naturally I did not think this out at the time.

(13) Now I did a squiggle and he made it into 'a snake curled up'. 'It is happy.' He gave this drawing a certain amount of attention and then he said quite spontaneously: 'I like that snake that is curled up.'

While this was going on he was beginning to finger his face and to play with his face with the pencil. I noted the feeling of a relationship between the idea of the curled-up snake and these infantile relics showing in his handling of his face. I also remembered that his mother had told me that when very young instead of using a transitional object he had tended to need her actual

34

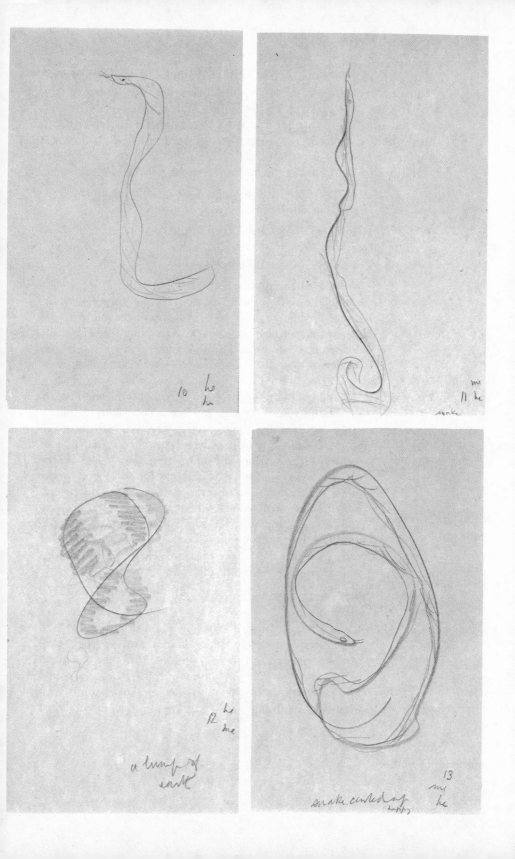

10 he
he

11 me he
snake

12 he
me
a lump of
earth

13 me
he
snake curled up
resting

face, the skin of which he would stroke until he went to sleep. I did not mention this because the mother and not he had told it to me, but I did refer to the happy snake in terms of himself curled up on his mother's lap, feeling safe and protected from the world. I felt confident that we now had reached a statement made by him of his conflict, a statement made in terms of going out into the world and growing up versus regressive dependence.

He now said: 'It's your go, isn't it'—and in this way gave the game a push forward.

(14) His squiggle which I turned into something that we called a ghost.

(15) Mine. He turned this into a goose.

We had all the drawings spread out on the floor in a line beside the table where we were playing or working together so that we could see them all at once, and we found that we had a farm—the snakes, the spider, the earth, the duck and the goose and a fish for the pond and a pig—and we began to wonder whether No. 9 was something lying around on the ground. He suggested it was a bit of wire. He added: 'And we have got a farmer'—referring to my drawing 6. I said: 'Would you like to be a farmer?' and he said: 'Well yes, but the trouble is there is a lot of work to be done on a farm.' It will be remembered that he had come from a farm to the consultation. And he could see that for a farmer the farm is not a 'found object'. In my mind was the question of making some kind of interpretation such as: 'You wonder whether to go out in the world and be a farmer and work or be where you can get back to mother's lap and curl up like the snake, and touch her when you feel like it, for pleasure. He accepted this idea without any apparent difficulty, and he drew

(16) saying: 'Well as we have got a farm we may as well call it a turnip.'

(17) I now drew this which was a series of coils. I think I did this rather deliberately without knowing why, perhaps with the idea of wire still in my mind. He took his pencil and played about over it as if stroking it. It was as if he found some kind of transitional object here, so I asked him about what he took to bed with him to keep him company when

36

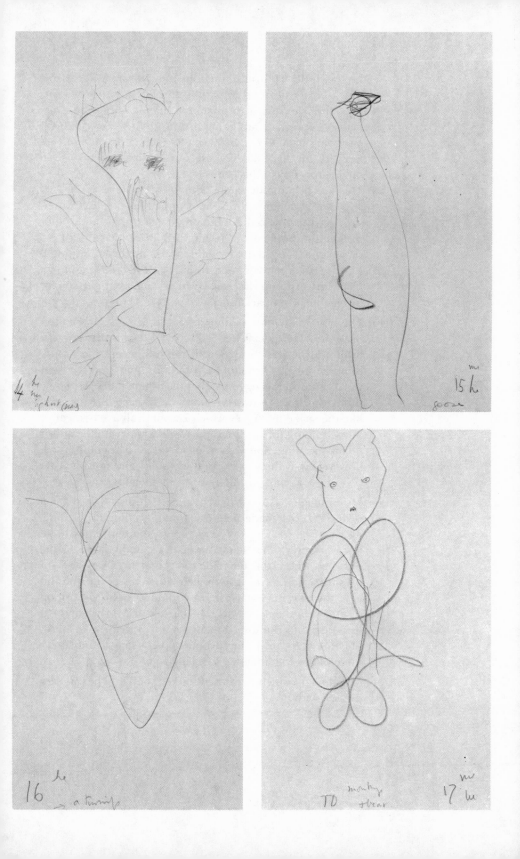

he was little. He told me about monkeys and a bear so I put a bear's head on top and it turned into a teddy bear. I persisted a little with my interpretation about the alternation between 'I am going forward into the world and I am going back to dependence and curling up on mother's lap'. (Naturally I did not use a word like dependence in talking to a boy of this age.)

(18) This was his, and he said: 'Oh it's an R but the wrong way round.' While he said this he dropped his pencil. I would say that this was rather obviously a parapraxis and full of meaning. I pointed out to him that R could stand for his own name. He had not thought of that and he was amused. I said: 'It is the wrong way round because R is afraid to go front forward into the world. He has to make quite sure of being able to get back quickly to mother's lap.'

(19) This was my complex squiggle. I said to him: 'Is that too difficult?' He quickly replied: 'No; I could turn it into a fish'—and he was pleased with the fish. There was something about this fish and he could not quite find the right word, but when I suggested that the fish might be proud he thought this was a way of putting it. It seemed to me to be like the snake in No. 11 which I would call a statement of himself going forward into the world, *I Am*, with the added quality of a direction of movement. It has to be emphasised, however, that the word proud was mine and not his. I do believe it was the word that he was looking for.

(20) His squiggle. This surprised him. He said: Oh that's a better R', so I made it into a robin, keeping up with the idea that he was drawing a picture of himself. There was a line, however, that could not be accommodated in the drawing. About this he made the comment: 'And he's got his little rifle,' so in this way he made sense of the line and gave the drawing a place in the continuity of his exposition of the main theme, namely the danger of *I Am* when it is a direction and the direction is one of movement forward, out into the world away from mother's lap. I said something of this to him in his own language.

(21) My squiggle which he turned into a rabbit and he was very pleased with this.

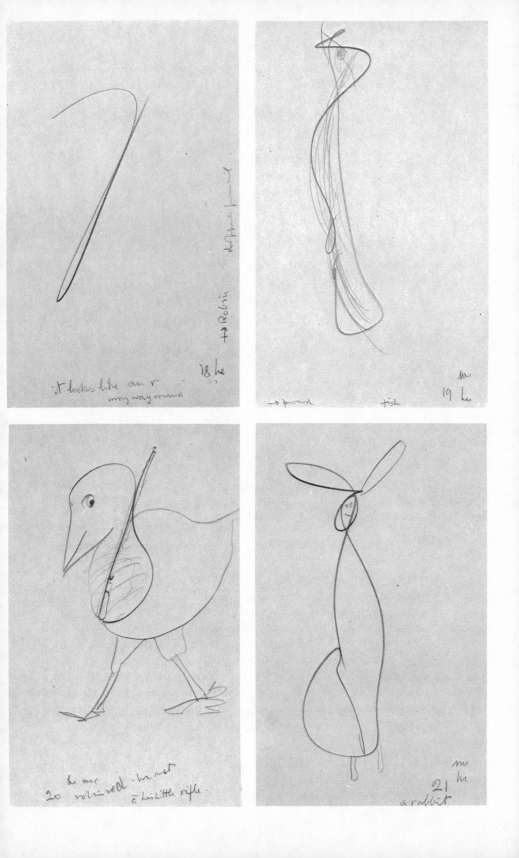

it looks like an r
wrong way round

18 he

→ Robin

→ proud   fish   19 he

20 he me
robin-red-breast
c his little rifle.

21
a rabbit

(22) I then did the last squiggle which he himself turned into another snake and he added: 'With his little rifle,' and we both laughed.

$22\,\underset{kc}{\overset{he}{l}}$

After this we knew we had finished; the statement had been made. As many children want to do he went over the material of the drawings again, and he had obviously dealt with the idea that he had been letting me know of his conflict whether to go forward into the world or to be prepared to run back to mother's lap. I took this as a picture of Robin at 5 years with a main problem associated with starting school, and with this the possibility of a conflict *in the mother* about finishing with babies. I felt confident that Robin was not an ill person; on the other hand I knew that the practical problem of getting Robin to school would depend very much on the parents and the way they might be able to adapt themselves to this special phase of the boy's development. As it happened, the parents were able to give themselves over to this early-morning problem in a way which was quickly fruitful. This included a big effort on the part of the boy's father who gave up some of his work in order to be sure to be available to take the boy to school.

Whether the parents discussed this problem more freely because of my report of what had happened I cannot say. In any case the problem resolved itself and, as I stated at the beginning of this account, I think the parents would have dealt with the problem satisfactorily without my help. They themselves feel that the therapeutic consultation helped them at this particular phase.

CASE III 'Eliza' *aet* $7\frac{1}{2}$ years

It would perhaps be appropriate to continue in this first section with cases in which the child is not ill enough to merit a psychiatric diagnosis. As with most of the cases described by me here I am batting on a good wicket, and indeed it is a feature of this work that if the wicket is not in a good state I do not go in to bat. To continue with this analogy it seems logical that, batting on a good wicket, we may knock up a few good scores. I would like to point out, even at risk of repetition, that in the vast majority of these cases the general atmosphere is favourable, and if one is able to give a little help to the child or to the ill person in the family or social group, then clinical improvement ensues by the forces of life and of the developmental processes. It is a matter of changing a vicious into a benign circle. The vast majority of potential cases are of this kind.

Here in Case III the parents already had reason to have confidence in myself as a person before they brought their little girl to see me and they were quite happy to leave the child with me without first talking about her. Afterwards the mother did not want to talk to me about what had happened for, as she said, she was interested in the result and not in how it came about.

The mother brought Eliza and the two waited for me in the consulting-room where I had placed several copies of *Animals* magazine. This no doubt influenced the material of the consultation at the start.

Eliza was the middle child in a mixed family of boys and girls.
In the few minutes that I had with the mother and Eliza together we talked about the *Animals* magazines. I got Eliza to go with me to the waiting-room which I had prepared for the mother complete with coffee, all of which interested her. She then came back into the consulting-room with me without any difficulty, and we settled down quickly to the squiggle game which I simply introduced and she acquiesced. She had not known about it as a game.

Eliza is a fair, slightly built girl, looking quite sweet as a child may do at 7 years, fairly independent and completely trusting in the context of the relationship which I had with her.

42

We started away with:

(1) My squiggle.

As far as I know Eliza had not been told previously why she was coming to see me. She was obviously much at home with a pencil.

> She took my squiggle and put another leg on it, leaving a space between the legs. (The line of the tummy was added later (see No. 9.)
>
> I said: 'What is it meant to be?'
>
> She said: 'Something gone wrong.'

It is not unusual in my experience for a child to plunge immediately into deep matters in the way that she was obviously doing. I made a mental note that the combination of the space where the belly might be and the words 'something gone wrong' might be giving me a definite indication, even at the very beginning of the session, that Eliza was aware of a problem, and that this problem could have to do with the belly. *I did not say anything.* Naturally I wondered whether there might not be some problem of the 'where do babies come from?' variety.

(2) Hers, which I made into a head, which she seemed to like. I did not do this for any reason, only because this is what I found myself doing.

(3) Mine, which she immediately made into a bird, and in doing so showed her capacity for self-expression in drawing.

(4) Hers, and I discussed with her what it might be. She was pleased with the idea of washing hanging out on a line although this does not come in the daily experience of her town-dwelling family. 'Everything goes to the laundry' seemed to be the comment, but not as a significant contribution from her as far as I could tell. It was more that she followed up my drawing with a reference to life at home.

(5) Mine, which she turned into someone with a long hat. She seemed to think it rather fun that the hat comes off the side of the head. It could be a boy or a girl she said when I made enquiries.

Interpolation

It is necessary here to refer to the fact that I had had a significant interview with the mother three months previously. This chiefly concerned the mother. Nevertheless in the course of describing Eliza the mother had told me of an incident that had had importance in Eliza's early childhood. This concerned *hats*. If I had let what the mother told me dominate the ideas in my mind I would have perhaps thought that drawing 5 indicated a main theme of hats; but as *I always take my cue from the child* I had already been informed in this interview with Eliza that the main theme would have reference to the space between the front and back legs (drawing 1) whatever that might come to mean. However, hats undoubtedly came in as a secondary theme. I shall describe the hat complex at the end of this description of the session with the child.

44

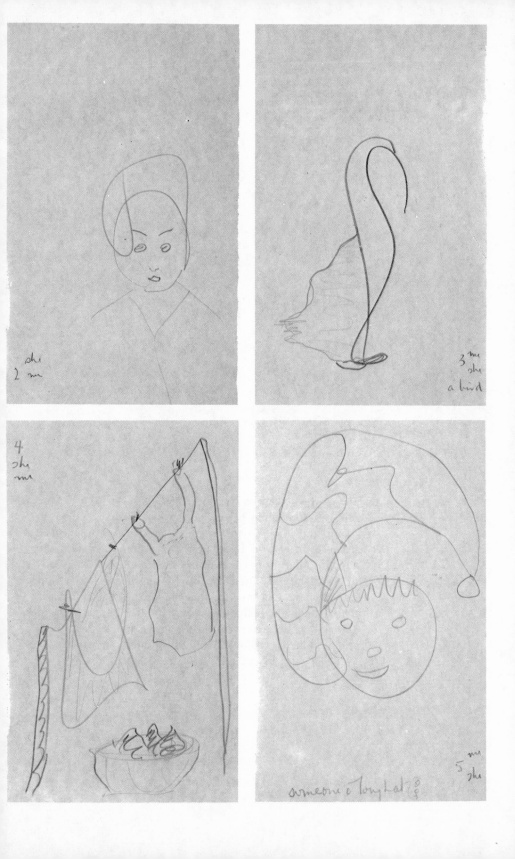

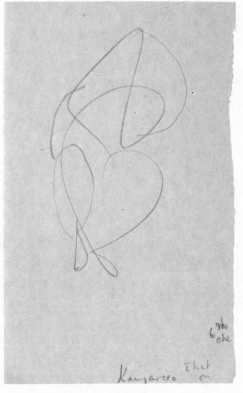

Kangaroo that on

7 me the hand (glove)

The Game, continued

(6) Hers, which she quickly saw as a kangaroo with a hat on.
She did something here which emphasised the kangaroo
theme and linked it to the idea of a place of significance
between front and back legs. She pointed out that the
kangaroo had its knees bent up in the way that kangaroos
do, and she illustrated this by drawing her own knees up
to her chest. One can see that one of the effects of this is
that it hides the belly, and in any case the kangaroo is an
animal that children often choose on account of the pouch,
and to indicate a visible instead of a hidden pregnancy.

(7) Mine, which she turned into a hand or glove.

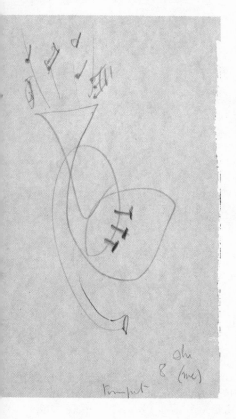

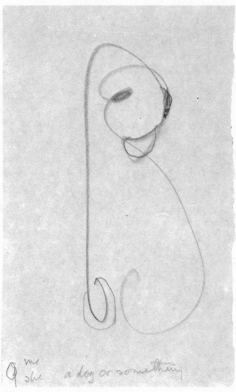

(8) Hers. Together we turned this into a trumpet.

(9) Mine, which she turned into 'a dog or something'. It will be noticed that this drawing also contains a space between the tail and the place where the limbs would be. Evidently she felt this *because she went back to drawing 1 and put in a line giving the tummy.*

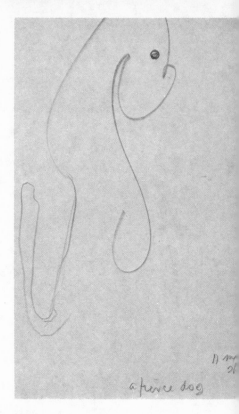

(10) Hers, which I discussed with her. I said 'that really is complete in itself; it doesn't need anything doing to it. I wonder if it isn't [and here I had to get from her the family name for products of defaecation] a "busy". If there is no tummy to the animal this could be the sort of thing that would drop out.'

Eliza looked at me as if she was interested but as if I was talking a language that was not hers, and she said it was a snake. So I put a plate round it and I suggested that we could have it for lunch.

(11) Mine which she turned into a fierce dog. She said that this dog seemed to be 'ready to punch somebody'.

This was evidence of Eliza's ability to get to something in her nature which essentially does not show in her usual behaviour or in what she looks like. (Incidentally I was thinking of joining the punching with the idea of the belly which was absent, and I made a mental note that of course she had had to witness developments belonging to the pregnancies that came after hers, especially the

48

second when she was $3\frac{1}{2}$–4 years old.)

(12) Hers, which I turned into 'an elf or something'. She thought that the elf was going to eat the leaves off the branch. She liked this one as a drawing and as an imaginative idea.

(13) Mine, which she dealt with in a highly imaginative way. 'It is something going under a tunnel. It might be a mole.' I felt that in this there was childhood symbolism of defaecation or birth or sexual intercourse, and I left the matter at that without interpreting.

(14) She made hers into a sort of duck that you see in the dark. This meant that we were near to ideas that turn up in the mind just before sleeping. *We were near to real dream material.*

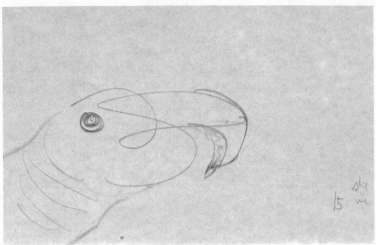

(15) Hers, which I turned into the head of some kind of a bird, and

(16) mine, which she dealt with in a similar way. She gave the bird feathers on its head.

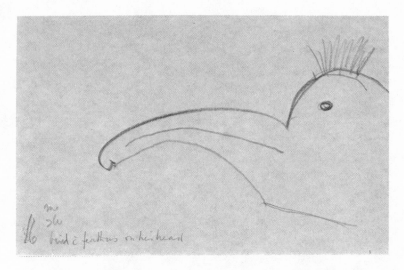

By this time there had developed quite a game which had to do with placing the pictures side by side on the floor; she was getting quite excited about taking each one as it was finished and putting it at the end of a row so that we now had pictures spreading into the other half of the room. When she went to put a picture there, or to check up on its number, I would say: 'Goodbye', and when she came back I would say: 'Hallo.' She was not over-excited, but she was vitally interested in what was going on, and we were both enjoying ourselves, playing together.

(17) Hers, which I made into a duck (imitating her and saying so). I gave it a fish to eat.

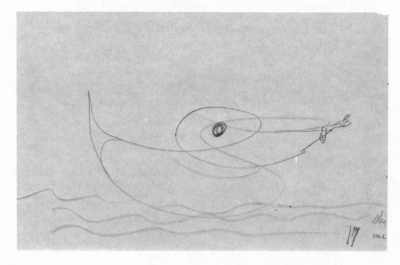

(18) Mine, which she made into 'a fierce something'.

By this time I had made some tentative enquiries about dreams that she might have had, but she was not finding it easy to tell me about them. She had ventured the comment that her dreams were horrid. I had pointed out that there was evidently something horrid that is part of herself but which she does not know what to do with, and I reminded her of the fierce dog (No. 11). The theme was continued in this drawing (No. 18) of the 'fierce something that has claws and big ears and one curious big eye so that it can see in the dark'.

I said something here about the way in which things would fall out of the inside if there was no tummy; perhaps something fierce would fall out like what she had drawn. (Body equivalent to mind.)

I also said something about the claws and her ideas of getting at whatever was inside mummy's tummy when her mummy was going to have one of the babies that came after her. This was quite a new idea to her. She was not quite sure that she remembered anything about mother being in a state of pregnancy. (We did not of course use this word.)

(19) Hers, which I started off doing something with, and together we turned it into an insect.

(20) Mine, rather unlike the other squiggles, and more concentrated. I said: 'That's a silly one, isn't it!' And she said: 'No!' and she turned it quickly into 'some kind of an animal with feelers'. 'It has a big foot and a tail. It can be nice *or* horrid.'

Somewhere here I tried to get from her some information as to whether the fierce and horrid things were male or female but I got no satisfactory indication.

(21) Hers, which I made into what she called 'a posh lady'. While I was drawing this she was doing the next one.

(22) Here she took a quarto sheet of paper. [Children often do this to indicate that what is coming up is significant.] This drawing was 'very difficult for her to do' and she said she would have to be 'very brave'. 'It is a frightening dream.' She started off with the dark and then put in the bed with herself lying on it. After this she got down to the details of the THING that plunges down on her. It has its knees up (in the way that she described when drawing the kangaroo and that she had also shown me with her own body). It has one

54

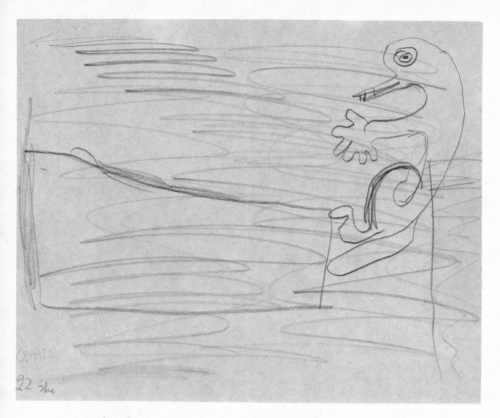

big foot and one small foot and one eye. From her point of view this thing is 'as horrid as possible'.

I tried to get from her what it would do to her if it got at her and all she could say was: 'it would be horrid to me'.

I explored round with the idea here of sexual stimulation either in the form of a seduction of some kind (which is unlikely in her family setting) or with the idea of some form of masturbation. I used words that she could understand. I did not force this issue at all but let her know that I knew about it and she looked at me with wondering eyes as if this was the first time that she had self-consciously thought about masturbation and guilt feelings related to masturbation. Obviously here I was speculating, basing my ideas on what I thought I saw going on. I went very carefully and made sure that I was in no way endangering the relationship that existed between us which had very powerful positive features which could be relied on to cover big risks.

At this stage I gave her the choice to do something else or to draw, and she chose to do two more in the squiggle game. In this

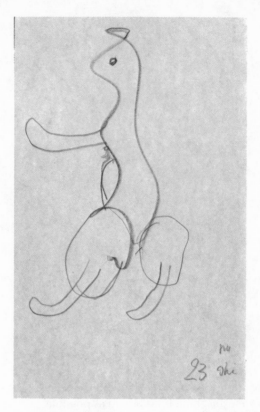

way I gave her every chance to get away, or to change the subject, or to play and see what might happen.

(23) Mine, which she turned into another kangaroo. This time the kangaroo had a big belly or pouch with a baby kangaroo in it. The knees were not up. I talked about the use of a kangaroo for thinking about a belly that has a baby in it but without actually coming directly to the idea of mother being pregnant. She talked about the kangaroo as an animal that does things with its legs and jumps. I gave Eliza some more of my own idea that this very awful thing that comes at her represents something that she has never properly accepted which is that she has feelings like that about the baby inside her mother's belly. The horrid THING would then be a return of something of her own that she could feel to be horrid but which she could not allow to be part of her own self.

(24) Hers, which I made into an animal which she liked. She seemed to want to continue, so I let the game proceed.

(25) Mine, which she made into a goat charging. [I assumed (but said nothing) that for Eliza as for other people a goat is a symbol of instinct, usually of sexual instinct in males.]

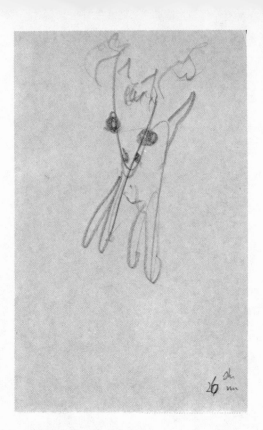

(26) Hers, which I changed into another little animal which pleased her.

(27) Mine, which she said was going to be a mouse. In any case it had a big ear.

We now came to what she said would be the last of the series.

(28) The final one. Hers, which she turned quite fantastically into a man's head. It started off with glasses and was fairly obviously a portrait of me. The man was reading a newspaper. 'No, he is crossing his arms.' She was very free at this point, and in fact she could now see whatever she liked to see into her own squiggles.

Eliza was now quite ready to go and I told her that we would fetch mother, so we gathered together all the drawings which she wanted to re-examine in their right order. We went over all the significant details, including the fun and the interpretative work. She took out the big quarto drawing of the dream and put it aside as 'different', and I think if mother had come in she would

59

have wanted this drawing to be kept as something private between herself and me. In any case I put all the drawings in the folder and said they were hers which she could have any time if she wanted them, but I would keep them for her. It is my usual practice to say this at the end, and the children very seldom want to take the squiggle game drawings home.

Now she fetched her mother. She went out of the front door in a very contented state and I said: 'Perhaps we will meet again one day.' She said: 'I hope.'

Comment

The reader who is studying this technique, and who is also trying to use the material for making an assessment of Eliza's psychiatric state, will wish to examine what has been presented without help. No doubt various opinions could be expressed, with the accent placed now on one aspect of the case and now on another.

Nevertheless a comment must be made for the reader to use after making a personal study of what transpired.

General Remarks

This intelligent girl comes within the meaning of the term normal, or she is healthy in a psychiatric sense. That is to say, she shows a freedom from any rigid defence organisation. In a more positive way, she is able to play and to enjoy playing, she easily accepts my playing and allows our playing to overlap, and she shows a sense of humour without being manic.[1]

Eliza is able to use her imagination, and after duly testing out the set situation she becomes able to give me a dream of significance, in which appears fierceness, the one feature that is clinically lacking and that is absent in her personality as it presents itself to those who know her.

There appear certain details which draw attention to areas in Eliza's 'total personality' organisation which give her some trouble because of conflict, ignorance and muddle. These details are as follows:

> Something wrong (1).
>
> Space instead of line for belly (1).
>
> Line put in later (at the time of 9).

[1] The term 'manic' implies, for me, that there is a mood of depression that is being denied, replaced by contra-depressive manifestations.

Kangaroo theme introducing confusion in respect of
pregnancy.

Genital pregnancy understood but pregenital (alimentary
tract) fantasy of pregnancy relatively under repression.

It is as if Eliza had been given information about babies coming
from the womb, but the information had not 'taken' because she
was still struggling with the concept of babies in terms of what
comes from the inside, the alimentary fantasy system. It cannot
be decided whether the fault here came from the mother or from
the child or both, because it is clear that the anxiety was organised round the horrid 'THING' in the alimentary-tract fantasy
system, and this was related to the horrid or destructive ideas
that she may have had towards the THINGS in the mother's belly
that periodically made her fat.

SECONDARY THEME (see Interpolation, after drawing 9)

There was a recurring interest in hats, and this may well have
been an aftermath of the significant episode to which the mother
referred, and which I have not yet recounted. It can be given here
without (I hope) interfering with the main issues of the case.

Near the end of the mother's interview with me, which was
mainly about herself, she told me of something that she felt guilty
about in the management of Eliza's early life. She said: 'It seems
ridiculous, but this is what happened when Eliza was only 10
months old. I had to go away for a few days, and I did so reluc-
tantly, but left the children (Eliza was the youngest then) in the
safe-keeping of a nurse in the constant surroundings and routine
of the home. I thought it would be all right, but I must have felt
guilty because when I came back I rushed into wherever Eliza
(the baby) was, *without taking off my hat first*. The awful thing was
that Eliza froze up. She did not react to anything I did at all. I
took her and kept her in my arms, and eventually (perhaps after
a whole day) she relaxed and then became just as she had been
before I went away. Gradually all returned to normal, except that
Eliza had developed and retained a phobia of hats. For a long
time, many months, the baby would not pass ladies with hats on.'

It was probably because of this phobia of hats, and the possibility of there being a residue of Eliza's three-day loss of her
mother at 10 months, that the mother decided to bring her for
psychiatric consultation, for the bed-wetting did not worry the

mother at all, and in fact the bed-wetting cleared up round about the time of the consultation.

But it was important, as has already been pointed out, that I followed the child's material, and not that of the subsidiary theme of hats which I could have recognised from what the mother had told me about the early months of Eliza's life.

THE MAIN THEME

Gradually the main theme became evident. It had to do with exactly the feature that was missing in Eliza's personality, the fierceness that appeared first in the 'fierce something' (No. 18) and then the 'thing' in the dream (No. 22). This fierceness had to do with her fear of the things that she imagined were growing inside her mother's tummy, based on an ingestion–retention–elimination (or pregenital) view of bodily functions. It also linked on to her own aggressive drives, her anger with mother who was withdrawing from her because of the new pregnancy, and her attack in fear of the imagined horrid objects inside mother. Behind all this was the overlaid attack on the mother's contents belonging to instinct-driven object-relating, or primitive love impulse, with a pre-history of the idea of attack on the contents of the breast, or greedy appetite.

The work done in this one therapeutic consultation was enough to free the primitive object-relating or love impulse from the secondary impulses containing reactive anger, and the consequence clinically was that the child's personality became more free in a general way, and there came about a greater ease in the to and fro of feeling between the child and her mother.

The main part of this work was the child's own discoveries, or ordered sequence of discoveries, culminating in her being able to use the dream which she had had but from which she had not been able to derive full benefit until she was able to produce it and to draw it for my benefit in the therapeutic consultation.

In other words, the interpretations did not produce the result, but they helped towards the child's own discovery of what was already there in herself. This is the essence of therapy.

Outcome

Eliza's arrival at these matters in the relationship to me had the effect of making her much more of a relaxed person, so that the parents were well satisfied with the clinical result of the consultation. This would point to the possibility that Eliza was ready for a more imaginative and childish explanation of the origin of babies than she had in fact been given.

General Comment

Once again it seems to me that this case may convey something of the richness and the potential of what I call the therapeutic consultation, or the exploitation of the first hour. In a discussion of the case one could take up the theme of the deprivation at 10 months and of Eliza's reaction to it, and her mother's management of her reaction. The main theme, however, must be the one that came (to Eliza's surprise) into the material and which I could in no way have predicted, even if I had had an interview with the mother about Eliza.

This is the kind of history-taking which I respect. I could put my view the other way round and say that I do not respect any other kind of history-taking. It is of no great value to know facts from the mother, and a patient's answers to questions lead nowhere except away from the central theme which in psychiatry *is always a difficult one*, and in fact is always the place *where conflict is exactly to be found*.

CASE IV 'Bob' *aet* 6 years

I wish to follow on with another case[1] in which a child of about the same age revealed in an entirely unexpected way the block that he found to his freedom to use the regressive aspect of the two-way tendency, one way which would lead him to the world and the other way which would lead him back to dependence. In this case the block was something that was in the mother, as the details of the case will show. Here again there was a favourable outcome.

The mother had been for some years in the care of a psychiatric colleague who is also an analyst, on account of panics and depression. She had obviously been a very ill patient and had been treated by psychotherapy. The father had also had depressive phases and both parents had attended for group therapy. They said they felt that the very existence of the family depended on the help given over the years by my colleague.

Preliminary Contact

First I saw Bob with his father and mother. I learned that in the household there was Bob aged 6 years, a brother aged 5 years, and another brother aged 1 year. There was also a girl of 15, the adopted daughter of the mother's parents. Bob's father worked in a factory. In the house there were three bedrooms, which were not enough. Bob and the next boy slept together, often in the same bed.

Already I was finding out what Bob was like. His words were shortened and many of them were difficult to understand. Nevertheless he communicated freely. He had come in an excited state and he took up his position in one of the little chairs, eager for whatever should happen. It could really be said that he was full of some vague kind of hope.

At this point the parents went to the waiting-room and I had Bob alone with me in my room for forty-five minutes.

Interview with Bob

Bob was easy to meet. He expected friendliness and helpfulness.

[1] First published in the *Int. J. Psycho-Anal.*, **46**.

I had provided paper and pencils and I suggested that we should play a game and I proceeded to show him what I meant. He was talking in an excited way and on one occasion there was a stammer, on the word *punch* (p . . . p . . . p . . . punch). This was when he was talking about the first drawing.

(1) I made a squiggle for him to do something with. He knew what he wanted to do and he carefully filled it in with shading and called it a bull. It took me a long time to realise that the word bull meant ball, but to help me he gave me a long story about pumping (? bumping) up and down, and punching. I made a mental note of this boy's capacity to conceive of a whole object, and also I began to doubt the diagnosis that had been assumed to be correct, Primary Defect.

I now suggested that he should make a squiggle for me to turn into something, but either he did not understand or else he could not make a squiggle. He said: 'Can I make a car?'

(2) This is his drawing of a car.

(3) I offered him a squiggle and he seemed bewildered. He said it was a hand, but he added: 'It's too hard', meaning he could not play this game.

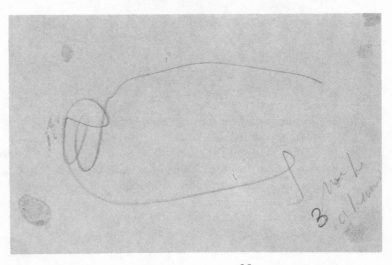

(4) He chose to draw the sun.

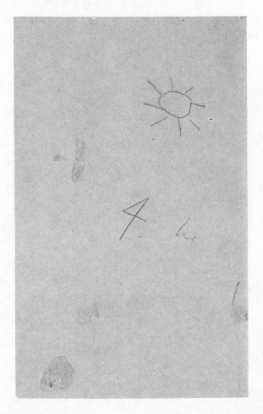

This was the end of a very cautious first phase in which he used the aspect of his self that tries to comply and to conform, but which does not carry feeling nor does it employ impulse.

The *second phase* started with

(5) His version of a squiggle. It was a drawing by use of a wavy line, and it may have been a person or a ghost. I added the moon.

It was now my turn and I did

(6) My squiggle. He put in the eyes and called it Humpty Dumpty.

The theme of Humpty Dumpty alerted me to the idea of disintegration, related to premature reliance on an ego organisation. At this stage I had no idea that his putting in the eyes had significance, but in the critical drawing (No. 26) this Humpty Dumpty theme and the eyes came to make sense.

It should be noted that in this work I do not usually make interpretations, but I wait until the essential feature of the child's communication has been revealed. Then I talk about the essential feature, but the important thing is not my talking so much as the fact that the child has reached something.

(7) Bob made a new characteristic squiggle composed of a wavy line; he quickly saw what he himself wanted to do with it and he turned it into a snake, 'dangerous because it stings'.

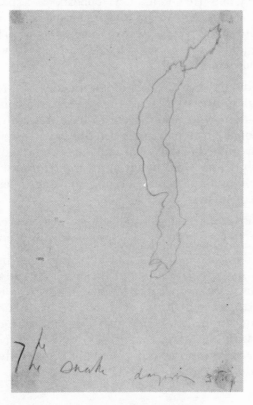

Here was now a drawing of Bob's own, based on his own

squiggle, and very different from the drawings of the objectively perceived car and sun (Nos. 2 and 4). He was pleased with his own drawing.

At this point he became interested in the numbers that I was putting on the drawings, and he told me all along the number of the next drawing.

> (8) My squiggle which he said was a hair. Then he said it was an 'ephelant' with a big mouth. He put in the eyes. (Eyes again!)

I am not attempting to reproduce the curious distortion of speech which made it very hard for me to understand what he was saying. It was always possible to understand in the end.

> (9) This was his squiggle, done by the same technique of the wavy line. He said it was a 'roundabout', a 'puzzle place'. I found that he meant a maze, but he could not use this word. It was horrid. He went with his Daddy. In fast speech he told a story of this visit to a maze, and he was anxious while remembering it.

Here I made another mental note of the idea of a reaction to environmental failure. In this case the idea was of a failure on the part of the father, who would seem to have not realised that a maze would touch on archaic anxiety in Bob. I had got into touch with Bob's threatened confusional state, his potential disorientation. Naturally I was building up in my mind an idea of his illness as one of infantile schizophrenia, showing a tendency to recover spontaneously.

> (10) This was my squiggle, and he went over it and emphasised everything. He said it was a 'roundabout like mine'.

This seemed to mean 'like his' but it became clear in the context that Bob meant 'a roundabout like *nine*'. He did not mean *mine*. This illustrates the peculiar language distortion to which I needed to adapt myself, in order to receive his otherwise very clear communication. (I assume that this language distortion corresponds with the glass or perspex (or whatever) that the schizophrenic often reports as a something between the self and the actual world.)

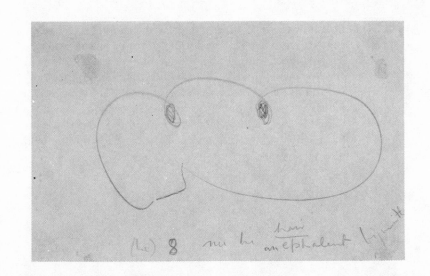

(b) 8 *see the* *than* *anophaleut* *lijourt* #

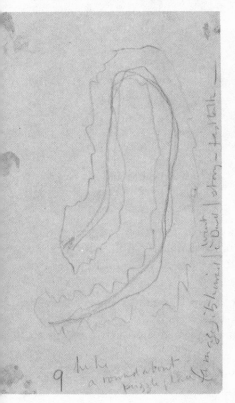

9 *see the*
a roundabout
puzzle plant

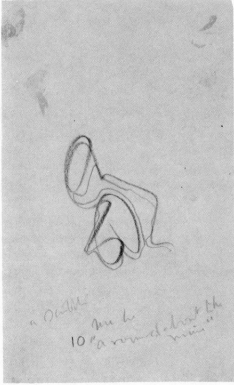

a double
see the
10 *a roundabout the*

(11) Bob now chose to draw. He drew the sun in his characteristic way and a jet plane by the other technique (after he
had made its outline by the wavy line method). Bob said:
'Twelve comes after it.' He was now numbering the drawings, and was correctly using the words 'he' and 'me' which
I put next to the numbers to denote the order of events. He
was able to call himself he, and me me, allowing for my
having my own point of view, or identifying himself with
me in the game.

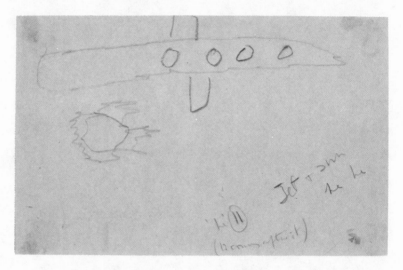

Talking about No. 11, I asked Bob if he would like to go in
a jet plane. He said: 'No, because they may go upside
down.'

From this I gathered further evidence that Bob was letting me
know of his experience of environmental unreliability during the
period of his own near-absolute dependence. I continued with
my policy of not making interpretations.

I seem to have asked at this point: 'Do you remember
being born?' He replied: 'Well, that was a long time ago.'
Then he added: 'Mummy showed me where I did be a
baby.'

I found afterwards that his mother had recently taken him to
see the house where he was born.

While we were talking in this way we had continued with the drawings.

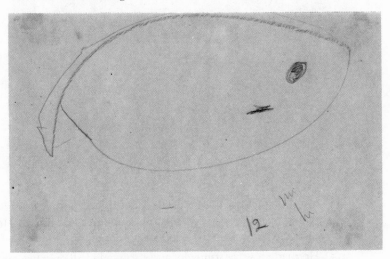

(12) My squiggle which he turned into a fish. He put in *the eye* and mouth.

(13) Here was one of his characteristic squiggles, which he turned into a boat. He told me a long story of someone who had gone in a big boat to Australia. He then said: 'My lines are all wiggly, wiggly.'

(14) My squiggle which went off the page on to another sheet of
paper (see No. 18), which amused him very much. He
turned what was on this sheet into a hand.

(15) He made a wavy squiggle, and I squiggled all over his, and
we were deliberately making a hopeless mess and muddle.
Then he saw it as a Donald Duck and *put in the eyes*.

(16) My squiggle, which he turned into a 'lephelent'. He added:
'It has a beak and it can catch me.' He dramatised this.

(17) He turned his own squiggle into a shoe.

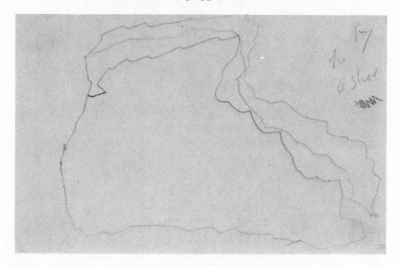

(18) Here I offered the spines which came from the spilt-over parts of No. 14. He made this into 'an animal that will eat you'. At this point he put his hand to his penis, feeling danger there. I pointed this out to him, else he would not have noticed that he had made this gesture.

(19) His drawing of a tiger.

He had now mastered his immediate anxiety about retaliation based on oral sadism, and he talked about numbers.

'Shall we go up to 100?'

Actually he was only capable of counting to twenty, or a little further with effort.

We were now in a doldrums area, between the second phase and the next phase. I did not know, of course, whether there would be another phase.

(20) He wrote his name at my request, putting one letter round the wrong way. He wrote the number six (his age), because he could not spell it.

(21) His squiggle, which he said was 'a mountain; you walk all round it and get lost'.

Now we had entered the third phase, and we began to get down to the significant detail. The content of No. 21 made me prepared for a new version of environmental failure producing threat of primitive anxiety of the type of falling, depersonalisation, confusion, disorientation, etc.

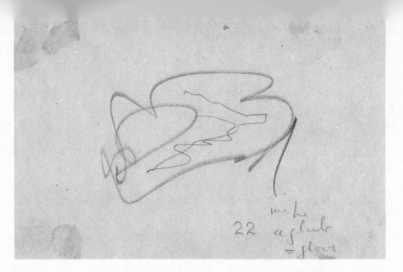

(22) My squiggle. I said, in a challenging voice: 'I bet you can't make anything of that.' He said: 'I'll try', and rather quickly he turned it into a glub (glove).

Bob now asked for a bigger sheet of paper. He obviously had something important to draw, and he used the larger sheets until the end.

(23) His deliberate drawing of 'a big hill, a very big one, a big mountain'. 'You climb up there and you slip; it's all ice.' He added: 'Have you a car?'

From this I felt sure he was telling me about being held, and about being affected by someone's withdrawal of cathexis and, of course, I wondered if this could be a picture of his mother's depression, and its effect on him when he was a baby. I continued to refrain from making comment, and asked him if his dreams were about this sort of thing.

He said: 'I forget them.' Then, remembering one: 'Oh, an awful dream about a witch.'

I said: 'What awful dream?'

He said: 'It was last night or another night. If I see it I cry. I don't know what it is. It is a witch.' And here he started dramatising.

'It's horrid, and has a wand. It makes you pee. You can talk but you can't be seen and you can't see yourself. Then you say "one, one, one" and you come back.'

The word 'pee' here does not mean micturate. 'No, not wee-wee!' It means disappear. When the witch 'pees you' he 'makes you vanish'. The witch has a hat and soft shoes. It's a man witch.

While all this was going on Bob was drawing

79

(24) He was now drawing an illustration of what he wanted to tell me at this point. He was dramatising horror and his penis got excited and he screwed himself up because of anxiety.

(25) Shows himself in bed having the nightmare. When he saw
the big stairs he said: 'Oh! oh! oh!' and he was very much
in the event he was describing.

He now told me that the drawing was about two things.
The awful one was the nightmare; but there was a real incident which was not horrid, it was nice. He really fell down-
stairs, and there was Daddy at the bottom of the stairs, and
he cried, and Daddy carried him to Mummy, and she took
him and made him well.

I now had the clearest possible evidence of Bob's wish to tell me about a lapse in the environmental provision which had been 'good' in a general way. I therefore started to talk, and I drew

(26) A mother figure holding a baby. I scribbled out the baby in arms; and while I was starting to put into words the baby's danger of being dropped, Bob took the paper and *smudged in the woman's eyes.* (See No. 6. Also Nos. 8, 12 and 15.) *As he smudged in the eyes he said : 'She goes to sleep.'*

This was the significant detail in the total communication. I now had his drawing illustrating the holding mother's withdrawal of cathexis.

I now put the baby on the floor in my drawing, wondering how Bob would deal with the archaic anxiety associated with falling for ever.

> Bob said: 'No, the witch came when the mother shut her eyes. I just screamed. I saw the witch. Mummy saw the witch. I shouted: "My mummy will get you!" Mummy saw the witch. Daddy was downstairs and he took his penknife and stuck it into the witch's tummy so it got killed for ever, and so the wand went too.'

In this fantasy can be seen the material for a psycho-neurotic organisation set up and maintained in defence against the un-thinkable or archaic or psychotic anxiety produced in the child by the failure of the mother's holding function. The recovery from the trauma depends on the father's help.

> (27) His drawing showing himself in bed and the male witch and also the wand which 'makes you pee' (disappear).

The communication having been made, Bob was ready to go. He seemed to be very satisfied with what had happened, and his excited state had calmed down.

Bob now went to his father in the waiting-room while his mother gave me the following account of the family problem.

Mother's Description given Me after My Interview with Bob, with Bob and His Father in the Waiting-room

At $2\frac{1}{2}$ years Bob was taken to a children's hospital because of continuous crying. At the time the mother was depressed. A paediatrician said he was frustrated. After brain examination and various tests the parents were told that there was no disease but that Bob was six months behind in development. The parents were told they must expect him to be *simple*.

A year later, at $3\frac{1}{2}$ years, Bob was taken again and the parents were told once more that he 'was simple'. At 3 years Bob did not speak at all. To help things forward the mother herself started a day nursery. Bob showed up as the slowest in the class and he was obviously tied to his mother. The parents had accepted the fact that Bob would be 'simple', but recently the mother's psychiatrist had suggested that they ought to question this diagnosis because of the wide range of Bob's interests as reported by the mother in her sessions with her. He was always talking about space and God and life and death. He was very sensitive and obviously the word 'simple' did not cover the whole of the diagnosis. On Intelligence Test Bob had scored 93 (Stanford-Binet).

There had been thumb-sucking throughout. A period of masturbation, erections, and day-dreaming seemed to have passed. At times he would get his penis out both at school and at home, but everyone tried not to make too much of this.

Talking about her childhood the mother herself remembered being unhappy at home at the time of her secondary school; she felt picked upon. It was better at a grammar school, when she got on to dressmaking and cooking. She does not give the impression of high intelligence, but evidence seems to show that she herself is not by any means limited. She achieved School Certificate.

The father, an only son, 'spent his childhood in dreamland' (mother's description), being unhappy at home. His parents were difficult people and indeed the mother ascribes the beginning of her illness to her having to be in contact with her in-laws. The father's mother had died a year ago.

Bob's mother did not suffer from panics any longer, and Bob's father had settled down to being a quiet personality. The family had times when there was a shortage of money. It was a severe blow to the father that his son should be simple, whereas the mother did not mind much. The father is an engineer.

BOB'S EARLY HISTORY

Bob's birth had not been difficult. Breast feeding was complicated by what the mother called a doctor's mistake. The mother had said to the doctor: 'I know this baby is ill.' Then at 2 weeks it was discovered that he had pyloric stenosis and he was operated on immediately, being away a fortnight. The mother had tried to forgive the doctor for not believing her that the child was ill, but had not entirely succeeded.

At 4 years 9 months the boy underwent tonsillectomy; here it was very evident to the parents that he was backward because they knew that although they could tell any other child what to expect they could not find a way of telling Bob. Bob had five days in hospital, with daily visiting. He was distressed during this period.

The mother said that she had this first baby in hospital but decided to have the others at home. In the third pregnancy the mother used the National Childbirth Trust methods. The birth was 'absolutely painless'. The father was present. They found the experience 'inspiring and lovely'. It was possible to detect here in this positive statement one side of the mother's illness, the idealisation which all the time carries with it the threat of the opposite. Contained in all this is her potential depression.

At the time of Bob's birth the mother feared hospital although the pregnancy was all right. The labour was in fact a short and easy one. *It was after the second birth, when Bob was 14 months old, that she started her panics and psychotherapy. I asked: 'How did you first become ill? In what way did your depression show itself?' She answered: 'I kept finding myself going to sleep while I was engaged in doing something.'*

It was when Bob was 14–16 months old that she was starting to get sleepy and this was the beginning of not being able to cope; later the panics supervened. This information coming at the very end of the consultation interested me very much because of the

85

evidence that I had already got of this from the material supplied by Bob himself.

As Bob left my house he said to his mother: 'Did you see how I rubbed in the lady's eyes?' This had obviously been the high light, for him, of the therapeutic interview. (Actually I had not shown her the drawings.)

The parents visited me three weeks later, not bringing Bob. Here I learned much detail about each parent, and also more about Bob. At home his difficulties were compatible with a diagnosis of infantile schizophrenia, tending to spontaneous recovery. His main trouble was a learning difficulty.

FOLLOW-UP

After 7 months. 'Learning at school has seemed to be released since the time of the consultation. At home, Bob makes steady growth in spite of father's illness (hospital) and mother's hospitalisation with the baby, who had an illness.'

Comment

It would seem that this boy retained a clear idea of the beginning of his illness, or of the organisation of his defences into a personality pattern. He was able to communicate this, and he did so with some urgency once he had felt that I might possibly understand and therefore make his communication effective.

The work of this therapeutic consultation is made more interesting by the fact that this boy did not use words at 3 years, that he had a learning difficulty, and that he was generally considered to be 'simple' by paediatricians, by school authorities and by the parents. It is unlikely that Bob could have told me what he did by verbal reply to verbal question. Gradually, however, he unfolded the etiology of his symptom-complex in the play-procedure of the therapeutic consultation.

The diagnosis became changed during the consultation from one of relative (primary) defect to one of infantile schizophrenia, with the patient tending to make spontaneous recovery.

It is interesting to note that schizophrenia, or the psychotic condition that resulted in a severe learning difficulty, is in fact a highly sophisticated defence organisation. The defence is against primitive, archaic ('unthinkable') anxiety produced by environmental failure in the stage of the child's near-absolute dependence. Without the defence there would be a breakdown of mental

86

organisation of the order of disintegration, disorientation, depersonalisation, falling for ever, and loss of sense of real and of the capacity for relating to objects. In the defence the child isolates what there is of himself, and attains a position of invulnerability. In the extreme of this defence the child cannot be traumatised, and at the same time cannot be induced to rediscover dependence and vulnerability, and a return of liability to archaic anxiety (Winnicott, 1968).

In the case of Bob the ego had known a certain type of disaster, limited in quantity, and had experienced breakdown, had reorganised itself against being retraumatised by developing the feeling of being traumatised all the time except when withdrawn. All details of experience had been retained and have been subjected to classification, categorisation and collation, and to primitive forms of thinking. It is to be presumed that as a result of the work of the therapeutic consultation this complex organisation around a traumatic event became transformed into material that could be forgotten because it had been remembered, that is to say, it had become available for a sophisticated thinking process that is relatively detached from psycho-somatic functioning.

Sequel

This case had a surprising sequel. The change in Bob continued. About a year after the consultation Bob said to his parents, out of the blue: 'You know I once went to see somebody in London . . .' And they reminded him of my name—'Well, I would like to take my brother to see him.' The consultation was fixed and without interviewing the parents I let into my consulting-room two very lively children. Bob seemed to remember everything about the place and the table where we did the drawings, but I think he did not remember the drawings themselves. He was proudly showing his brother what it was like coming to see this man, and to my amazement he decided to take his brother all over my house, which is a tall house going up four storeys. He took him up and showed him the roof garden, which I hardly thought he had noticed although he could have seen it from the window where we had sat a year previously; and then he took him to all the rooms upstairs. It happened that no-one was in and he was able to explore the whole house. In effect what he was doing was to show his brother that he knew the geography of my house, and both the children were interested in every detail. The tour of inspection included the bedroom. When they got down again they did a certain amount of drawing, but this was not important, and they then seemed ready to go.

I had to assume that Bob was finding a way of remembering what he felt had happened a year previously when he was a withdrawn introvert, hardly able to talk intelligible English because of the speech distortion. A year ago it would have seemed to the observer that he was not noticing anything, yet one could see now that he not only had noticed a great deal but that he 'knew' a great deal that in fact he did not know. I think it could be said that he was in process of objectifying me, and that I was emerging (for him) out of the category of subjective object, or dream come true.

I am informed that the change in Bob has persisted in the five years since the consultation. The reader should be reminded that both the parents had had psychiatric help before the occasion of Bob's first visit, and this had continued in the interval between then and now. No doubt this was responsible for some of the psychiatric health attained and retained by Bob.

Added Note

For purposes of economy I am not giving the sixteen pictures that we did *à trois* because it seems to me that they do not add any significant feature to the case. We ended with a squiggle of his which was like a w, and I put ENT (WENT) after it because we were near the moment when he and his brother could go. He said: 'It is a thing you put in a word', and I was interested in this because of the fact that he had originally come to me with a marked speech defect which had disappeared, but which certainly involved what he put into words, almost as if deliberately distorting them.

CASE V 'Robert' *aet* 9 years

Here is a very simple case. We will call the boy Robert. He belongs to a family which is very much a 'going concern'. At the time of the consultation, fifteen years ago, Robert was 9; he had a sister of 7 and a sister of 5. There is a very definite sense of responsibility in the parents, and they are both able to tolerate bad times if there is the hope of a satisfactory outcome.

I interviewed the father first; he seemed to want this so I acquiesced. Usually I see the child first. He said to me: 'The trouble is this boy is too much like me.' The father said he himself was a late developer. Robert always hated school. He refused to work or to reach out for things. At home, for instance, with his Meccano set he would not read the book of instructions although he very much wanted to be able to make something described in the book. Instead of working from the book he would ask his father, and then get angry. In fact he hated reading. Or he would not learn the names of things. He had been expected to do well at school but he was becoming a disappointment. He was at the local primary school with fifty in a class. The parents were perturbed because the school reported that Robert had 'got stuck at the stage of being a baby'.

The paternal grandfather was constantly testing the boy's scholastic achievements and the father himself did this occasionally, being horrified to find that the boy could not subtract 9 (his age) from 1953 (the year). His mother had said she would like to have a routine Intelligence Test because 'either he must be allowed to be a dunce or we must chase him'. The Educational Psychologist's test report was: 'Taking an average of tests of wide range given in two interviews, the I.Q. works out at about 130.'

The father told me about the boy's early history. The child was born when the father was away in the army. He was breast-fed, but at the time the mother was at the mercy of everyone. An air-raid at the time of the birth caused delay in the arrival of the doctor. Fly-bombs complicated things further and the father came back and took the mother and her infant to the Midlands. There the infant was fed by the clock and allowed to cry in the intervals because there was too much anxiety to allow of experimentation and trial. The mother is a good mother and with

89

support she would have started better with him, and she did better with the two girls. For instance, with support she could have been enabled to adopt a technique less strict, more adapted to the infant's early needs.

In further description the father said: 'Robert has always been very fond of his mother, and he and his mother were very much together in the early years.' When he was 2 years old (while the father was still at the war), the first sister was born, and Robert became violently jealous. This jealousy has continued. In relation to this sister 'he gets a devil in him', and constantly provokes her. She on the other hand is 'incredibly sweet'. The father said that Robert knew about babies being inside, and when the mother came back from the nursing home he made remarks like: 'Now your tummy's the right size again' and 'Now you can come and play again'. When the mother was not able to go into the garden with him or play with him in the old way he would get into a mood. There is a garden to the house that they all live in now and he likes to play in it, but he is unlikely to play for long periods on his own. He does, however, persecute newts and in this way he works off feelings about human beings. He shows what he is doing by calling this one a fat mother newt and that one a father newt. He can be endearing to his mother while being incredibly cruel to the mother newt. The father, being fond of newts, is at a loss to know what to do. Perhaps a few newts must suffer, he sadly conceded, in the cause of the gradual socialisation of this boy? In playing with other children Robert is able to use imagination, but usually the imaginative idea goes wild. He is a bad sport and in a game he constantly adapts rules to his own needs in the way that domineering children do, so that he is the only one really able to fit in with the rules and the other children are always, so to speak, offside.

At one time Robert showed a good deal of constructiveness in his play, but this has lessened and he has become slowed up generally. The slowness seems to be a symptom of a mild depressive mood which affects the child both at home and at school. The school put down the difficulties at school to the home situation, but the home is essentially a good one and the trouble must be put down to difficulties in the boy's own nature, inherent difficulties belonging to emotional growth.

All the children have been free from sleep disturbances and to account for this we must accept that the mother really does give herself adequately to her children. She provides them with a very good setting indeed. The other two smaller children are more able than Robert to make use of this setting.

On the whole people like Robert. He can be friendly, effusive even, without being bashful. He is not only like his father, but he copies his father too. He is handicapped in play by the fact that the father is an intellectual. He was heard to say that he wished he had 'an ordinary father', by which he meant a father who was a soldier or a bricklayer, or something you could tell people about or copy in a game. There is a maleness about the boy which is satisfactory, but there is also a very obvious envy of the mother's productive capacity, and his latent woman-identification is closely bound up with his affection for his father. In regard to sexual matters he seems to be unable or unwilling to ask for information, and the parents have never found the right position from which to tell him about sex except in regard to the growth of the baby inside the mother. They think that possibly he is wanting information and that he cannot make use of them, and they admit to being rather shy of these matters. He can get excited, and excitement does not make him ill. Masturbation is not a problem with him as far as the parents can tell.

In regard to school, which he always enjoys, he tends to be in a rage against it on Sunday evenings and at the ends of holidays. Once he ran home from school. Life was at its worst for him probably when he was 6 years old. The father was away and the mother became very depressed and the whole family got caught up in the mother's depression. The family doctor was of great help and saw the whole family through this era. Out of this phase of strain the family moved to a new district with the father at home and Robert going to the local primary school. This is how matters stand at present.

*   *   *

It was some months after my interview with the father that the mother actually brought Robert to see me. I could see immediately that Robert resembled his father in a certain slowness of action going along with superior intelligence.

First I had a talk with Robert in front of the mother. The details are very ordinary but I suppose they do add up to a technique of human contact. In making such a contact one must be free while keeping to a professional relationship.

Here was the boy standing beside me, with the mother sitting in the comfortable chair. The boy was all polite smiles. I immediately pointed to his badge and he was glad to speak not about himself directly but about the activities and interests represented by the badge.

I spoke about school, and he made it clear that he could only work at his own pace; and he was at his worst in examinations where hurry is important and work is done to the clock. I asked about the garden and found he works a small part himself. He made the rather odd spontaneous remark about his gardening: 'It brightens up a dull patch.'

The mother was revealing herself to me as a depressive kind of person, serious and somewhat anxious in the situation of the consultation. I suppose she first of all wanted to be sure I would find the boy nice, good, and polite, because you never know with doctors what they will say if a child acts naturally. However, she gradually came to see me as someone who is not concerned too much with surface phenomena.

I made a mental note that perhaps the dark patch to be brightened up would turn out to be the mother in her depressions—especially as I had already heard from the father of a phase (when the boy was 6) in which the mother's depressions had presented a definite problem.

We soon came on to the subject of reading and I asked about comics. The boy looked at his mother and I had clearly hit on a controversial matter. Robert said he was not allowed to read comics. I spoke to the mother afterwards about this, because I felt that the boy would learn to like reading from comics rather than from good books carefully chosen from the library. Robert said: 'I try to read the good books, but there are always long words I don't understand.' He also said that comics circulate at school as an under-the-counter activity, a mild pornography.

I did not want to see the mother long on this occasion as a long talk would have ruined my chances of getting into touch personally with Robert, so I took the mother to the waiting-room and got in a word there about the way she and her husband were trying to implant their own religious moral standards and taste on to their boy, which was a pity since this boy was capable of developing his own morality and his own taste if left to it. The mother saw what I meant, and she seemed relieved not to have to feel responsible henceforward for her boy's goodness.

I returned to the boy and he was co-operative in playing the squiggle game with me.

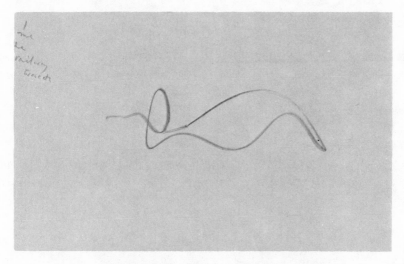

(1) My squiggle, which he said was a railway track.

(2) His, which he said was another railway track.

These two drawings revealed his main interest, which is railways, which he plays with his friend. His sisters play at dressing up.

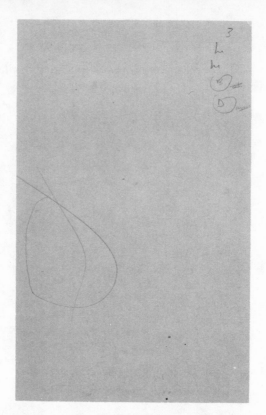

(3) His, which he said might have been a B, but it became a D. B would stand for badness.

(4) His, which I turned into a kind of bird, perhaps a bat (bad bird).

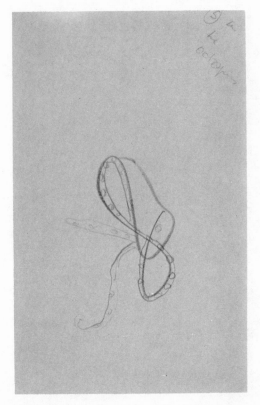

(5) Mine. He turned this into an octopus, and the important
thing was that one of the loops came back to the octopus
and had no end to it rather like the railway line that he
always is using.

I interpreted this as a kind of thumb-sucking on the part of the
octopus, which is of course covered with suckers. He said that he
was never a thumb-sucker, but he volunteered the information
immediately that what he did was to suck a horrible filthy dirty
rag called Tissie. Eventually his mother could stand it no longer
and she burned it and he cried a lot till he forgot it. It had holes
in it because of his biting and constant sucking. It was a floor
cloth.

(6) His drawing of Tissie, showing two of the holes. He clearly remembers at the age of one, as he said, taking it out of a bucket while his mother was cleaning the floor, and from then onwards it was always 'my Tissie'.

(7) His drawing of himself at 1 year taking the rag out of the bucket. He was very surprised indeed to find that he had a dress on, and it seemed that he had reached to a deep memory.

He was now ready to talk about nightmares.

(8) His picture of a house on fire in a dream.

I interpreted this as sexual excitement and he understood because he gets an erection associated with the dream. At this point I gave him some sex information for which he was longing. I told him to go and ask his father if he wanted to know more.

His other nightmare was of burglars who steal jewels and he said he could not draw, so I was prepared to leave this aside. But he said: 'Can you draw a burglar getting into a house?'—and he was obviously wanting to go further. I carefully hid what I was doing so that he could also be drawing a burglar getting into a house.

(9) My drawing, which I kept out of his sight while he got on with his own version of the theme.

(10) His drawing. I was able to point out that the pistol that broke the glass was a picture of his erect penis. I said that as he was not yet able to have the emission that belongs to grown-up men he has to use the magic of the pistol shot.

We then looked at the three drawings. Here was a hole in the window from the pistol shot. I joined this up with the first thing he said to me, which was that his garden brightens a dark patch. I then said: 'You see at first you were a baby and you loved mother and you bit the holes in the Tissie. One day you will be a grown-up man like Daddy and you will marry and have children. Now you are half-way between. You love someone and you dream of the house burning up because it feels so exciting. And you shoot your way in because there is no emission, and instead of giving babies you steal the jewels.' I went on: 'There is someone you love when you are dreaming these dreams', and he said: 'I think it's Mummy.' So I said: 'Well, if you were a burglar and you got into the house you would have to knock down Father.' He said: 'Well, I would not like to do that.' I said: 'No, because you are fond of him too and sometimes because you are fond of him you wish you were a girl.' He said: 'Only a little tiny bit.'

We then got on to the very difficult relationship with the sister. From the parents' point of view he is actively and violently jealous. He described what happens between them and I said: 'Well, it looks to mother and father as if you and your sister are jealous of each other, and I would say you are jealous of her for being a girl, and she is jealous of you for being a boy. At the same time you are in love with each other, and as you are not grown-up the nearest you can get to making love is to pester each other and fight.'

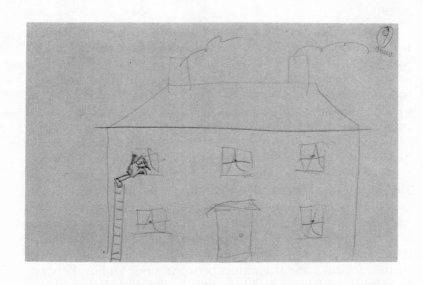

He seemed very relieved about all this, and decided that he had finished all that we wanted to do and that it was time to go, with which I fully agreed.

The important moment in this psychotherapeutic consultation was when Robert was surprised to find himself in a dress when he took the Tissie out of the pail. At this point he was back in the original situation, and probably not much older than 1 year.

Of comparable importance was the link that I was able to make between the words: 'It brightens up a dull patch' with Robert's sense of responsibility for his mother's depressive phases, especially the one that affected all the children when Robert was 6.

A third detail of importance was the separating out of the love of father and the identification with the girl (or woman) that goes with this, from the rivalry with father that belongs to the boy's (heterosexual) love of his mother. This makes free the other matter, which is the friendship between a boy and his father or between boys that is possible in health, and that is a natural sublimation of normal or healthy homosexuality.

I consider that this boy was very much needing an objective statement of the home situation, which the parents were not able to give him. I felt that the interview might well be a healing one for him because of what he was ready for and because I was not dealing with illness. At the end he said to me: 'I don't suppose you can answer this one. When I'm away from school, like half-terms, I don't want to go back, and then when I go back I like it very much indeed.' I had the material for the answer to this question and I said to him: 'You see, when you are at home you love your mother and you love being with her, but more important than that, you have to deal with the fact that she is unhappy and most of the time rather depressed.' He said: 'Yes, and she worries such a lot when I and my sister fight.' I said: 'When you are at home you wonder how mother will manage when she has not got you to worry about. When you get to school you get away from mother's anxieties and worries and depressions and you are able to forget them and then you are able to enjoy school.' I laid special emphasis again on the need that he had to take his time over things and to see to it that nobody rushes him. If he is rushed he just cannot manage. Actually at school he had been greatly helped by being allowed to stay two years in one class, although this had made him feel awful because his sister had gone up two classes all at once.

He went away from me with the feeling that there is a natural growth in everything. He said: 'My electric train has a certain speed; you switch it on or off; you can't make it go faster although of course you could make it go slower by the use of a transformer.'

It will be necessary to ask the parents to try to lift from this child the burden of their own religion, morality, and anxieties, if possible. I have no doubt whatever that he has it in him, if left to himself, to make a good job of life.

A tentative appointment was made for a second visit, but the mother rang up to say that she would like to postpone this as the boy seemed very much relieved after his visit. When he came out of the door he was obviously very pleased with the result of the consultation and he said, as if he could hardly believe it, 'We even talked about Tissie.'

Naturally I communicated with the parents, giving my view that they were tending to forget that this boy has his own innate processes, his own speed of development and his own capacity for eventually making a social contribution as well as a good life for himself. The parents themselves have a rather set religious and cultural pattern derived from their own upbringing, and they were really quite relieved to be reminded that they need not plant this on the child. On the other hand, of course, it is helpful to the child that there is a definite setting in which he is developing and which he can use or reject according to his own growing personal philosophy.

As a result of the consultation there was a new attitude of the parents towards the school, and the boy was now allowed to take his own time over things without anyone fussing him. The consequence was that there was a quite marked clinical improvement. Robert is still backward in reading and he has a considerable reading inhibition which distresses him, but the parents are not worrying him about it. He actually asked his parents to get out a library book for him, but they could not take it for granted that he would read it. I think the parents became more prepared than they were previously to find the boy reading low literature (comics) like the other boys at the school. The jealousy of the sister continued and he and she fight a good deal, but sometimes they seem to be on good terms. The idea of this boy as a problem seems to have died down.

Comment

I have described a very simple case. I think a point is that this child might have been your child or mine. Perhaps the most important result of the consultation was that the parents had met psycho-analysis in the sense of having consulted a psycho-analyst. They had naturally been wondering whether a psycho-analyst would say: 'Your child is very ill and if you do not provide psycho-analytic treatment for him now he will be a failure and it will always be your fault because the emotional difficulties of adults always have their roots in the childhood era.' I did not advise psycho-analysis, which in any case was not available.

It was very important for me to find the normality rather than the illness in this case although this meant that I had to pull out for inspection the abnormalities in the parents and in the school situation. I particularly drew attention to our system whereby we may require children of 11 years old to show that they can swot for an examination.

The danger of this kind of case-description is that it avoids the whole huge subject of the emotional development of the individual, a continuous process starting from birth or just before birth. It is not possible, however, to do more than give a reminder of the vastness of this subject even in so far as we know about it at the moment. As I have already said, this subject of dynamic psychology has the dimensions of physiology.

On the positive side I have chosen this case because it introduces an aspect of child psychology which one can immediately follow up and use. This is represented here by the Tissie. I have referred to these very early objects employed by infants as *transitional objects* and I have given reasons for the use of such a name.[1] There is a vast amount to learn from a study of the use of transitional objects and it is almost true that in every case-history the positive and negative aspects of the transitional objects and their use provide important information. Moreover, not only do parents like to remind themselves, which they do if they are given time, of these early infantile techniques, but also children get back to their infancy by the route of the transitional object more easily than by any other route.

In regard to the psycho-analysis of this child, I want to make it

[1] 'Transitional Objects and Transitional Phenomena' (1951), in *Collected Papers*, Tavistock, 1958.

quite clear that if these parents could afford and could easily manage a five times a week treatment over a long period, I would advise psycho-analysis, not because the child is very ill but because there are enough troubles to make a treatment worth while, and the more normal a child is the more rich and quick is the result. Experience makes me know that we would find a good deal of illness in this boy as well as health in the course of psycho-analytic treatment. The child is, however, not in any way a psychotic child. There is a depressive tendency, but this would turn out to be more related to the burden of the mother's depression than to the child's own anxieties of depressive type. The boy has passed through all the early emotional developmental stages well enough and is not liable to psychotic breakdown. His problems are in the rich field of interpersonal relationships and of the bringing together of the two types of relationship, the affectionate and that which rides on waves of instinct. In my remarks to this boy I brought in sexual matters, and in dealing with children who are developing well we fail if we cannot follow the children wherever they lead. This child had a conflict of an ordinary kind in regard to his love of his father, and alongside this his hate of him which belongs to the dream in which his instincts are directed towards the mother. Complicating the situation is the boy's hereditary resemblance to the father, which makes an identification with the father a tempting way out of this dilemma.

Thus we get a quite good picture of the situation from letting this case take its own course without trying to force it into a framework which would give a more complete case-history. There is much that we would like to know. We could try to work at the case and have the answer to everything written down; but in fact if we want to know more than we know through this consultation we can only do it usefully through the analysis of the child, in the course of which the world of the child would become displayed before us. Otherwise we may as well leave it as it is. The parents have shared their anxieties with me in a professional way, and if fresh troubles arise the parents will naturally tend to come back to me rather than to brood over them in an unuseful way at home.

Follow-up

After two years Robert went to boarding-school and he enjoyed this. After three years the parents reported :

He continues to do well. Excellent (school) reports (boarding-school). Nice to sister in holidays, even generous to her. Could be said to be a normal boy doing well. Has passed through some crisis associated with temporary strain at home.

Later By the time of his coming of age he had found a girl-friend, and he seemed to be going ahead towards independent adult status. His learning difficulty has gone and he reads normally.

CASE VI [1] 'Rosemary' *aet* 10 years

This child was seen once, and in her personal interview she found a clue to her symptoms. She was brought because of 'black fits of depression'. She also had blinding headaches, nausea and photophobia, lasting two or three days and sending her to bed. She had lately become withdrawn. Along with this was a bad temper in the morning.

All these symptoms cleared up when she arrived at the drawing of the dream in which her mother got run over.

Rosemary is one of two children in a good working-class family.

The interview was as follows. There were two visitors and two Psychiatric Social Workers present. This was a routine clinic case.

Rosemary started drawing[2] and showed some ability.

    (1) She drew a girl.

    (2) We then played squiggles and she turned my squiggle into a head.

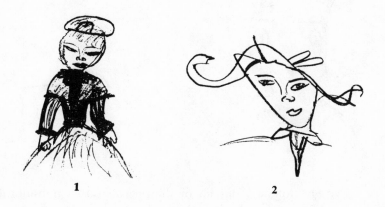

     1   **2**

[1] This case was first published in the *St. Mary's Hospital Gazette*, Jan./Feb. 1962, under the title 'A Child Psychiatry Interview'.

[2] Her original drawings are no longer available. They are reproduced here from the *St. Mary's Hospital Gazette*.

(3) Hers, which I turned into a landscape.

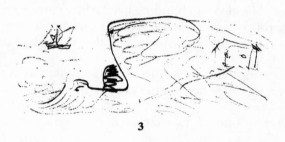

3

(4) She and I together turned her squiggle into Bruno which is a *transitional object* of hers.

4   **5**

(5) She followed this up by drawing an earlier transitional object, called Doggie; it is broken, and the drawing shows this.

She said her brother took her teddy. Her brother is nice and very naughty. She doesn't hate him but she gets very cross with him. She wanted a sister.

6

(6) Is her drawing of the brother?

Apparently her father draws cartoons with her, and some of her drawing technique is influenced in this way by her father.

She talked about nice dreams but she said: 'Last night I and two friends were in the tower waiting to be executed.'

7

8

(7) Is a bad dream of this kind?

She said at 5 years old (when her brother was 3) she had a horrible dream, which she drew.

(8) Her drawing. It was a wicked stepmother who broke the glass slipper, herself being Cinderella.

9

(9) Gives a picture of Cinderella. To some extent she is the Prince, although she would not want actually to be a man.

A sad dream would be a nightmare of mother getting killed.

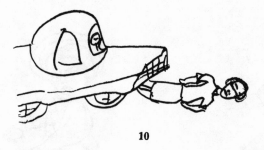

10

(10) Her drawing. She drew this with great intensity of feeling and very quickly, showing mother being run over by father's car.

I made an interpretation here about the hate between her mother and herself which makes sense in the context of the triangular situation with the father.

After this she was able to tell me about a weird dream.

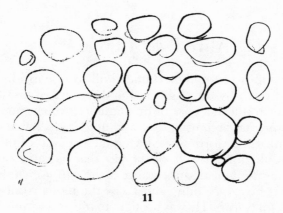

11

(11) Her drawing of a weird dream, showing bubbles coming
at her, making a funny noise like an ear-ache noise; they
are white. This dream is somewhat influenced by science-
fiction and links with the idea of comets and meteors which
presumably are met with in space.

I suggest that these white bubbles that make a funny noise give
a picture of a coming alive 'inside', following a phase of deadness 'inside' which is represented here by the dead mother of the
dream.

In this case the girl's depressive mood was the clinical manifestation of the death-wish towards her mother which was under
repression. This death-wish was experienced in the context of
strong positive feeling towards both parents, who together built
and maintained the good home that she lived in.

CASE VII 'Alfred' *aet* 10 years

This group of cases could be rounded off by one in which some light was thrown by the child on the dynamics of his stammer. This did not result in a cure of the stammer, which continued to vary according to circumstances as stammering is liable to do. It would seem to be worth while giving the material of this therapeutic consultation in spite of the fact that its value cannot be proved in terms of the disappearance of the symptomatology.

I saw this boy once only, and I saw the mother once. There was a sister of 6 years. He was brought to me on account of stammering. His father works in the office at a mental hospital. He was referred by a friend of the parents, but with the full knowledge and the goodwill of the general practitioner. The parents provide a satisfactory home. This consultation had to be fitted rigidly into the framework of one hour and ten minutes, that being exactly what I had to offer.

I went to the waiting-room and, making sure that the mother was agreeable, I took Alfred alone into my room and started to make contact with him, which was easy. He and I had a table between us and paper for drawing. As he answered some questions about his father and his father's work a stammer turned up, and I realised that I must not ask questions, because if I did he would gather himself together to give answers, and there would be a stammer. So I asked no more direct questions about environmental facts, and during the rest of the hour in which he was in my room there was practically no stammer. He agreed that we should play a game and I made a squiggle. I explained to him that in the squiggle game I make a squiggle which he turns into something, and then he makes a squiggle which I turn into something, and so the game develops. A game without rules.

(1) My squiggle which Alfred made into a face. First he said it looked like a bee. As he drew the face he named each feature. I noticed while he was doing this rather deliberate work that every time he breathed out *he made a little push with his breath. This occurred throughout the hour.* Eventually I talked about it with him and it proved to be a significant feature.

110

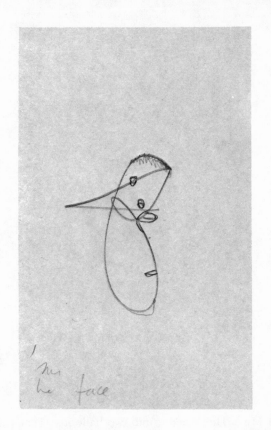

(2) His, which I made into a man's bow-tie.

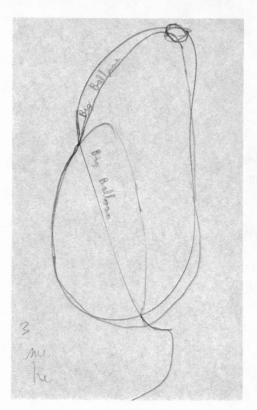

(3) Mine. He turned it into two balloons. 'That's all I can do,' he said, as if I might expect more of him. (The significance of this remark was hidden at this early stage.)

(4) Mine, which he said was like a treble-clef sign, and so he left it at that, without altering it or adding to it.

(5) Mine, which he turned into a fish, and he rather enjoyed himself doing this one.

This sequence already indicates, I suggest, how contact between two people is made in this way, and I made a note that he was now quite at ease. I was making notes on the back of the pieces of paper which we let fall on the floor when finished with; there is an advantage in this squiggle technique in that one has time to make notes while the drawing is going on, and the drawings themselves provide a valuable record.

(6) His. He was rather pleased with this one, which I turned into a road-sign for motorcars (this was a sort of superego symbol, but I did not do this deliberately; it just occurred to me to do that on the basis of his squiggle).

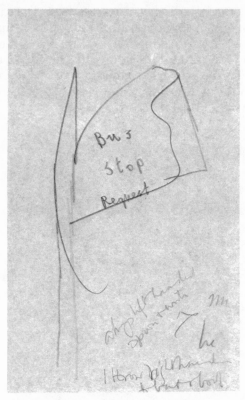

(7) Mine. I said: 'Oh, I think that's impossible', but he said: 'Oh, I dunno; I've got one, I think.' Then he went on and made a request bus-stop sign, following on with the idea that I had already given him.

At this point I talked about his writing left-handed and he said he had always written that way, and he used a spoon with his left hand when he was little. In cricket he throws and bats and bowls with his right hand. 'It's funny, isn't it?' he said. (When I enquired he said that nobody had ever tried to make him use his right hand. I made this enquiry because of the theory that if a child is made to use the right hand when he naturally uses the left this may cause a stammer, but it did not seem to apply here).

114

(8) Mine. I said that I thought it was too complicated. 'Oh, I dunno; if I turn it round till I find it; oh, I've got an idea, I'm trying to make it into a lady's hat, a sort of bonnet. I'll put someone's head in it.' And he put into the bonnet the head of a lady with long hair.

One of the aims in this game is to reach to the child's ease and so to his fantasy and so to his dreams. A dream can be used in therapy since the fact that it *has been dreamed and remembered and reported* indicates that the material of the dream is within the capacity of the child, along with the excitements and anxieties that belong to it.

At this point I began to talk about dreams. He said: 'Oh, I dream about things I've been doing. I'll do a squiggle with my right hand.' He seemed rather pleased about that idea.

115

(9) His, done with his right hand. I turned this into a witch with a broom and a hat. So then he talked about racing cars and dreaming about racing cars, but while he was doing that he turned

(10) mine into a racing track with a grandstand, and with people in the grandstand. 'Yes [he said], I do have frightening dreams. *A few years ago I had one.*'

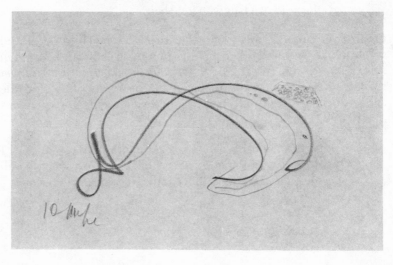

While he was telling me this I was turning

(11) his squiggle into some kind of complex face. He had given me a muddle of lines and it could have been anything or nothing (he deliberately made it a muddle of lines and looked at me while he was doing it), so I said: 'That's a muddle, isn't it!' He had intended that it should be a muddle, and a challenge to me, and I worked it into a face.

We were still liable to get a delayed response to my query about dreams. It will be observed that my questions about dreams have as their aim an extension of my ordinary interest in him to an interest in his deeper self.

Now he told me the dream of a few years ago. 'Witches came and took me away.'

I said: 'How funny I did that drawing about witches.'

At this point I began to wish I had not drawn the witch, because the idea was perseverating, and I feared lest the boy's personal process had been distorted, in which case I would not reach to the area of principal distress which I was seeking.

> He said: 'Oh no, that's nothing to do with this. This is a frightening dream that I had a few years ago which I've never forgotten.'

> (12) His drawing which illustrates the story in the dream. The witch comes in at the open window and takes him out to a den like a coal-mine.

> *He said that when he had this dream several times he was about 6½ or 7 years old. He told me the year; he knew this, he said, because it was then that the family moved from another town to the place where the father now works.*

This illustrates the way in which the child's account of the past-history takes the psychiatrist to the period of strain, and gives him opportunity for accurate understanding.

> He said that life was now quite nice, that he enjoyed himself, but he was sad to leave his old home because it had a bigger garden, and as it was not near main roads he was more free to play. He missed the freedom of it all now.

At this stage I did not know that he was also referring to freedom from anxiety related to a specific event.

> I said: 'Perhaps the witch was taking you back to the old town or house.'

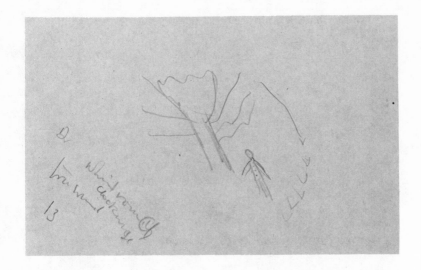

This was not meant as a psycho-analytic interpretation but it was a comment that the witch *might* be taking him from something to something in a significant way.

> He told me then about his two grandmothers, each of whom had died, and about his grandfather, who still lived in the house with them. I tried to find out what was difficult about that time when he was 6½ or 7 and *he was not able to tell me*. It did not seem that he was sufficiently disturbed by leaving the old house to need the witch to take him back or to take him away from the present one. He was quite clear about one thing, however, that this (recurring) dream belonged to the particular time round about 6½.

> He then told me about another dream that he dreamed at this stage.

> (13) This drawing illustrates the other dream although, as he said: 'You can't draw this . . . there are a lot of arrows coming round to the right . . .' In the dream he is whirled round and round clockwise, as if rolled over in bed. 'It's not really a frightening dream.'

After this, at my request, he drew the next one.

(14) This is his drawing of the place the witch took him to, the
coal-mine. There is a fire in the coal-mine, and the witch
has pots and pans on the shelf; she has a pointed hat and
she has a tail. She can be seen sitting on a three-legged
stool.

This is a dream that is full of symbols that belong to myth and
fairy-story: the three-legged stool, the fire, the tail, the witch
with tall hat: the pots and pans indicating something cooking or
being concocted, and the darkness, indicating the unconscious.
The whole thing goes right down to deep unconscious material,
but not of course to the deepest; the deepest unconscious material
is indescribable. As soon as one has found ways of describing it
one has left the deepest layers. Society offers names, verbalisation, fairy-story and myth to the child to help him or her to deal
with the unnamed fears that belong to the unnameable.

I asked whether the witch was likely to eat him (because of
the pots and pans and the fire and so on) and he said: 'I
don't know, I wake at that point. The trouble about telling
you these dreams is that if I have a dream and it goes
horrible, then I wake.' He added: 'Sometimes I would like
to go on with it and find out what was horrible, instead of
waking'; and then he laughed at himself, saying again that
he would rather go on and be frightened than wake.

I was being invited to take him to the worst, if only I could find out how to do so.

> At this point I talked about his breathing tension. I said that all the time that he had been drawing, although he did not seem to be making a great effort, yet he was pushing with his breath every time he breathed. He was able to recognise that this was true. I said: 'I wonder what it is that you are trying to do so hard all the time?'
>
> He had no idea. He now talked about his stammer. He said: 'Because when I try it's then that I stutter. If I don't try then I'm all right. It's like here, I'm not trying at all and I'm not stuttering. It's if I don't know, perhaps, then I try hard, and then I stutter. If I don't know something well . . .' But he seemed puzzled.
>
> I said: 'It's as if you've got steam[1] up and you're trying hard, and you don't know why you have to make such an effort.'
>
> To my surprise he said: 'It's a re-iteration.' (I don't know where he had heard this word.) He went on: 'It's only started recently.'
>
> We talked about school, where he had been trying hard. I said: 'It sounds, too, as if you are trying to pass faeces. It took a long time for us to get a common language here. The word 'shit' was no good. Eventually we reached the family term 'go to the lavatory', the nearest we could get to a naming of the act of defaecating. (Indicating a family pattern of denial of anal-phase matters.)
>
> He then said: 'I'd like to stop to try hard.'
> Then he did the next squiggle.

[1] It was still in the days of steam engines.

(15) His, in doing which he was very free, and he turned his
own squiggle into a drawing.

It is always satisfactory when a child uses his or her own
squiggle, so that there is a drawing which is entirely personal.
Such a drawing done by a child and based on the child's own
squiggle is quite different from any drawing that he or she would
do as a drawing or a picture.

> Here was a man with a violin case which has a strap round
> it. Alfred's father plays the violin. He was rather pleased
> about having done this all himself, but I was not able to
> use the specific material in the drawing. I said to him: 'If
> you don't try, one thing you have to do is to take a risk,
> and of course it might be that nothing would happen at
> all.'

The contact had now come to an end and had lasted an hour;
Alfred was quite satisfied to go to the waiting-room while I had a
brief talk with his mother. I knew that I had failed to discover the
clue, but I had something important to lead me towards it,

namely *the special state that the boy was in at the age of 6½, at the time of the dream of the witch taking him away.*

Actually the next quarter of an hour was rather dramatic in this case. I now saw the mother and explained to her that I had purposely given up the time to the boy. I had about eight minutes with her. She seemed to me to be a rather pleasant woman and someone who liked to be a wife and a mother and to run a home. She told me that Alfred had been starting to stammer recently. No-one tried to make him work hard, or to use his right hand, and she agreed with Alfred that the difficulty must come from within himself. He had won a scholarship recently and she said that it was in himself that there was this anxiety to do well, and to try hard all the time.

I told her that I had formed an opinion that this boy had been through a difficult time after the move from the old house to the place where they lived now, that is to say, at the time when his father changed his job. I said: '*I am sure that we must get to what happened when this boy was 6½.*'

The mother said: 'Did he tell you that at that time his father had a mental breakdown? You see, his father found his new job exacting, *and he got caught up in a tremendous effort to succeed,* and this made him obsessional and he became a case of agitated depression. The father was worrying all the time, and he went into hospital as a patient for a few months.'

I said that I was sure that this could be the clue to Alfred's illness. As we now had only three minutes left I asked her to let me see Alfred again for a moment and then to take him home, and to write me a letter letting me know what sort of reactions he might have to the visit. She agreed to all this quite easily.

I had Alfred back in the room, and he sat in a chair. I said: 'I've been talking things over with your mother and I asked her about the time when you were 6½, the time when you said you had nightmares. Do you remember that just then Father had a sort of illness, a breakdown?'

Alfred's head suddenly went back and he jerked himself into a memory of this illness of his father *which he had completely forgotten.* He looked immensely relieved. I said: 'You see you've been trying all this time, not because of your own need to try, and you have told me that things go better if you don't try. *You've been trying hard on your father's account,* and you are still going on trying to cure father of this worry about his work when he couldn't do it

123

well enough. So that's why you push every time you breathe out, and as you told me, it's this pushing and trying that interferes with all your work and your talking, and that makes you stutter.'

At this point we parted and he went off with his mother, seeming to be quite happy and at ease.

Interview with Mother

Two months after the interview with Alfred I saw the mother and gave her an hour to herself. (The evolution of this interview has an interest of its own but it would be out of place for me to describe it in detail here and now.)

In the history of Alfred's case as obtained from the mother attention was drawn to earlier compulsions in Alfred's life, including a form of compulsive eroticised moving about, which started when Alfred was $1\frac{1}{2}$ years old and which was at its worst when he was 3. It seems to have started along with walking. There were various kinds of compulsive activities so that the mother constantly found herself saying: 'Relax, Alfred.' Now this drive took the form of working too hard at school, when no-one was pressing him or expecting him to do more than he could easily manage. (He was not pressed in the matter of toilet training.)

All these details would be important if the aim were to arrange for a long-term psychotherapy; the history as taken from the mother could not, however, have given the clue to the crisis in Alfred's life when he was $6\frac{1}{2}$. This clue, given by the boy, enabled me to see that the special effort was on father's behalf and belonged to father's mental breakdown.

The mother was able to give a clear account of the way that the father's illness impinged on Alfred when he was 5 years old. There was indeed a crisis which Alfred witnessed, and this was followed by the father's hospitalisation, his obsessional neurosis having gone over into an agitated depression. In fact it was at this point Alfred had started to stammer.

The mother reported that as he left me after my interview with him he said: 'You know, I'd completely forgotten that time when Daddy was ill', and he seemed relaxed and relieved. A few weeks later, when my name came up in conversation, he said: 'That doctor was bang-on.'

Result

My therapeutic consultation with Alfred had an effect both on

Alfred and on his mother. On the principle: how little need be done? there was no need for me to do any more. The stammering ceased to be a problem, and the boy became released from some of his compulsion to make excessive effort.

One more detail concerns the meaning of the last drawing. It transpired that Alfred's father has a general sense of frustration because he is involved in an administrative office job and has had to suppress his need to be creative. He has a violin, and the strap round the violin represents the fact that the father has not been able to develop his musical interests. It could be said this way, that if I could undo the strap of his father's violin, then his father could be creative and could get into contact with his deeper self; then, with the father happier, Alfred would be able to give up pushing and overstraining in a hopeless attempt to boost his father's effort to make a success of a hated routine job that is the reverse of creative. I did not understand this at the time that Alfred made the drawing, and therefore I had no opportunity for making this comment. However, it was unnecessary for me to verbalise this, since the boy's recovery of the memory of his father's illness produced the required effect. The good effect of the therapeutic consultation has lasted one year, and if new troubles arise the mother will bring Alfred to see me again, as is appropriate in the limited field of child psychiatry.

Further Comment

The mother said: 'You know, the improvement in Alfred started not when you saw him, but a week earlier, in fact, it started the moment I knew I was coming to see you.' This may well be true, and in child psychiatry it is quite usual for symptomatic improvement to be related to the mother's or the father's change-over from hopeless bewilderment to hopefulness. Nevertheless it is also necessary for the child's psychiatrist to be able to do the job that presents itself at the time of the interview.

Summary

A therapeutic consultation is described which illustrates the use made of history-taking through the child. History-taking in this context does not mean the collecting of facts; it means that the psychiatrist makes contact with the child in such a way that the process in the child leads the psychiatrist towards a significant area of distress.

Follow-up

Seven years later the mother reports, in response to my enquiry, that Alfred's stammer 'causes very little inconvenience these days'. Nevertheless in certain circumstances it threatens to reappear, and he says he has disliked telephoning.

His development has been steady, and he likes to act and to give talks at a Youth Centre. He seems to have no fear of the university entrance exams, and it is his own plan to read law.

The mother adds that he seems well balanced, enjoying the occasional dance and social event, mixing quite well with others of his own age.

It is not my claim, of course, that the one interview produced all this, which is a mixture of the boy's growth process and of the family provision and management. But when he came to see me he did need help, and he got it.

Part Two

INTRODUCTION

The therapeutic consultations described in this, the second, part will involve the same principles of technique as those in the first part. The reader who is probably doing somewhat similar work will be prepared now for cases in which the issues are more complex. Certainly in some of the cases the background issues have great complexity. Nevertheless in the total working out of a family or social situation there seems to have been a place for the one or perhaps three interviews in which a communication is made with one child. A communication of this kind that I am describing differs from that which is made in the familiar home setting, as between children and parents and among the children themselves. It is also, of course, quite different from the communication that takes place between the child and the teacher at school.

In several of the cases other agencies are at work helping either other children or perhaps the parents themselves, so that the therapeutic consultation as described needs to be thought of as simply one of many things happening in a wider casework issue. It often happens, however, that parents become able to cope with their own problems and the problems of the family when relieved just to the extent that a loosening up in the child's defences follows the therapeutic consultation. In some cases, of course, even where the child makes very good use of the therapeutic consultation, there is no outcome, and this usually means that the problems of the parents or the family were the main issues, the child being caught up in a sick family situation and presenting symptomatology which, although seeming to belong to the child, really does belong to the family. All these are familiar issues in social work involving families.

Once again here in these cases is illustrated not so much a new idea as one example after another of communication with the child, sometimes useful and almost always providing the student or a group of students with material for consideration and discussion. Often big issues are involved which lead the student on to the theories or to the basic theory as accepted at the present time concerning the emotional development of the individual in the given environment.

Attention is drawn again to the fact that in this type of case-presentation the reader, that is to say the student, knows as much about the case as the psychiatrist knows, and therefore is not at a disadvantage in discussion. The student must be at a disadvantage if the psychiatrist has a great deal of information up his sleeve which he has not been able to give because of matters of time and space.

It should be noted that these cases, although representing all kinds of diagnostic types, do not contain illustrations of the anti-social tendency. The reason for this is that I present a group of cases illustrating the relationship between the antisocial tendency and deprivation in the third section of this book.

CASE VIII 'Charles' *aet* 9 years

The following case illustrates the way in which the understanding of a detail was necessary. The main principles hold, that the child gradually gets a sense of the emotional climate in the interview and unfolds himself. This boy had been referred by a colleague who also had an interview with him, and a Child Guidance Clinic had not succeeded in making useful contact.

Family History

Sister   11 years.
Himself   9 years.
Sister   7 years.
     Family intact.

This boy complained of headaches and of 'thoughts'. It was his mind that was troubling him and he was beginning to have ideas about his thinking apparatus. He had said that one bit of his brain was taking over the rest of him. He had started to make vows and he tried to keep them, but these vows made no difference even when he swore by the Bible.

We settled down to the squiggle game.

(1) Mine, which he turned into a fish.

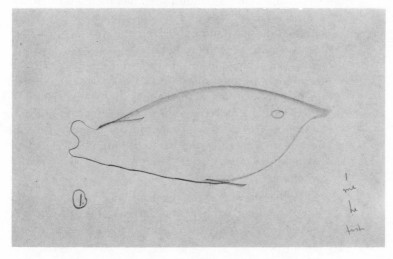

(2) His, which was in three parts, and I turned it into a land-scape.

(3) Mine, which he turned into what he called a girl, 'because she has a skirt'. 'It's probably my [7-year-old] sister.' We talked about girls and I asked if they were lucky to be girls. He said: 'No, I would not like to be one. We have awful fights.' While he said this he was breathing hard. He went on: 'There is one rule: "DON'T HIT GIRLS!" but this doesn't apply when I am fighting my sister.' He talked about having a governess for some lessons and not going to school. This is an arrangement made at the wise instigation of my colleague who had seen him. He is glad about having this holiday from school, though he does love swimming.

(4) His. While drawing this squiggle he talked about fights and how they don't happen when he has only got one sister with him. It is only when they are all three there that the fighting starts up.

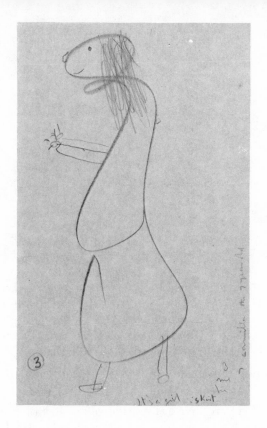

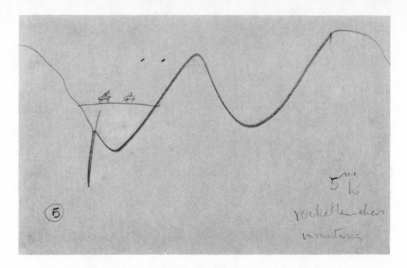

(5) Mine. He turned it into mountains with rocket launchers. There is a big platform. He is fond of rockets but they are top secret so probably he will have to fly a 'plane instead. He said: 'I like battleships', and he talked about war. In his room he draws on the floor with chalk.

At the time I had no notion that he was already talking about his mind.

There are four or five nationalities and a lot of minefields and little roads, one for each nationality. He described the intricacies of mine-detecting and the war in which each nationality has to get back to base, or perhaps there may be no roads. He has got hundreds of soldiers and mortars and grenades, and while describing his games to me he made all the appropriate noises belonging to these and to rifles. He has a grenadier with a bazooka. Of the Russians only one has a mortar. And so on.

(6) His drawing of his game that he plays on the floor at home.

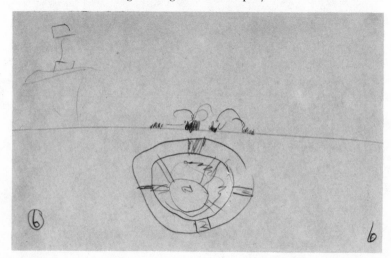

I used the material of this drawing, joining it up with his first remarks which were about his mind. I told him quite dogmatically that he was giving me a picture of his mind with the various compartments. The mind represented all the mustnots, and in the game the bad was attacking the good. In quite a natural way he helped me along with this interpretation. He said: 'It is like a switch and when it is on it starts up everything.' He added: 'Only a tiny bit of the brain is in control of the limbs.' He feels controlled by this tiny bit when it is switched on.

(7) A further drawing of the same game and also, as he now consciously intended, a diagram of his mind.

By this time we had reached to a communication which he had needed to make but which he could not make except to a person who understood that his diagrams on the floor and his war games were for him diagrams of the mind.

We continued with the squiggles.

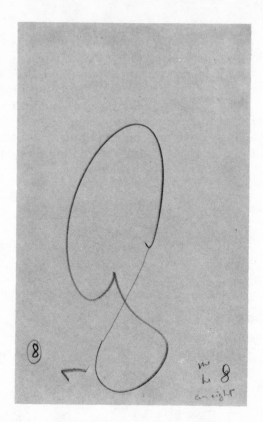

(8) Mine. He said this was like an 8, and a 7, and a 9 too. I reminded him that he had said that he would like to be 9, but
he said that 14 would be best because he would have left
school by then. He would get a super car. He would not be
working. That would be the best time of life 'or possibly 16
so that I could play'. He then went over school life. 'School
is $9\frac{1}{2}$ hours working out of the 12. It ought to be 4 hours'
play. You only get 4 months' holiday as compared with
8 months' school time every year.' He seemed very much
burdened by this thought, the thought of play-time
obstructed.

One can see from this that here was a boy whose intellect could
be exploited. He could be helped a little by being given opportunity for playing, but the question would arise as to whether he
would be able to play and to leave the management of his mind
alone.

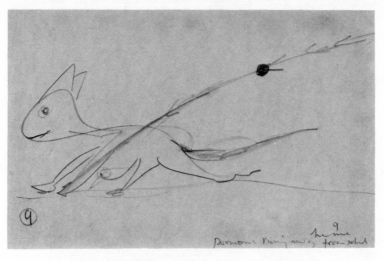

(9) His, which I turned into an animal running, and he said it
was someone running away from school.

I then asked him about dreams. He said he had a lot and
they were all in colour. 'They are all nasty and some are
doubly nasty. There is a spider very vividly coloured which
is more than nasty.'

(10) He told me to draw a mosquito and then he drew something on the top of it which would have very vivid colour-
ing in the dream, a gigantic spider or daddy-long-legs. He
was anxious even telling about these things. He told me
about his fear of daddy-long-legs and spiders. 'When you
are abroad these can be poisonous. I don't mind tiny ones
but some have long bodies and wings and those are the
ones that come into the dreams. Sometimes between waking
and the end of the dream there is a flash and then there's
someone looking at me. It is always the same woman and
then I wake. It's awful. I can't draw her.'

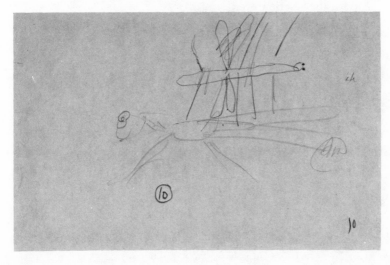

(11) He did, however, manage the shape of the head and the hair down the back. The frightening woman has long black hair. 'Yes, it could be Mother.'

(12) His squiggle which looked like an erect penis, but he turned it first into a finger, and then into a 'plane. He said: 'It is not well drawn.' The squiggle was so much like an erect penis that I asked him about his own organ and he said: 'It stretches.' He added: 'I can't talk about this.' I asked him if he had ever talked about his penis and he said: 'This is the first time ever.'

(13) His, which was deliberately muddled, and I managed to make it into something like a 'plane, letting his conscious idea perseverate.

(14) Mine, which he made into a bomb.

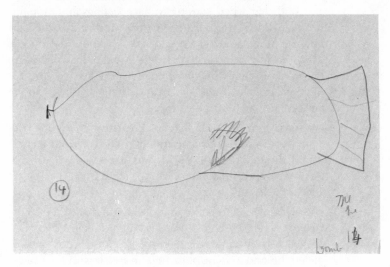

(15) His. He quite deliberately made a muddle and I now went
on with the interpretation which I had started earlier. I
said: 'This again represents your mind. The other drawing of the mind was an attempt to organise it into compartments when really the trouble is that you are in a
muddle.' (Acute confusional state.) He agreed about this
and said that when starting to have feelings and thoughts
it was awful. He told Father to tell Mother and then she
told the other doctors. He said he knew about the muddle
which he split into two parts. The losing part is bigger. All
the thinking bit is on the winning side. The smaller bit is
in control of the limbs, etc. (some details lost here, and in
any case he had a variable theory).

I wanted him to know that his great fear that he carries
round with him is of being totally confused. I put a circle
round the muddle and said it was like spaghetti which I
was prepared to make into a meal. He was eager to go on
and said: 'It's my turn to squiggle again.'

(16) His, which was 'a terrible muddle', and I turned it into the
face of a man. He said it was Sir Walter Raleigh. Here in a
sense I was offering a reassurance of a distraction. Nevertheless he and I were both fully in touch with the central
theme of muddle and I was helping him to recognise and
to come to terms with the acute confusional state which is
his form of unthinkable anxiety, something that constantly
threatens him.

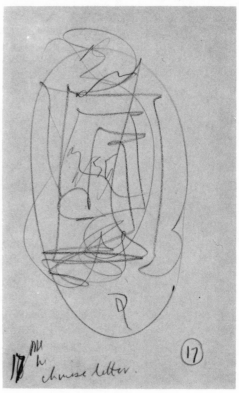

chinese letter.

(17) I made a muddle purposely and he saw it as a Chinese letter and so again he was making something out of a muddle. He said: 'I could have made this into spaghetti but that would be copying what you did with No. 15.'

I asked him about dreaming of a muddle. He began to tell me about such a dream but he yawned as if exhausted. He managed to say: 'In a dream like that I was walking near the school. A huge wave came and sucked me into the water. I shouted for help. I shouted "Llewellyn" twice. That was the name of the other boy in the dream.' Then he added: 'I didn't see the woman that time between sleeping and waking!' This was important to him because the woman comes so persistently into his frightening dreams. He said that the woman was there with the spider dream. Then he made the comment: 'Perhaps I was only 7 or even younger when I had this dream so the woman had not come yet.'

It was quite easy in the relationship to ask him here whether the dreams belonged to sexual excitement, masturbation, erections and so on, and he said: 'No, they don't.'

(18) His, and I turned it into a cat. This led him to talk about his mother's wedding anniversary because this happened to be the cat's birthday.

(19) Mine. He made it into what he called modern art.

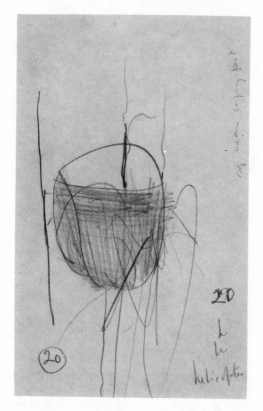

(20) His, and he made his own squiggle into a helicopter. He said it was a pot before it turned into a helicopter. Perhaps it was his need to get away from the pot that made me ask if he ever wet the bed, and he said: 'Yes, I do, because in the dream I am having I go to the lavatory. I have wet the bed once or twice that way.'

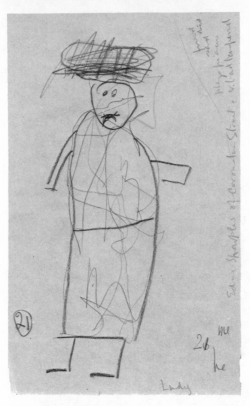

(21) Mine, which he seemed to find difficult. He said: 'I will
try.' After crossing out the top part he drew Ena Sharples
of Coronation Street (TV current series). The point about
Ena Sharples was, as he said, that her friend had died and
she was sad. Someone was very bad-tempered playing the
piano. He had now reached the idea of a bad temper and
this clue took him to *the memory of a cook* that they had had
at home who was very nasty to everyone, even to mother.
This cook evidently broke some of the children's toys, including his sister's calculating machine. 'Girls lose their
tempers. They get on my nerves.' He then started to describe the way that his sister forces people to come over on
to her side. He said: 'She invents sanctions such as: the
donkey will die if you don't . . . and the donkey did die of
pneumonia.'

I noted that he was very easily in touch with the concept of a
woman with magical powers like those of a goddess.

As it turned out, a secondary theme had appeared which was to have prime importance. In talking around the subject of squiggle No. 10, he referred to a special quality of the feelings that may belong to the moments between waking and the end of the dream. 'There's a flash, and then there's someone looking at me. It's always the same woman and then I wake. It's awful! I can't draw her.' I had no idea what could be the meaning or significance of this piece of acute self-observation. In (11) he did manage to catch something of what he saw—the shape of the head and the hair down the back. Long black hair.

In (15) the idea of an acute confusional state appeared, and I now see that this threat was associated with the fear of losing the hold on fact and on sequence in the memory system from which sense could be made of something that could not be understood by him at the time.

We went on with our experience of playing together, and then in (17), after telling me the dream, he made the observation that the woman was not there when he had this dream and when he woke from it. He now became able to place the dream, '7 or younger', and 'before the woman came'.

I still failed to understand, and I went ahead as if I had not heard.

Now in (21), by using the material of a current TV series, he reached to the idea of a bad-tempered cook, one who was nasty even to mother, and who seemed to him like the idea of a witch come true.

After the interview had ended I was able to find out from the mother about this woman, who seriously upset the household and who had to be sent away. Charles had correctly placed the trouble at the time just before he was 7 years old.

It was not until after the interview that I saw the acute confusional state as related to the presence of this woman, who was a witch from his point of view, and specifically when she was present at the time of his waking from a dream, especially an exciting dream producing an erection or a strong urge to micturate (see material of (12) and (7)). The confusion would be between dream material and the experience of life when awake.

This provides an interesting comment on the universal difficulty in human beings that is associated with waking from sleep, a subject that deserves study of the kind that is given to the more obvious difficulty at the time of going to sleep, just there where what I call transitional phenomena have significance. (This theme of waking from sleep recurs in the next case, that of Ashton.)

I felt that we had now come to the end of what we could do together in this one consultation, but as there was time to spare I took him over to the subject of what I call transitional objects.

> (22) He now drew his 'lovely teddy bear'. It had no eyes. He said: 'It is easy to draw this.' He told me that his mother had been afraid that the wires that held the eyes would hurt him so she took them out and that is why there were no eyes. He said, however, that he was so young at the time that he did not realise that there ever had been any eyes. He also told me about a very big teddy bear that his father seems to have retained with one leg off, and this he drew alongside his own. He also told me about one of his sisters and her addiction to little animals and how she sometimes adopts his teddy bear. In other words, he knew that we were talking about comforts that are available at moments of strain such as when one is going from the waking to the sleeping state.

Before stopping we talked a little about his relationship to his father. Here he was very definite. 'The two girls ought to leave father to me. They have got each other.' He obviously felt very much deprived in terms of father.

He then went over to a new version of the malignant goddess. He described how one of his sisters spoiled the whole day by losing the dog. She would spoil anything with ear-ache or something. His final statement was: 'I ought to have the best of father and I haven't got it. It's terribly boring.'

I saw the mother for a few minutes and I learned that my colleague had already wisely arranged for Charles to have a holiday from school.

Subsequent History

In the course of the next six months I saw Charles four times more, but the first interview remained the significant one, after which the parents became able to manage Charles' life and eventually to find the right schools for him.

Four years later when he was 13 I had a report that Charles was doing well at public school. It is necessary for me to omit detailed reference to the tremendous amount done for Charles

by the family and by the family doctor after my initial significant contacts with him. From the parents' point of view what they all did subsequently depended a great deal on Charles' communication with me in this first psychotherapeutic consultation and the lessening of the story of the threat of acute mental confusion.

The school magazine has recently published a poem by this boy which I have permission to reproduce on the next page:

'I have to live'

'I have to live,' they declared,

'But I don't want to live,' I said,

'They dragged me from the pond,
Gave me life,
But I want to die.'

'Nowadays everybody lives.'

'What's wrong with dying?' I said.

'Everything,' they said,
'It's nothing, blackness, evil,' they said.

'But it isn't,' I said,
'I want to die, I've done all I need,
Here I am a hindrance,
There, dead, I am gone.
I have fulfilled my purpose,
I want to see God,' I said.

'What is God?' they said.

CASE IX 'Ashton' *aet* 12 years

The next case that I wish to present provides an example of a therapeutic consultation which carried itself forward by its own momentum, and the boy and I reached surprising places. There was a significant result to this consultation in that the boy, who had become more and more blocked in his emotional development, and was developing into a schizoid personality, was able to go forward in his development. Both at home and at school he could now be helped.

In this case, a great deal depended on the result of the therapeutic consultation. Had this not been effectual, then, it would have been necessary for the boy to have been moved from his school and his good home environment and for him to be in someone else's care, living near a psychotherapist. The burden of the case would then have been a very heavy one to be borne by the psychiatrist or a team and special school, and of course paid for by the parents who would not have been able to understand what they were paying for. In fact the boy used the consultation in a productive way and became changed in that he now was able to make use of help that was actually available. The parents were easily able to pay for the work done by me and they were encouraged and indeed delighted to find themselves in the new position of being able themselves to offer effective help to their son and to gain the co-operation of the school.

If an attempt were made to give a psychiatric label to this case one would have to think in terms of incipient schizophrenia, but there is a limit to the value of labelling cases in child psychiatry and especially labelling children in the stages just before puberty and in early adolescence. The schizoid quality of the case rather rapidly disappeared from the clinical picture in the new phase that followed the work that the boy and I did together. This work as usual consisted in little more than communication, communication at all levels including a very deep level, communication made possible by the gradual development of the boy's trust in the quality of the professional setting which he met in my room.

Ashton was referred to me by his general practitioner, who wrote:

. . . exceptionally intelligent but unfortunately with most of the snags of the people who approach genius. He is very irritable, nervy and worried about his health. He invariably becomes ill and runs a temperature prior to returning to school. Recently he has developed habit spasms and has become rather difficult to manage at home. In addition he has been having great difficulty with sleep and a lot of trouble with nightmares . . . the parents' views on coping with the situation are opposed . . .

I saw Ashton first (except for a few minutes at the start when I saw him along with his parents). The interview lasted an hour and a half. At the end I saw the mother for two or three minutes, explaining only that I had not seen her because I had had to give the whole time to the boy.

Ashton turned out to be a very exceptional person, as a description of the course of the interview will show. He had a married sister who had two children; he was therefore an uncle.

Note. I give the minimum of information in order to make the case suitably disguised. Inevitably a great deal is lost by this, but the main features of the boy's communication remain clear.

It was not difficult to form a contact. I quickly got evidence of the fact that this boy has a high intelligence, and in fact this also applies to both parents and to the boy's sister. I had arranged paper in front of us, and Ashton and I started by playing squiggles.

(1) He turned my first squiggle into a fish.

(2) I turned his into a snake with a snake-charmer.

(3) He turned mine into a fish swallowing a turtle or a large jellyfish. He was very amused at the squiggles, which seemed to mean something special for him.

(4) I turned his into a kind of dog.

(5) He turned mine into a rabbit sitting down.

(6) I made his into a face.

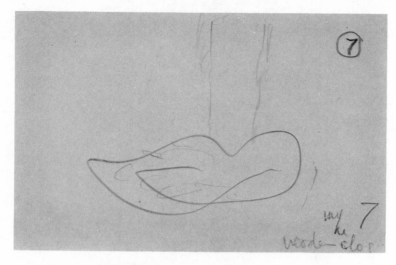

(7) He turned mine into a wooden clog.

(8) I made his into a pound sign.

(9) He turned mine into a bottle-opener.

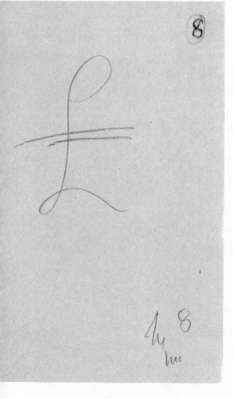

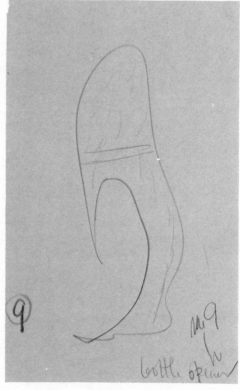

(10) I turned his into a kind of figure or doll and from this we
discussed objects that people take to bed with them to
keep them company. He told me about his having had two
teddies.

(11) He turned mine into a fish-head, like one in an advertisement he knew.

At this point I could introduce the idea of dreams. 'When you dream do you see things like that (fish-head)?'

So he drew.

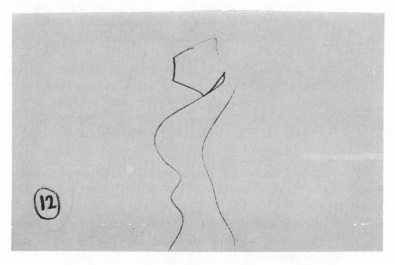

(12) A detail of 'a weird dream, very difficult to describe or to draw'. It is ghostly and moves. 'It tied me up with pieces of string. When I broke the string it looked at me rather nastily.'

In a way that is difficult to describe Ashton now took over the interview. He spoke in a highly sophisticated rather stilted way like a much older and even an erudite person. He operated, so to speak, through the intellect, and had a quick grasp of intellectual concepts and of the relationships between ideas.

Ashton went on to talk about his dreams and about nasty noises. 'You can't draw them; it might be as if a house were falling down.' 'Once I had a nasty experience. I was in bed and as I could not go to sleep I was listening to music, that is to say, going through a Beethoven symphony in my mind. I must have been half asleep because when there was a break in the music the next bit came as a weird noise instead of as the bit of music that was due.' This seemed to him to be a very frightening state of affairs and it was quite clear to me by this time that music meant a great deal to him because of the way that it deals with chaotic and unorganised noise. Music for him displaces hallucinations.

There was a pause here, and he recounted how in physics he once made a machine 'which was supposed to make sand pictures if you made a noise'. He went on to describe something that he said was very frightening. 'I turned over in bed and saw the curtains drawing themselves to and fro. The worst thing was that in the dream the curtains were left drawn to, but on waking I found they were *not* drawn to.' Then he said, as if to get away from the deep meaning of dreams: 'Dreams, you know, are often governed by the day-before happenings. For instance, the bathroom light went out so I had a dream the next night that the bathroom light went out.'

In this way he kept his escape lines open. After this we talked about music and painting as a way of getting control over hallucinations.

Then he said: 'Recently I did an abstract; it was a rather complicated painting but I will take this bit out of it to show you.' At this point he drew

(13) A detail that he chose to give me from the abstract painting.

(14) This is the whole of the abstract painting, and I know I could not have picked out the significant feature myself.[1]

As it turned out this was the main thing in the interview. I felt he had trusted me with something sacred, he had given me the clue to his abstract, although an abstract is by nature a secret hiding place as well as being a demonstration of a constellation in the artist's mind. I felt challenged at this point. Something had become due from me. I therefore ventured to make an interpretation, hoping it might be right to some extent. I knew I must speak in terms of primitive mental mechanisms and I said: 'It could be a representation of *simultaneous acceptance and refusal*.'[2]

Ashton was very excited about this interpretation. He exclaimed: 'When I drew this picture I had no idea it could mean anything. I know that it had to do with a picture I

[1] The parents sent this to me at a later date.
[2] I could have gone on to say that the object is himself, in between the opposing attitudes of the parents—see the letter from the referring doctor.

154

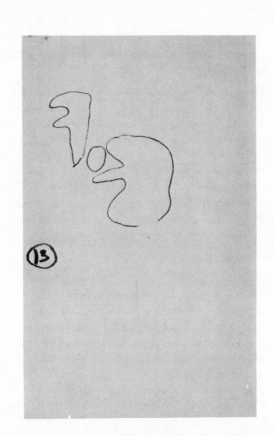

had seen the day before, of a monster with a lady on the tip of its tongue.'

Then I made another interpretation. I said: 'This painting that was the stimulus for the dream had a meaning for you, it had to do with your love of your mother which includes primitive features like eating her. The monster in fact is yourself.' I said that the object in the abstract could be the breast or the nipple, and that the simultaneous acceptance and refusal could be a conflict in him (Ashton) because of protecting the mother from being eaten and destroyed, because of his primitive love of her.

This was a long interpretation for me to make, and I hardly expected to be understood.

To my surprise Ashton said: 'I understand perfectly what you are saying, but it is new to me.' Then he went on to describe watching his baby nephew taking the bottle. I found he had not been told about breast-feeding (or he had not assimilated the knowledge) and he was very pleased to have the chance to discuss breast-feeding with someone. As if to clinch the matter he added: 'That reminds me of a story Father told some people, and I could not see why it was thought to be funny. This was of a small child who had said: "If I like something I eat it."'

Here I felt encouraged to go on talking, because of his exceptional grasp of ideas, and I gave him all I knew about the theory of oral sadism and early object relationships, including the beginnings of the sense of guilt arising out of the ruthlessness of primitive love feelings. I knew that he was interested and that he was using my little lecture.

Ashton was now eager to communicate freely about things that interested him. He told me of a dream in which there was a ghost in the house. To get rid of the ghost he used a magic formula which he was able to tell me exactly. Some of the words were familiar ('invisible', 'spurious', 'matured'); others were invented words. I could not make accurate notes of this formula.

Next he told me of an earlier dream in which there was a car travelling along with a man in it. 'There was another man in the car, either in front or behind, and one man attacked the other. I rushed to his aid. *The frightening thing was that I realised that both the men were myself.'*

I knew that this had been remembered and had been given specifically for me to interpret.

> What I said was: 'That nicely gets you out of the clash between you and father when you both love mother. You are father and he is you. You each lose your separate identities, but you don't have to kill each other.'

I could tell that this was what he wanted by the way he went on to tell me another dream of early years, a dream of a level crossing.

> He said: 'A train ran across a level crossing and killed an animal.'

From my point of view the symbolism here was clear. It was a dream of the danger to the child of intercourse between the parents. I said nothing.

> He went straight on with his own comment, which gave the characteristics and the build-up of his own personal defence organisation. He said: 'Now I can see that the important thing was the death of the animal, but what I remembered until now was not the death of the animal but the noise of the train coming; and then I forgot that and remembered the music which keeps the noise away.'

Here then was a clear statement of music dealing with noise, and noise remembered in avoidance of the death of the animal (child). Here death means conception.

> Together Ashton and I linked up this noise with the sound that he knew of parents in intercourse. He had heard the father's laboured breathing in intercourse. This led on to the further exploration of the antagonism between son and father. In his curiously stilted way he said: 'Is the son jealous of the father's adult relationship to the woman or is the father jealous of the infant's infantile possession of the mother and his intimacy with her?' He added: 'I think that in my case the accent is on the second of these two alternatives.' He then reconstructed the child's position in between the parents in bed: 'Up to a certain stage the child would be in possession of his mother; then after a period

157

of time the father resumes his adult relationship with the
mother and the child is the one eliminated, as the animal
was in the dream of the train and the level crossing.'

It will be agreed that this boy's ability to take up ideas and
develop them was out of the ordinary. But it was not just an intellectual exercise, as can be deduced from the fact that the interview had a profound effect on his whole personality structure,
taking away its bizarre quality.

I had to terminate this one-and-a-quarter hour interview
because I was exhausted and because it seemed unlikely to end
by natural process. Ashton was quite willing to go, and he was
obviously very satisfied with what had happened.

Subsequent Procedure

Four months later Ashton had his second interview with me. He
and I communicated again through a squiggle game, but there
was no significant feature arising out of the game. This interview
was necessary because of the patient's need to get me down to my
real size. In other words I can do nothing except on the basis of
clues offered by the patient, and in this abortive type of session
the patient gets rid of the idea of me as a magician.

The parents came for a long interview and they showed that in
spite of the fact that each had high intelligence they had not
understood deeply what was going on in their son. They made
good use of what I was able to tell them of the interview. Also
they gave many important details which cannot be reported here
because of the need to keep the case unrecognisable. Fortunately,
it is not necessary for me to give these additional details, because
this is not a case-report but is a description of a psychotherapeutic interview in which significant things happened which led
to a clearing up of the boy's main symptoms and the essential
block preventing him from using his family and his school.

A full description, if it could be given here, would show Ashton
as a boy who had (as I stated at the start) many of the general
features of a schizoid personality, and who is a near-genius. He
had been degenerating prior to the date of the consultation, and
after the first interview he went forward in all respects, and especially in the art form in which he is creative, which is music; moreover he lost his feverish bouts that regularly prevented him from
getting to school from home, and he made excellent progress

scholastically, being in all ways in advance of his age.

In this sort of case the interview cannot do all. At best it un-hitches something at the place where the patient's development is hitched up. Here, the parents' increased understanding follow-ing my letting them know how he had used his hour with me was of special importance. Also, very important in this case was the school's special effort to understand and to tolerate this odd boy's personal struggle and to appreciate his special talents.

It was with great relief to the parents that the case could be managed with the boy still living in his home.

Summary of the Case

    (*a*) Case of a boy, 12 years old, presenting clinically as a schizoid personality, with good home, and with a school that wished to co-operate. High intelligence.

    (*b*) Preliminary phase of play.

    (*c*) Imagination leading to dream.

    (*d*) Dream leading to report of auditory and visual hallucina-tions.

    (*e*) Second phase in which the boy risked exposing the central theme of his 'abstract'. The interpretation of this in terms of conflict proved to be the dynamic moment of the inter-view.

    (*f*) Subsequent phase in which the boy followed up with rich material which he had never hoped would be understood. This led to the Oedipus complex.

    (*g*) The boy used this interview in such a way that his main symptomatology cleared up. He remained somewhat schizoid in personality type, but his tendency to psychiatric degeneration changed into a definite forward movement in respect of his emotional development.

Conclusion

Attention is again drawn to the unique opportunity which a first interview affords in psychiatry. The immediate effect of the first consultation was that Ashton stopped having a raised tempera-ture and feeling unwell whenever the return to school came near. He went back to school and quite quickly found a new place in the local community. At the end of that term he was able to play one movement of a Beethoven piano concerto at the school con-cert with success.

In fact Ashton quickly became like the other boys at this school in that he was not separated out from them by oddities and peculiarities of personality. His interest in music developed and it could be said that he was left with one main symptom, an indecision as to his career, should he be an executant musician or a composer?

Six years later Ashton asked to see me again. He was now a serious music student. He probably did not remember any of the details of the first interview. What he brought to me was a conflict, the same as the one that he was left with when he was a schoolboy, should he develop his talent as an executant or as a composer? All that I did on this occasion was to remind him of the germ of this conflict that was already evident when he was a schoolboy, and indeed in the material of the initial therapeutic consultation. From my point of view this conflict was present in his nightmare in which he was both the driver of the car and the passenger, and in his uncertainty as to which was the more mature, himself or his father. I was contented to leave him using life itself in the solution of this his personal problem.

CASE X 'Albert' *aet* 7 years 9 months

I now wish to give another case which illustrates fairly obvious material obtained by this natural method of history-taking. The boy hated his brother.

It is of the nature of this case that there was no question of any difficulty in the initial stages. He came straight in while mother went around with the brother in the car trying to park it.

I had been told by the mother in a letter about Albert's satisfactory development except for certain difficulties which included nightmares; also I was told that he had a preoccupation with ideas of good and bad. 'He is almost too untroublesome.'

This was obviously a case in which the squiggle technique could be employed, and so we immediately settled down to playing this game.

(1) Mine, which he turned into a duck.

He told me about his family.

Brother	8 years 9 months.
Albert	7 years 9 months.
Sister	$5\frac{1}{2}$ years.
Brother	$3\frac{1}{2}$ years.

161

About school he said that it was funny that a little while ago he was the eldest in the junior school and now he is the youngest in the senior school.

He was sitting on the adult blue chair that I had put for him and I was on the child chair which I use because it is convenient for writing notes on the couch.

He interrupted what we were doing to say: 'You had better have the blue chair because the little chair will be uncomfortable for you.'

So on this basis we rearranged matters. This considerateness, though pleasant, seemed to join up with the words 'too untroublesome'.

(2) His. I made it into a flower. He said he would have made it into the sea.

162

I did know at this time that here was already the important theme and I wondered how the squiggle could have been turned into the sea.

(3) Mine, which he turned into an illustration to a story. The squiggle part had on top of it a metal man. Down in the sea which he put in at the bottom of the cliff was Sir Lancelot in a fight with King Arthur. In the story somehow or other the metal man falls down off the cliff and kills someone and hits a man who comes out in the course of the war.

By this time I had come to the conclusion that there must be something special about the sea, and the hills and the mud, because they could not possibly have been suggested by the squiggle, and because of the perseveration of the idea. I had no clue as to the meaning for him of these things.

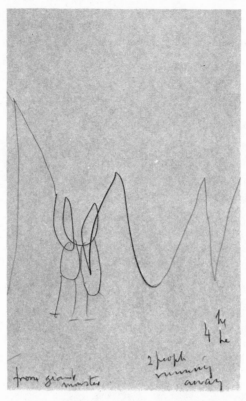

(4) His, which he made into two people running away, 'from a giant monster'.

(5) He chose to draw. It was an aeroplane.

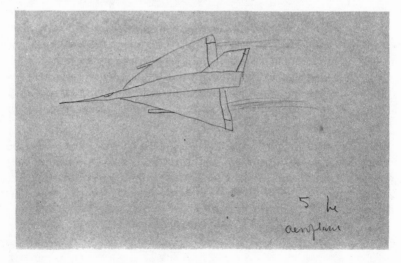

I had tried to get on to dreams from the idea of the monster. We talked about dreams and he referred to bad dreams. But he soon was talking about playing with his older girl cousin who seems to be mixed in her sex as if she would like to have been a boy. Also his sister says she wants to be in the army. She says that girls do fight and if she were a boy she could do boxing at school. She wants to do boxing because she is good at it. He then gave her a consolation prize and said 'but she really can do ballet'. They have dressing-up materials given them by some friend and they dress up a lot. In dressing-up games his sister likes to be a princess or a fairy. Somebody said that she ought to be put on the top of the tree in Trafalgar Square. When he dresses up he dresses up as anything–'but I have not been a dragon yet'. He has been a giant and a prince, and then he plunged into the idea of dressing up as a girl, illustrating it.

(6) This is a back view, and shows a cloth over his head. The buttons on the shirt do up at the back because it is on the wrong way round. He is carrying a net. This seemed to be rather important. 'You pop it on somebody and then you put them in the larder.' He went on to talk about cooking fish, implying that these people are kept in cold storage until the next meal. This idea seemed to be connected with the idea of dressing up as a woman.

(7) He wanted to draw this on the back of No. 6, because it is the front of the figure. Here the shirt is patched. That shows it is old. You can see the skirt, he said, and his feet just poking out at the end. 'That is me from the front,' he explained.

Rather a funny kind of woman seemed to be represented here, which led on to the idea of a witch, and he is concerned with witches. 'They are wicked. And they have a lot of jewels. That belongs to another game. There was a bad woman who stole treasures and hid them. My brother came and killed me. I was the good man and he was the bad one.'

This was the first clear evidence of the fight-to-the-death relationship which is included in his total relationship to his brother.

'Then there is another quite funny one. There is a bad giant.' Albert's brother is chasing the bad giant. They go all the way round the garden. All their clothes fall off and his brother landed on his face. He got a spear, two daggers, and a sword. He went 'woof! woof! woof!' pointing them in all directions. 'One hit me and I was dead.'

He felt it to be rather funny that he should be dead in his own dream.

I asked him about good and bad. Once he was 'half good' in a dream because he was bad but pretended to be good. A giant, dressed to look like one of the princess dolls, captured the princess. He locked her up and kept her as a hostage. This princess was himself. The brother rescued her. In one play his younger brother threw a bomb which was a football. 'I was the wicked woman. It hit me and I was dead.'

I said: 'You seem to have died a lot of times.'

Here he took off his coat and said it was hot and the idea occurred to him that I would be able to see his school uniform. He said: 'I am the tallest'—that is to say in his family—'but not the oldest. It is useful; my brother tells me what school is like so I know how to behave.'

I asked him again about good and bad and he said that bad is kicking and punching people when you lose your temper. When he loses his temper he punches everyone, especially his friends.

(8) Here he did his own squiggle which he himself made into a space-ship.

(9) Mine, which he turned into a fish.

(10) His, which I turned into something.

We then got nearer to the subject of real dreams. A nasty one has to do with a witch.

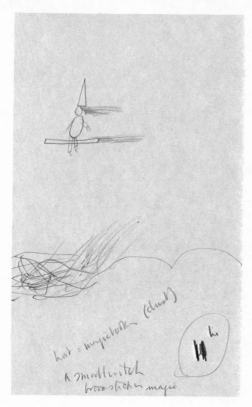

(11) This is his attempt to draw the witch; it is rather a small one but there are big ones. She has a big hat because that is where she keeps all her magic books. I said: 'I think you drew her small because you can be·so frightened of the idea of her.' The broomstick has to do with her magic.

(12) This is the wizard. He drew this big as if less frightened (according to my view). There was a whole lot of story around this; how he lives in a castle; he finds the castle spooky because there are human bones in it. (Substituting the idea of spookiness for humans for castles with spooks in them.) The wizard bumped his head on the door. This of course altered the door because of the magic. There is a big wooden door fastened with iron bolts. No-one knows where the handle is. He opens it by his magic. Up at the top you can see one of the magic monkeys that have wings. They catch people. The wizard has a long beard.

I tried to get at the connection there might be here between the wizard and his father's laboratory work, but he was neutral about there being a connection. This idea led nowhere.

He talked about the witch as always wanting to fly over to the wizard. I took this to mean that he was not deeply involved in witch symbolism and I have no means of telling whether this detail was because of a very deep fear of the witch idea or because of Albert's having come forward from witches and wizards to the idea of woman and man, and parents.

'The witch went three times round the moon. It only took a few seconds. She stayed five years on the island that Napoleon died on. Yes, Elba. She liked Na [meaning Napoleon].' Here he put in a bit of spooky language, including a funny way of pronouncing Napoleon Bonaparte. 'She wanted to die on the island too.' Apparently the wizard is on the same island.

He then talked about nice dreams which are of fairies, and he drew

(13) This shows a fairy. 'Boys are not fairies; they are angels.' At the end he put clothes on the fairy. The wand is to make magic so that what you want comes.

Here he wanted to switch over to another game, a 'hat game', so we had a session of 'heads, bodies, legs'.

(14) and
(15)

It turned out that each of us, when it came to naming the unknown quantity, had used the word Henry, his older brother's name, so we were laughing at his elder brother.

I asked him if he knew why he had come and he seemed to have no idea. The main thing was that he had missed history by coming, his worst subject.

> He said: 'I did want to come so as to miss the history lesson.' He then explained to me another game he wanted to play called hangman.

172

(16) Illustrates this but he did not really know how to play it.

We seemed to be near the end, especially as he could now see his mother's car outside the window, but I asked him once again about good and bad. Good means satisfied, bad is horrible. He allowed the word horrible to take him to the most horrible thing in his life. He seemed quite clear about this.

(17) Illustrates horrible. 'When I was nearly drowned.' He named a certain river. Here was the material which had intruded itself into the first part of the squiggle game—a river, an island, hills and mud and a bridge with a metal object going across it, a lorry. He explained how his father rescued him. The drawing is not really a drawing of the real incident which he said was not too bad. He would not have drowned even if his father had not rescued him. The drawing was like an imaginative elaboration of the incident in which the lorry falls off the bridge and kills Henry. There was a clear representation here of his rivalry with his brother in relation to the father.

I was getting a real incident described as a dream.

I took him to a further description of his love of his father and of his jealousy of his brother 'who is a teaser'. He was quite willing to enter into some verbal play in which we agreed it would be very convenient sometimes if his brother had been killed somehow or other. It was really a metal knight and that fell and hit Henry, and this joined up with the Sir Lancelot game.

He had finished now what he wanted to do and he went off and fetched another volume of the Asterix books and would have occupied himself with this if I had not said it was time to go. He seemed to know this cartoon and he said he could speak French but not read it. He said: 'I think they want to get rid of the Romans', which is really an accurate comment on the whole Asterix idea. I said: 'Why?' and he said: 'Well, they don't like paying taxes [to the Romans].'

In the waiting-room the mother was drinking cold coffee and the younger brother was very happy eating the sugar. Albert joined them, eating the biscuits. There was a quite simple and friendly exit and not a lot of looking back and saying goodbye.

After this consultation Albert seemed to have lost his uncertainty about his identity. The parents have kept me in touch with his case over the last two years and there has been no dropping back into his old state of being 'almost too untroublesome'. He has made good progress scholastically. It came out clearly in the material that he had a hatred of his older brother which he had not acknowledged either to himself or to any other person, this having resulted in a general suppression of aggressiveness affecting his whole personality.

An interesting feature of the case was the way that water obtruded itself into the second and third drawings of the squiggle game, and then at the end appeared surprisingly in the real incident given in dream-form.

CASE XI 'Hesta' *aet* 16 years

This case provides another example of a communication of the kind that belongs specifically to the professional interview. The work that the girl and I did together did not lead to a clearing up of her symptomatology. What did happen was that the parents and the family doctor, who was actively in charge of her case, felt that following the consultation they were now at last in a position to do what they felt they needed to do. They had been hampered previously by the girl's inability to accept the fact that she was ill. After the consultation she seemed to want, as well as to need, help. She abandoned her unstable assertion of her own capacity to manage and became rather childlike; perhaps it could be said that although she was 16 she became like an 8-year-old. The parents were able to find a girl to act as mental nurse for her, someone who was not trained in mental nursing but who had a natural understanding and tolerance, and this plan worked well because Hesta had now become able to let herself be an ill person. She continued, however, to insist that her various doctors were friends.

I have now had further interviews with this girl and I find that she continues to use me in a special way as someone available on demand. In the meantime she is heavily dependent on her parents and on the G.P. The future of this case is not yet clear, but a significant change in the total situation was brought about by the therapeutic consultation which I propose to describe.

Hesta is the third of four children in an intact family. I now present the case in detail, and I wish to carry you with me through the therapeutic consultation. All I knew about this case was derived from a letter from her family doctor. The main trouble was that Hesta, now 16 years old, had been nervous since her first menstrual flow, which happened when she was 14. At this time the relationship between the parents was in a state of crisis, and this crisis in the home has since been resolved.

At the age of 15 Hesta was sleepless, over-sensitive about what others thought of her, and carried a sense of inadequacy both at school and in her personal life. She feared she was lesbian. Here psychiatric abnormalities became manifest in phases, each phase apparently resolving or turning into another phase. A manic-depressive swing could be seen clinically. She herself claimed that there was nothing wrong with her.

At 16 she was acutely ill, with bizarre symptoms. There was a fear that she would kill herself. She refused hospitalisation. Nursed at home she gradually lost her generalised hostility and she became fat; it was felt that she was behaving as if she were 10 years old, making faces and talking to persons not present. The I.Q. had already been estimated at about 130.

Hesta and her mother seemed friendly, and after a few minutes in which we all three talked together about the family the mother decided to go for a walk in the district. I was left then with a rather heavy 16-year-old girl, potentially hostile and a bit dressed up, so that one felt she had been told to put on her best things because she was to see the doctor.

It was a very hot day. I was in a mood just after my holidays in which I was reluctant to work; I let her know about this and it seemed to suit her very well. She talked a little about herself. There is some trouble about the school and she said she might have to move. It seems that she did not take her examination and in any case she might have failed because she had done no work. This was as far as I could get in the description of anything abnormal. Hesta's attitude was a fixed one, that she was herself all right and quite normal; the only trouble was that she 'had abnormal parents'. She told me that the troubles had to do with her mother and father. She said: 'If I were left alone it would be all right.' And she added: 'There was a time when father and mother did not get on well together when I was 13, or 12, but the main trouble was when I was 14 when I had rather a serious depression.' She was not impressed with the theory that she was ill at that time because of monthlies.

Everything became easy when we settled down to the squiggle game. This is something that she has been playing with a boy in the country. She loves the country, and hates coming back to London. It was evident as soon as we started the squiggle game that she was capable of applying herself to a job seriously, if interested in it.

Once again I wish to put in a reminder that the squiggle game is not the essential part of the interview. It is simply part of the technique adopted, and it has the advantage that it provides its own notes, thus facilitating recapture for the purpose of presentation.

177

(1) Mine. At first Hesta could see nothing in it, but she said: 'It will take time', and she worked at it, soon producing a mouse or a mouse-dog.

It will be seen that many of the drawings have comments made by herself. These comments were written in by Hesta at the very end when she wanted to go through the whole series to get quite clear in her mind what each was about.

It was significant that Hesta applied herself to the job, being interested and at ease in her relation to myself. She could work.

(2) Hers, which was made in two phases, a circular movement and an added V. I made it into a girl. She was screaming 'Help', which led to our talking about the Beatles.

This idea came out of myself, and was not in any way suggested by her squiggle. In this work I allow myself freedom to be spontaneous and impulsive. This does not interfere with the process in the child. The reader is entitled to any view as to what I may have had in me, making me use this theme.

(3) Mine, which she turned into a fish springing out of the sea. Eventually she labelled this 'Dancing Fish'.

This showed Hesta's capacity for creative imaginative play. She used some of the strength of my squiggle for giving strength to the fish. This can be discussed in terms of 'ego-support', which of course can be excessive. This drawing made me feel that Hesta had courage of the kind that would enable her, in the course of time, to use her instinctual experiences rather than to be scared by them.

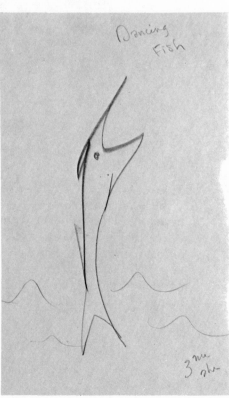

(4) Hers, which she herself saw as a face. Later she labelled it
'Sinister man'.

This, of course, was all her own work, and therefore important
as showing a theme of her own. A sinister man is what I might
have turned out to be. One can think in terms either of the father
as a sexual figure or else as a man with evil intent, as for instance
a doctor trying to work on her on behalf of the parents, that is,
to cure her in a way that would threaten her individuality. I made
no interpretations, and in this way allowed all the various mean-
ings to exist alongside each other.

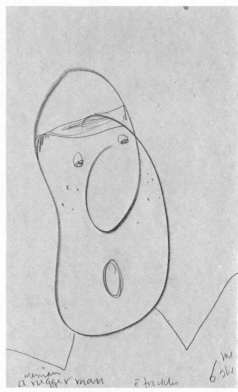

a rugger man *ō freckles*

(5) Hers, which I turned into a telephone. She and I were playing together and I felt we were at ease. I said at some point, as if we were a bit naughty, 'I expect mother thinks we are *working*!'

(6) Mine, which she made into 'a rugger man with freckles'; later she added 'American'. She was persevering with the idea of a man, this time allowing comicality and derision.

At this point I asked her whether she would have chosen to have been a boy or a girl and she seemed to know the problem, and talked about it rather philosophically, the basis of her argument being that people like to be what they are. This left open the idea of fantasy and she said to me: 'Which would *you* rather have been?' I said: 'Well, it's like that with me; I am a male and I like being one, but I know what it is like to think along the other line'—etc. etc.

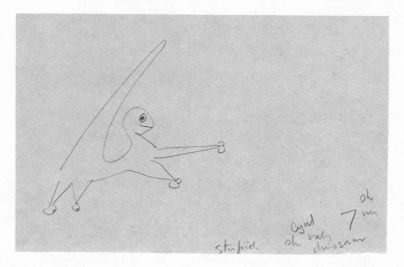

You will see here again how I give myself away freely in this sort of interview.

(7) Hers. She knew what it looked like to her, but wanted me to have my own way of working it out. Eventually I tried to draw her idea. It was a baby dinosaur. 'It's stupid.' Later she named it Cyril. She was very pleased indeed with this drawing and thought it might be the best we would do. Here again is fantasy about males and perhaps penis envy, but again I did not interpret as I did not want to pin down the communication to a specific symbolism.

(8) Mine, which she in a very imaginative way turned into Jack and the Beanstalk. Later she gave Jack a mouth and at the very end she came back to the drawing and put in the beans.

One could say that Hesta became active in her creative expression, this being something that a girl can do as well as a boy. A penis is not necessary. She gave the boy a male achievement, climbing the beanstalk, and perhaps took him down a peg or two in the end by underlining the pregenital or oral aspect of the theme (mouth and beans added). I did not interpret anything.

(9) Hers, a two-phase squiggle again. I turned it into a boy and a girl together. This she thought 'very good' and at the end labelled it Tango.

Jack + the
Beanstalk.

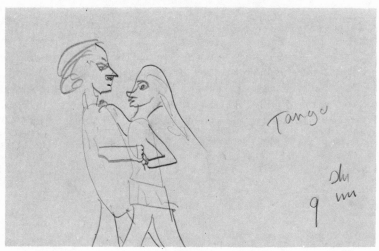

Tango

It could be said that my theme was a kind of interpretation, an observation on the two-part nature of her squiggle.

(10) Mine. She knew immediately what she wanted to do with this and she turned it into a schoolgirl with a hat. Eventually she said that it might be herself, and when I looked at it I could see that it was a rather good self-portrait. I was astonished at the way in which together somehow or other we had achieved a portrait of this girl.

At some time or other she said how much she liked one of the pictures on my wall, and we did a tour of the room examining all the pictures. She obviously has ability in drawing. Some of her curves were undoubtedly beautiful. From my point of view there was a link between these curves and the curves of her own body, taking into consideration the fact that she is very large and plump and yet not really fat. I felt that she was aware of her physical self in a quite natural way and in a way that indicated self-acceptance.

It is possible here to see the play with the hat as part of Hesta's acceptance of herself as a girl, and the diminution of her penis-envy into fun with hats and other symbols of the male organ that appear naturally in woman's clothing and in their intellectual attainments and in a hundred ways that give the signal to the boys and men that the penis-envy theme is becoming manageable in a girl, along with her full discovery of woman's use of her female body and personality.

At this point I felt myself becoming convinced of Hesta's capacity to accept puberty and to grow to be an adult woman.

> She thinks that she will be a nursery school teacher. She might of course just try out acting, but she does not expect this to lead to anything.

(11) Hers. I noticed that in many of her squiggles there was a
two-phase movement and I wondered if use could be made
of this. While thinking around this idea I hesitated, and
Hesta suggested that we should introduce into the game
the following rule: if you can't make the other person's
squiggle into something you challenge them and it is up to
them to make it into something. So I challenged her and
she made this two-phase squiggle of hers into a person
with a child in a canoe. 'The person is obviously happy but
the child is indifferent.'

This was again all her own work, and the theme is therefore
significant. I knew that here was a picture of some important
aspect of Hesta's relation to her mother, the mother being happy
and self-contained, and Hesta feeling left out and alone. This

was probably a comment on the game, since in the game Hesta felt involved, so that she and I could be said to be playing together, each having opportunity to be creative. Here are conditions to which I have referred in my paper on Playing (Winnicott, 1968), in which I claim that 'psychotherapy is done in the area of overlap between the playing of the patient and the playing of the therapist'.

(12) Hers. This was another squiggle with the same two-phase, rather deliberate drawing, one pointed and the other round. I turned it into a girl drying herself after bathing. She was very pleased with this and eventually labelled it 'Lady at Plymouth', where she knew I had spent my holiday. She thought it was a very good picture.

187

At some point I try to get to a deeper layer by asking about dreams. If I choose my moment well, the child having already reached to fantasy of a highly personal quality, I usually find the child eager to communicate a few dreams, perhaps one 'dreamed last night', as if in preparation for the consultation. So we had a bit of a talk here about dreams.

> A funny one: she was taking O-levels with Jimmie. Instead of cubicles there were tables which seemed to have names like 'roast beef' and 'cod roe'. Probably she went to the wrong table.
>
> In another dream she had twin fathers.
>
> In a third dream an aeroplane crashed. 'Flying dreams have unfortunately stopped because I suddenly realised that I cannot fly.'

We talked a little about what a shame it is that she cannot actually fly, and in a way we were discussing the whole matter of the reality principle and its boring qualities as compared with the freedom of dream.

> She said that she remembered about the flying dreams when talking to her father about birds, so there was an actual moment of disillusionment at a specific moment when she was in the company of her father.

I noted in my mind the fact of her having with difficulty come to terms with the split that exists between dream and waking reality. I did not interpret or refer to these matters.

> (13) Mine, which she turned into Harpo Marx. She was very fond of him and at one time felt identified with him. He died but he wrote a book called Harpo Talks. He had hardly any hair at all but he always wore this curly wig.

Here then she had allowed a male identification, getting value out of Harpo's success and lovableness and childishness; also the wig and the dumbness made provision for the remnants of her sense of inadequacy at the phallic phase, a trouble which had also showed in her school work in spite of her superior intelligence.

13. Harpo Marx

Contrast

(14) Hers. Here was another in this series of squiggles with the two phases. I just simply said: 'Let's leave it at that. It looks to me like the male and female principles.' She understood what I meant here and was pleased to leave it, and she said we would label it 'Contrast'.

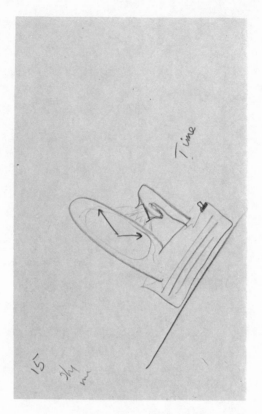

(15) Hers, another two-phase squiggle, which I rather quickly turned into a bedside clock with a lamp. She was very pleased at my having the ability to make something of this squiggle. Eventually she labelled it 'Time'.

If asked about this clock coming in here I would say that we were both thinking that it must be nearly time to stop. But we were also dealing with the time factor which the adolescent feels as a major manifestation of the reality principle. As I have said elsewhere 'the only cure for adolescence is the passage of time'. (Winnicott, 1965).

We were now getting near the end of what we could do together. She asked me, did I know various people she knows? I was able to say that I knew some of them, and we talked about these. The world is full of quite nice people, but there are three *impossibles*: her two parents and the doctor that she saw at the

Adolescent Unit. The latter seemed all right at first, and then she went there and he kept her an hour every time and neither of them said anything and it was a terrible waste of his and her time and she hated this. It was clear that I must let her go as soon as she had begun to feel she wanted to go, else I might suffer his fate. And in any case the hour was nearly up. So we did our last squiggle.

(16) Mine, which gave her trouble because she said: Oh dear, it could be two things, a camel or a negro lady.'

Here was another version of two, the basic dilemma, which includes the manic-depressive swing. She seemed to know well the paralysis that arrives when there are two possibilities, and I of course was thinking, among other things, of the two possibilities of the male and female principles of her squiggle technique.

191

With a sigh she said:

> 'So it will have to be something else.' First she said it could
> be a negro camel, but then she made it into a puppy and at
> the end she labelled it 'Hippopotamus puppy'. In one
> sense she had solved the problem by producing a baby. In
> another sense she had avoided the problem by grasping at
> a distraction. Before finishing she told me that she had
> had a frightening dream about a fire.

It was now time to go, and we went over the whole series giving
them labels and we were very pleased with ourselves.

> When she grows up she will have children—two or four;
> 'you can't have one because it gets spoiled, and it's not fair
> on the world to have more than four because of the
> population explosion'.

She rather expected me to see her mother and she was very
relieved when I said that I was going to tell her mother that I did
not want to see her. I said: 'Of course I can hear mother's point
of view and it will be very different from yours, but at the moment
I am interested in your point of view.' The mother fitted in with
this very quickly and the interview ended with my making an
appreciative remark about the necklace the mother was wearing,
and so we parted with mother perhaps feeling she had had some
personal attention from myself, although she would have to wait
before my being able to give her a personal interview.

After this I received this letter from the doctor:

> I think your interview was a great success, and not only with
> Hesta. Her mother was not at all offended at being to some
> extent left out of it. I am happy with the programme you outline,
> but I think I am so because Hesta is considerably better than she
> was. It is possible now for her to be treated as a 'normal' person
> and even as somebody who is right while everybody else is wrong.
> Twelve months ago I think this would have been absolutely im-
> possible for her parents, her friends or me. She seemed very ill
> then and absolutely unable to recognise this fact. One felt then
> that it was right to try to get her to accept that she was ill, and
> that if she could have asked for help, this might have been the
> beginning of getting better.
>
> I am not really quite sure why I am saying this to you. Perhaps
> it is just to rub in that you are lucky to be seeing her when she is
> so much better! But I expect you will see what I am after.

The parents also wrote in appreciative vein, and readily agreed to a programme of my seeing only Hesta, and of my seeing Hesta as little as possible, perhaps not seeing her again at all. The matter could be left open, and if Hesta wished to see me I would comply as quickly as possible according to my timetable. The mother added:

> She has, in my view, been changed by her first visit to you—especially in her attitude to me. For instance she said to me 'I would like to come away for the weekend with you [she paused]. Oh, but I'd better not because we're not getting on very well at the moment, are we?' This is the first time for months that she has been able to (kind of) see herself in relationship with me. At least that is what I felt about it.
>
> I do understand too about the fact that you don't want to be asked for advice. So I'll just tell you what we are doing about her education. We have decided (with the help of the family doctor) that Hesta should not go back to school this term. I have found her a coach who will take her once or twice a week depending on how Hesta feels about it.

So there the matter lies at the moment. My point is that very little was done, and to do it was economical (one hour); also the parents and the doctor have not had the case wrested from them as would inevitably happen in a psychotherapy.

After this first interview the mother said: 'This is the first time anyone has communicated with this girl since she became ill at 14.'

Follow-up

This case continues to be managed at home with the help of the family doctor and a girl who acts as nurse. Hesta uses me 'on demand', so that I have seen her half a dozen times in a year. There is a diminution of the manic element, and a manageable depression is often the chief clinical feature. There has been a voluntary return to school work.

The first interview that I have described here continues to be the basis for the teamwork on the case that is now being done with some success up to date.

The outcome cannot be predicted while the rapid and violent changes of puberty dominate the scene.

CASE XII 'Milton' *aet* 8 years

I end this second part with the case of a boy who went home after the first therapeutic consultation with a developmental block removed. The various members of the household found themselves with a child who had been released and who could use them more freely, and they behaved differently towards the child. The family does the cure of a child like this in the course of the subsequent weeks and months, although without the therapeutic consultation they would not have been able to do this, but would have remained available but unused.

Family History

Milton, boy	8 years.
Twins, boy and girl	6 years.
Girl	4 years.

The mother of this boy wrote to me a letter in which she stated the problem as seen from her point of view. The main trouble as she saw it was that Milton, who was the eldest child, had never really accepted the arrival of the twin brother and sister, who were born when he was two years old. She wrote: 'Their birth threw him into utter turmoil which manifested itself in many obvious and wretched ways. He became and has remained heavily dependent on me and involved with me.' There were certain other pathological features such as a predilection for sado-masochistic situations and the beginnings of a pleasure in the idea of whipping. Also he showed a potential for pervert tendencies such as a compulsion to look at and to feel girls' pants. While he tended to be bullying and aggressive at home he was on the whole placatory and nervous at school, and not very popular. In his actual school work he was doing well, showing a special interest in history and English. The mother added that she had had some treatment herself, and that although this had enabled her to deal better than previously with the other children, her improvement had not made a difference to her management of these tendencies in Milton which she was reporting.

Psychotherapeutic Interview

The two parents brought Milton to the therapeutic consultation. After a few minutes in which we all talked together they retired to the waiting-room and patiently waited the one and a quarter hours which elapsed before Milton had finished his contact with me. They had to go home without having a talk with me, but I had warned them of this possibility. Several weeks later I saw the parents together, and I was then able to give them my full attention, which it would have been a bad thing to have done immediately after my interview with Milton.

The Personal Interview

I found Milton to be very lively and one could almost say that he was eager for something. He was restless and during the drawing games he was often standing rather than sitting, and the game was always liable to degenerate into an activity which contained winning and losing. My aim was to enable him (if possible) to play at squiggles, but first I had to concede a period of noughts and crosses, a game which (as I soon found) he did not really understand. (See Pre-1 drawing.)

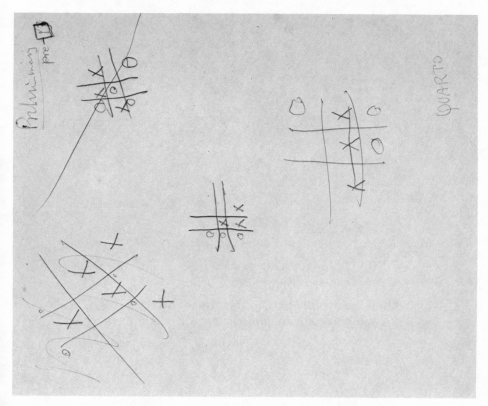

It seemed to me in the early stages to be unlikely that we could make use of the session in terms of playing of the kind which would naturally lead to contact between him and me of a deepening kind. I went forward, however, and in the end I was rewarded.

Squiggles

I explained the game to him, letting him know that first I make a squiggle which he can turn into something if he wants to do so, and then he makes a squiggle for me to turn into something. Then I made my first squiggle:

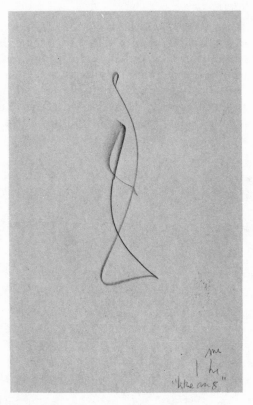

(1) Mine. He said: 'It's like an 8', and he had no impulse to turn it into anything.

On this occasion, perhaps because of his restlessness, I deemed it advisable to come in immediately with a comment which might or might not lead to a development in the tenuous relationship between us.

I said: 'That's you'—because he had just told me that he was 8 years old. He immediately entered into the game and did:

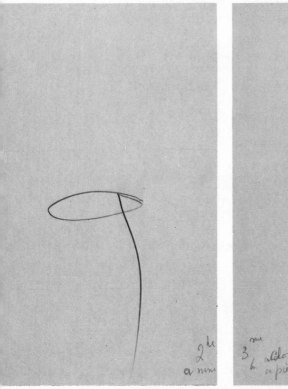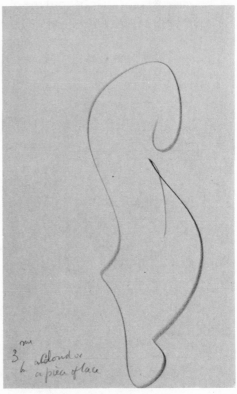

(2) His, which was a vigorous squiggle done like mine as if un-directed and not deliberate. He looked at it, and quickly said: 'That's me too; it's a 9 and I will be 9 in a week's time.'

We were now in communication with each other in terms of the game but there was still much restlessness. I had begun to feel hopeful.

(3) Mine. He had no desire to alter this or to make it into any-thing. He just said: 'It's a cloud or a piece of lace.'

This made me think of the whole area of fantasy and of what I have called *transitional phenomena*, things that belong to the transition from being awake to being asleep, and I explored round this area, fishing for information from him about transitional objects or techniques that he might remember. This led to nothing in his particular case (although it might have done in another case) except that he told me of a teddy bear that he had had when he was 3. So we continued with the game.

(4) His. I noted that he did this in two separate parts so I turned one part into a head and the rest into a figure which eventually resulted in a drawing of a girl with a handbag. He made a comment in two layers. In the superficial layer he said: 'You draw well!' and then with more conviction he said: '*Really* it was a lantern.'

He meant that if I had let him turn the squiggle into something he would have made it into a lantern. This carried the implication that therefore I was not magically in touch with his thoughts. Incidentally he made the handle of the handbag more securely joined to the bag. He was restless here and walking round, bending down to draw on the low table without sitting.

(5) His. He sat down to this. It was simply four lines and he immediately said: 'I know what it is', and he turned it into a volcano. I said: 'Well, that's you again', and he seemed to accept this idea with a good grace.

6 [in a bush or snail.]

(6) Mine. He said it was a bush or a snail and the only thing he would do about it was to decide which way up it ought to be.

Note the laziness which is an indication that he feels that the result should come by magic, not by work and skill. This squiggle game allows for the operation of this principle, until the child begins to feel like active participation.

(7) His. I made this into a plant in a pot, but he said that was quite wrong. He said: 'It is a whirlwind.' I said: 'Well, that's you again.' I added: 'They all seem to be about you, except perhaps the girl, but of course it was I who drew that one.' We talked a bit about his being a boy or a girl and his preferences. He came down heavily on the side of being a boy. When asked for reasons he became rational and said: 'Well, girls are all right but I happen to be a boy.'

(8) His. *He was now quite happy to be playing the game that I had instituted.* He said: 'That's a book; that's me again because I love books and I read all the time.'

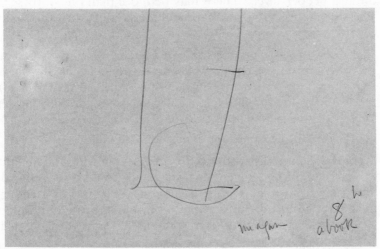

201

(9) Mine. He said it was a funny plant. I said: 'Well, if that's you there is something funny about you. What could it be?' And he answered: 'Well, my sister's always laughing at me.' Contemplating what he might make this squiggle into he said: 'Do you recommend anything?' I said: 'No, I had nothing in my mind when I did it.'

I felt that there was an indication here of his having some fear of spontaneity and free fantasy and of his wanting the support which I might offer by giving ideas of my own.

(10) His. He said: 'It's got a collar.' This gave me the clue, and I filled in the face and again we decided that it was a picture of himself.

The Period of Reassessment

We were now in a period which occurs in many of these therapeutic consultations, in which nothing much seems to be happening. At one time in the past I might have thought that we had come to the end of our contact, but I have learned that this marking time is a phase in which the child is reassessing the situation. On the basis of what has happened the child is (unconsciously) weighing up the reliability of the professional relationship and is taking a little time to decide whether to accept the risks that belong to deeper involvement. It is a kind of changing gear, and if the consultation proceeds one finds regularly that the work goes on at a deeper level.[1] There may be more than one of these reassessment areas in a consultation of this kind. During this period we did:

(11) In this can be seen a type of game which is his own distortion of noughts and crosses. He called it 'crosswords'. I could see here that he was nearer to dream than to reality and therefore entitled to be in control, and I let him win. He shouted: 'I've won!' and was very pleased.

(12) His, a continuation of this distorted game.

I now began to fish around for dreams, knowing full well that we were on a knife-edge. His restlessness would very easily take him away from manageable discussion, yet he was near enough to fantasy and to dream for me to be able to invite him to look *into* himself as he had looked *at* himself. As it turned out he

[1] See especially Part Three, Case XIII (the Hands Case).

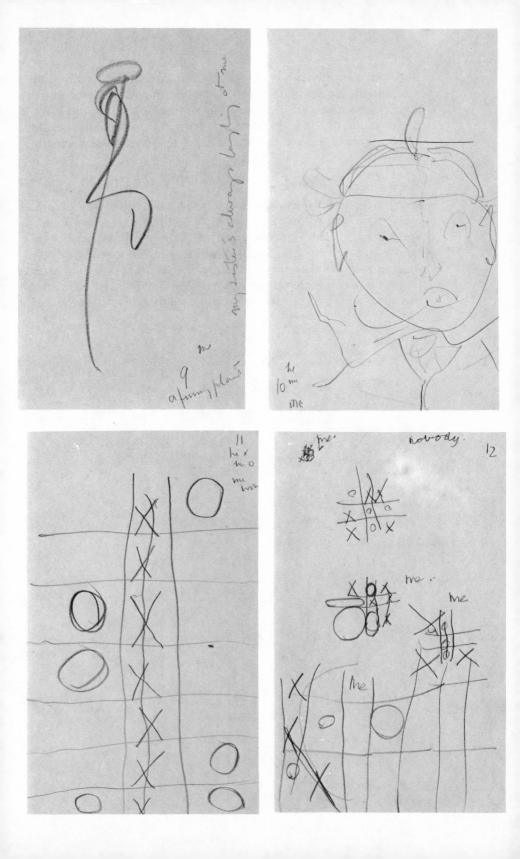

responded positively to my query about dreams, and from that moment the consultation proceeded without my having any more anxiety about its turning into a fiasco. I knew that I could leave the dynamic of the interview to the process in the child, which would drive him to communicate with me in terms of his main problem.

Work at a Deeper Level

In response to my query about dreams he said: 'I have one dream every night, but I don't know what these dreams are. I could tell you a *funny* dream' – and he liked my suggestion that he should take a large sheet of paper in illustrating it. He started to draw on one side and then turned the paper over and continued as if doing the second attempt on the back. (I have learned that these tiny details have to be taken seriously and that this meant that he

13 QUARTO

was talking about the back of himself. From the mother afterwards I learned that Milton compulsively asks about the birth of
babies, and that he has a fixed idea that they come from 'behind',
and not 'from the front' as he has been repeatedly told.)

(13) and (14) The thing about this dream is that he dreamed it
when he was 'very little, probably 3'. He said: 'At the time
when I dreamed it, it was very frightening, but in the course
of the years it has become funny.' I made an attempt to
join up this early age of the dream with the arrival of the
twins, although I knew that it was at 2 that the twins had
arrived.

The dream as given by him at this stage was obscure. First
of all there is a chandelier and there is a 'red lady' hanging
down from it. As the dream goes on there are toboggans
down the sand which slopes to the beach and to the sea—

'and they all landed in the sea'. There appeared to be lots
of red ladies in the dream. The red, he said, was the colour
of blood. He kept saying how silly it all was, and from this
I could infer that he knew that although the dream had
turned into a funny dream, originally it was not funny and
was of great significance. He went on: 'These characters in
the dream do acrobatics and things with skipping ropes;
that is not in the dream, though; that is what came into the
dream later when it became funny. At the time when I
dreamed the dream, at the beginning, I was very little, and
there was nothing nice about it. It was only frightening.
Everything was red.'

At this point I got the feeling that he was remembering having
the dream and being very frightened, and he was only a little boy.

He now turned the page over and continued drawing (No.
13). (This was the side of the page that he used originally,

13 QUARTO

before he turned it over to draw on the back.) Here he drew an 8 (obscure in the picture because of the subsequent elaboration). I said: 'Oh, that's you again.' And he filled in the details of the face, giving himself glasses. I made a comment about this and he said: 'Well, I may have to wear glasses one day because, you see, I read such a lot. I really do love books. I read in the night all the time; history and the men and women in history.' He went on to talk about Lord Nuffield, 'who gave away £30 million; so what he must have made I don't know. He was an experienced engineer.'

For the moment I abandoned the dream, feeling that he had gone as far as he could for the time being towards being frightened again. So I asked him what he was going to be, taking up the idea of Lord Nuffield as an engineer. 'Well, maybe a scientist. But at school science is not very interesting.' He then told me about the literary occupations of his father and mother, obviously being proud of them. While he was talking he was doing something very dark on drawing 13. I asked him about it and he said: 'See me picking up the telephone.' But it seemed to me that the original idea was to have something very dark on this page. I assumed that this was an obscurantist move, a symbolic representation of repression, an almost deliberate black-out to deny something frightening, as for instance the blood-red ladies. The telephone, however, has a positive meaning as a symbol of communication.

It will be observed that I am not making interpretations. I allow the rich material to develop in its own way, and work in confidence that the patient will use his trust in me and in the professional setting to reach to the reliving of being frightened of the dream, as it was dreamed when he was 3 years old.

We were in a second period of marking time, but I could guess that there was another stage to be reached. I occupied the time by saying to him: 'Who do you love best?' I followed this up quickly with the comment: 'I know.' I think I did this because I could see that he was at a loss, and I wanted to make use of the fact that he had not yet decided how to deal with my question. If I had waited he would have given an answer based on rationalisation. He seemed puzzled at my saying that I knew, and he asked me to tell him. So I said: 'Yourself.' Naturally I was influenced by the way in which in many ways he himself had come into the material of the drawings. He reacted to my answer with a display of indignation. 'No, I don't love myself at all; I don't love *anybody*.' He went on with the theme, however, and told me that he probably does love his grandparents, and no-one else. He gave me a picture of home life in which the girl twin plays with the little brother and the boy twin is of no use. 'He never plays with me. I have no-one to play with.' He then told me about one boy friend. The basis of this friendship seemed to be that the boy bullied him. We were now heavily on the masochistic side of the sado-masochistic organisation. Apparently these two boys do achieve quite a lot of playing together, but the playing is liable to degenerate into some kind of antisocial activity. He illustrated this: 'Once I got into trouble climbing into school through the window and opening the teacher's desk, but there was nothing in it.' I followed this up with the question: 'Do you ever pinch [steal]?' 'No, but I play at pinching things and I always give the things back.' The marking time was coming to an end.

He now returned spontaneously to dreams with the statement: 'I have a dream every day of my life but the dream never comes into my vision.' This seemed to be his way of describing a consciousness of dreaming without cognisance of the content of the dream, or alternatively the way that he can remember a dream, but when he wakes fully he forgets it. He went on: 'I have only seen two dreams in full vision in my life; one had to do with horses and carts and it was nice, and was connected with the book *Black Beauty*; the other one I only half saw and it was very nice indeed, about Norse Gods who all came true; it was great.' And he went on to tell me that he had read about Norse legends. He had obviously collected a great deal of information from the books that he reads in bed.

Things were still hanging fire a little and I said: 'Are you a happy person?' to which he replied: 'Not at school; I get bullied.' And he went on to describe the way that the boys are beastly to him. On the other hand, on the particular day that he was talking to me the boys had voted for him to be one of the editors of the class magazine. I said: 'Do they actually hurt you?' 'Oh no,' he said boastfully, 'they can't hurt *me*; I know Judo, but they say nasty things, and they don't believe things that I have said which are true. They go about saying I am a liar.' And then he confessed: 'I used to boast a lot.'

We talked about school a little while, but I was waiting for an opportunity to get back to his drawings of his dream. At last he got back to it on his own. He said: 'It was a shock when the twins were born. You see, I was not very old; I was about 2. It brought about a change in my life.' He then made the comment: 'I don't really remember, but mother thinks I am still affected by this'—showing that he was not really back yet in the situation of having his life upset by the twins. But he went on: 'I don't like the world and I don't like living and it is horrible at school.' And then he gave me a rather excited account of the way that a belief in God is needed at his school, and he cannot manage this himself.

I said: 'Do you believe in anything? Do you believe in yourself, for instance?'

'What do you mean? I don't really understand.'

At this point he was trying very hard to come to grips with the idea that I was putting forward about a belief in himself as something that was related to the belief in God. I tried to help him out by saying: 'Well, do you feel that you are important to someone?' To which he answered: 'No.' Then he tried to get out of the position that he was in by boasting: 'Oh, I can have fun; I know the right TV programme to turn on.' And then he became very serious about God again and discussed the philosophical problem that if God is the Father then who is God's father and who is the father of God's father? He ended up by saying: 'You could go on for millions of years like that till you were dead.' So I said: 'Is your own father important to you?' He responded with: 'Well, naturally he likes having a son, but I like nagging my father.' And then he went back to the question of belief in God.

I found out later that the parents, who agree in most matters, have a permanent disagreement in terms of religion and a belief in God. Here, perhaps, comes the word *crosswords* that he used to describe the game he had invented.

> He told me that he had read all about religion 'in the encyclopaedia where they do try to be scientific'. At this stage he entered a phase in which it could be said that he was identified with God. For a while he was saying things like: 'I found out for myself all about everything, how all the planets work, how everything was formed', and so on and so on, which led me to make the remark: 'So in a way you are God and God is you.' He reacted to this sharply. 'No, I don't want to be God! I hardly know anything! I don't know a trillionth of one of what the world knows!' After this extreme retreat from an identification with God he gave me a description of Leonardo da Vinci, the cleverest man, as he said, because he invented things that were beyond his time. He gave me a very good description of Leonardo's position. Then he returned to something more personal and said: 'My brother never plays with me; I am lonely.'

It was now necessary for me to make a final attempt to get to the analysis of the dream, and I knew that I must get Milton to reach over to the sadistic side of the sado-masochistic organisation because in the position where we were at that moment the main defence was his liability to get bullied and badly treated and neglected.

> In answer to something I said he told me that he used to be always twitting his brother, so that the fact that his brother never played with him could be put down to the brother's defence against being bullied by him. Then he went on to say that he used to thwack his brother when he was little. Milton was now right back at 3 years old, with a little brother of 1 year, and (this time not quoting mother) he said: '*You see, I wanted to be the only one.*'

> He was now ready to look at the dream again, operating from the sadistic side. He seemed to know what everything meant, but he was not able to convey it all to me. 'The chandelier—well, not really a chandelier, a sort of lamp

hanging down. No. It's bosoms. A breast like a man.' He was seeing what he had called the chandelier as the torso of a man or woman looked at from the point of view of a baby on the lap. He was now able and willing to talk about the 'red ladies'. He said they were torn-off breasts. This was quite spontaneous. I think that he was using the idea of his brother at the breast to express his own very primitive sadistic fantasies towards the actual breast of the mother, ideas that dominated him as ideas when he was 3 years old. Of course they had origin in his own infancy.

He was now showing very great anxiety and he was able to convey some but not all of the fantasy content of the dream. The tobogganing and the sliding down to the sea had to do with birth. So the dream was now a mixture of a birth dream and a sadistic attack on the breasts. His mind was working at a terrific rate: 'Oh yes, there was another thing in that dream; it was like a film; there was an interval. Actually I loathe custard but, you see, I did love custard when I was a baby' (i.e. before the birth of the twins and the changed attitude to mother). 'This waiter came along; there was a piano there. Funny, isn't it! These people were dining. They called out: "Waiter!" and the lady said something, *only in the dream there were no words,* and the waiter brought the custard.' (He was in the pre-verbal era of his life.) He interrupted himself here to say: 'Me! Ugh! Custard!' And he went on: 'And they suddenly came to the chandelier; there were bosoms in a sort of a way on the tummy; a bosom or a breast.' He was pointing to the drawing and saying that he had the idea of the swollen belly of pregnancy as a central breast and that this was the object of his attack in the dream leading to the blood or the raw surfaces. (He was superimposing his attack on the pregnant belly on to his sadistic attack on the breasts.) He added: 'There were six or eight ladies really, all red.'

He was right there in an infantile relationship with his mother's body and he went on about bosoms (breasts), and then about man who, as he said, 'Gathers it all together in the penis, the thing that holds the seed.'

So now he had the sequence quite clear in his mind: breasts; pregnant belly; male with no bosoms but a penis. Everything was blood-red because of the sadistic attack.

He went on: 'Yes, they were bosoms, I remember now', and I had the feeling that he had now reached the frightening 3-year-old version of the dream, a dream which in the course of the years had gradually become funny. He was sufficiently in touch with sadistic fantasy and impulse for me to cease to worry about his masochism. He had re-experienced his angry attacks and had got behind these to his oral sadism that belongs to primitive relating and to excitement about the breasts; moreover he had reached to the pre-ambivalent object-relating to the breasts in the re-capturing of the love of custard which in his childhood had turned into a phobia of custard.

We had now spent one and a quarter hours together and we were both glad to finish.

Sequel

A month later both parents came to talk to me about their boy. I went over the details of the consultation with them and they found their view of their son very much enriched as a result of this information. I felt reasonably certain that they were mature enough not to let me down by reporting even indirectly what I told them. It has to be remembered that parents have no knowledge of what is going on when we do psychotherapy of a child and they are liable to feel that the whole thing is a mystery. When they hear a factual account of what transpires they can make use of the information that it gives about aspects of their child which do not become evident in ordinary home life. Incidentally, these parents were able to add one or two significant details which enriched my understanding of the case.

The parents were very impressed by one thing, which was that although it had always been evident to them that the birth of the twins had been a disaster from Milton's point of view, the first time that he ever actually said this himself was after he came back from the consultation he had with me. Also both parents had noticed a lightening of tension, especially between Milton and his brother. The very evening of the consultation they found Milton and his brother playing and fighting together in a boyish way on the sofa, and this was quite a new feature. The parents were well satisfied with the result up to date and were willing to wait for developments.

A month later I found the parents extremely pleased with what had happened. The father said that somehow or other Milton had 'found a key' in this consultation with me. The mother said that she kept on expecting something horrible to happen because she is so used to an unbroken series of disasters, but somehow or other the whole atmosphere had changed, everything centring round a great improvement in the relationship between Milton and his brother.

Soon after he came home from the consultation Milton said to his mother in astonishment and indignation: 'Dr. Winnicott said I only love myself!' The mother described the change in Milton with the phrase: 'It is as if he was turned inside-out.' She explained that whereas formerly he was always boasting about what he could do, he was now talking about things that he was actually planning to do, and the whole thing had become realistic. For the first time they were able to tease him, that is to say, without being afraid of his flaring up in a rage. He had been working well at school as before, but there was now less of a sense of pressure and he seemed to be more relaxed about secondary matters like marks and place in form. The parents realised that only two months had passed and that there was still opportunity for a return to the former condition. But they could not help noticing that the change in Milton had produced favourable changes in the whole of his environment, so that in a way he was now for the first time using his family and what the family could offer. Especially he seemed released for making use of his mother.

In a year I have seen Milton four times 'on demand'. Also I have been in close touch with Milton's mother, mostly by 'phone. A great deal has been lived through in this year, which could be described, but it would be out of place here; moreover, the more one reports the more is the case likely to become recognisable, in spite of disguises legitimately adopted.

The mother's remark seems worth quoting, as she is perspicacious and also she is familiar with the analytic routine through her own experience of being analysed. She said: 'This method that you have adopted with Milton, which seems so unorthodox, really seems to have worked in this case.'

I must add: has worked so far. No child case is finished. There may come a time, however, when a child grows up and becomes an adult, and even a socialised adult and an independent person, and then one can at last make an assessment in regard to health and to illness patterns.

Comment

This therapeutic consultation illustrates the sort of work that is appropriate in child psychiatry. This is different from psychoanalysis and from prolonged and regular psychotherapy. In child psychiatry the slogan must be *How little need be done in the clinic?* and obviously this slogan belongs to a type of case in which the family and the school are ready waiting to be used if the child is enabled to get past some block in his or her development so as to be able to use the environment. In this particular case there were unfavourable signs at the beginning of the consultation, restlessness indicating that the child had a great fear of deep feelings. Gradually by the technique employed the boy became able to gain confidence in the relationship and so to be able to play. Thus he could not only remember a significant and frightening dream, but he could reach back to *a reliving of the time when he was having it*, at the age when he was highly disturbed by the birth of the twins, that is to say, when he was 2 or 3 years old. Eventually he worked very hard at this dream and displayed insight, so that he was able to accommodate the great anxieties associated with the primitive love impulse and particularly with oral sadism. He even reached to pre-ambivalence, and the early good relationship to the mother (custard) that he had lost at 3. The immediate clinical result was satisfactory and indicated a real change in the boy's personality. Incidentally the changes in the boy produced favourable changes in the environment and the general result was beneficial.

In this work the therapist cashes in on the child's capacity to believe in human reliability. The therapist remains a 'subjective object', and the work is unlike that of psycho-analysis in that it is not done in terms of transference neurosis samples.

Interpretation is minimal. Interpretation is not in itself therapeutic, but it facilitates that which is therapeutic, namely, the child's reliving of frightening experiences. With the therapist's ego support the child becomes able for the first time to assimilate these key experiences into the whole personality.

Part Three

INTRODUCTION

In this section I continue illustrating the theme of communication with a child.

In this group I have collected together cases that illustrate the psychogenesis of the antisocial tendency. The antisocial tendency is represented in these cases chiefly by *stealing*, although other main symptoms that have *nuisance value* are included.

The Theory of the Antisocial Tendency

My intention here is to illustrate the theory that I have propounded to explain the antisocial tendency. This theory is obscured when the case has been mishandled or has become in other ways complex perhaps because secondary gains have become established as a feature. Research into the antisocial tendency is best carried out on the simpler cases or in those cases tackled early, and especially in those in which there is an environmental provision which can adapt itself to improvements that may take place in the child's character and personality as a result of a consultation. In all the cases in this series (XIII–XXI), therefore, it will be found that stealing or some other form of antisocial activity is a feature. This is the kind of clinical material on which I have based the theory that I have stated and which I will restate. It is also the kind of proof which I have used. When a child is stealing and after the therapeutic consultation there is no more stealing, then there is a strong presumption that the work done in the consultation was effective and therefore based on a theory which is not altogether incorrect. I am not dismayed by the fact that there is a vast number of very serious antisocial cases which I would not hope to change in the way that I am describing in this series. The first thing is to establish the possibility of understanding and dealing with the antisocial tendency as it appears in children who are of relatively good environment and, as it often happens, children of one's friends and colleagues.

The theory is not complex and I have been at pains to expound it in several papers since the time when it first became clear to me in the early forties. Up to a certain date in my career I avoided the antisocial case both in my clinic and in private practice, knowing that I had nothing to offer, and that the clue was missing. I simply saw antisocial children in a routine way in order to provide notes for a court. After a certain date, however, I found myself able to offer some kind of a service for those cases that came to me in which the antisocial tendency was the main symptom. Since then I have allowed myself to become involved in many of these cases that can give a great deal of trouble even when everyone is trying to be helpful and tolerant.

The theory is as follows: where the antisocial tendency, either in the form of stealing or being a nuisance, is the character disturbance for which the child is brought there is regularly to be found in the history an early period in which the environment enabled the child to make a good start in a personal development. In another language, the maturational processes have had a chance to become established to some extent because of a satisfactory facilitating environment. Then in these cases there is to be found an environmental lapse of some kind or other as a result of which the maturational processes become blocked, perhaps suddenly. This blockage or the child's reaction to the new anxieties cuts across the line of life of the child. There may be a kind of recovery, but there is now a gap in the continuity of the child's life *from the child's point of view*. There has been an acute confusional state in the time-phase between the environmental failure and whatever there may be in the way of a recovery. In so far as the child does not recover the personality remains relatively disintegrated and the child is clinically restless and dependent on being directed by someone, or restrained by an institution. In so far as there is recovery the child can be said to be (*a*) most of the time in a somewhat depressed state, hopeless but not knowing why, and then (*b*) the child begins to get hope. There is hope perhaps because of something good happening in the environment. It is at this point, the point where hope appears, that the child comes alive and reaches back over the gap to the satisfactory state that obtained before the environmental failure. The child who is stealing is (in the initial stages) quite simply reaching back over the gap, hopeful, or not entirely hopeless, about rediscovering the lost object or the lost maternal provision, or the lost family structure.

It will be seen that in every household there are minor instances in which a child has become a deprived child in a small way and is cured by the parents who (quite naturally and without instruction) feel that this child needs a phase of spoiling, as it is called. Spoiling here means giving a limited and temporary opportunity for the child to regress to dependence and to a maternal provision which belongs to an age that is younger than that of the child at the moment. Parents are very frequently successful in curing their children of these minor deprivations and this gives the clue to the hopefulness which the clinician may feel about getting some cures of the antisocial tendency when therapy can be undertaken before the child has started to organise secondary gains. It has to be remembered all the time that these things are going on in the forgotten past and apart from the child's conscious life, but it is a surprise to the worker in this field how near to consciousness conflict can be in this particular type of illness. Communication may be all that is needed.

Roughly speaking there can be said to be the two types of antisocial tendency. *In the one* the illness presents as stealing, or claiming special attention through bed-wetting and untidiness and other minor delinquencies which do in fact give the mother extra work and worry. *In the other* there is destructiveness provoking firm management, that is to say firm management without the added quality of retaliation. Roughly speaking, the former type of child is deprived in the sense of losing maternal care or a 'good object', and the second type of child is deprived in terms of the father or of the quality in the mother that shows that she has a man's support behind her; this includes her strictness or perhaps her capacity to survive attack and to be able to repair damage done to clothes or to the carpet, or to the walls of the house or the windows.

Needless to say there is no value to the child in history-taking which the psychiatrist or social worker may undertake which is done through anyone other than the child. It is of no use to know from the mother or from a social history that at $2\frac{1}{2}$ years a child changed in character after being in hospital for tonsillectomy. The only value in a therapeutic sense is in the discovery of these matters in the therapeutic consultation with the child. The child may be wrong in regard to details which can be corrected afterwards, and which are not significant, such as, for instance, the exact age at which a deprivation took place. But it is the child

217

who knows the essential and significant facts. Also what may have been a deprivation from the point of view of this child may not have been noticed by the parents.

These are well-known concepts. Examples are strewn through the whole of the literature of child therapy and social work. The thing that I am trying to present has to do with the technique for getting at these important details in the past history of the child *through contact with the child* and therefore in a way that can be used. These matters can be seen in a careful dissection of the vast amount of material that occurs in a psycho-analytic treatment. Nevertheless there is a tendency for the main features of truly analytic cases to be hidden in the quantity of material that is available. I feel that the student can best learn the beginnings of this important part of the theory which applies to the antisocial tendency by examining cases of the kind I present here in which there is a limited amount of material for description. For this reason I give seven cases in illustration of my thesis and of my technique.

As in the first twelve cases in this book I shall give these anti-social cases in the form of descriptions of what I call therapeutic consultations and the exploitation of the first interview. Where the case is complex the first interview may be reduplicated, or may be extended as an 'on demand therapy' over months or even years. It is convenient, however, to continue with the idea of the exploitation of the first interview in order the better to distinguish this technique from that of psychotherapy and psycho-analysis. Although there is no sharp line between these ways of dealing with a case, nevertheless if the interviews tend to take on the pattern of a series then a psychotherapy is starting up, and the work begins to take on a different quality. In psychotherapy the work becomes organised automatically into work which is done in terms of transference and the analysis of resistance, so that already after a few interviews the treatment can be better named psycho-analysis or analytic therapy.

In my first case there is one very simple fact which may per-haps carry the student through the detailed account, and that is that the child came to me for stealing and was a compulsive thief up to the time of the consultation, but she went away changed in such a way that the mother noticed the change immediately, and she has never stolen since that moment. She had rediscovered the mother of her early childhood. She could now reach for the breasts and she no longer needed to feel across the gap in a compulsive way and without consciousness of the motive. This result could not be obtained by pure chance.

Many of the cases are not as clear as this, but it is hoped that this one case may enable the student to gain an interest in making an examination of the antisocial tendency as an expression of hope in a child who is most of the time hopeless, hopeless because of a break in the continuity of his or her life-line, the break being due to a massive reaction in the child, automatic and inevitable, to an environmental failure.

CASE XIII[1] 'Ada' *aet* 8 years

I now give a detailed and complete description of a psychotherapeutic interview with a girl of 8 years who was brought on account of *stealing*. (There was also enuresis, but this was not beyond the parents' understanding and tolerance.) It is at the end of this long description that the reader will find the illustration of denial representing a dissociation in the child's personality structure. This is an important feature of the antisocial case, and explains the unconsciously motivated compulsion to steal making the child feel mad, so that at the start he or she seeks help.

Referral

The school had made it clear that Ada's stealing was giving trouble, and Ada would have to leave if the symptom persisted. It was practicable for me to see this girl once or even a few times, but she lived too far away for me to be able to think in terms of a treatment. It was therefore necessary for me to act on the basis that I must do everything possible in the first psychotherapeutic consultation. This was a hospital clinic case.

Technique Detail

I saw the child without first seeing the mother who brought her. The reason for this was that I was not at this stage concerned with taking an accurate history; I was concerned with getting the patient to give herself away to me, slowly as she gained confidence in me, and deeply as she might find that she could take the risk.

The Interview Described

Ada and I sat down together at a small table on which were small sheets of paper and a pencil, and a few crayons in a box.

There were two Psychiatric Social Workers and a visitor present, sitting a few yards away.

[1] First published in *Crime, Law and Corrections*, ed. Ralph Slovenko (Charles C. Thomas, 1966), under the title 'A Psychoanalytic View of the Antisocial Tendency'.

First Ada told me (in answer to my question) that she was 8 years old. She had a big sister, aged 16, and also a small brother of $4\frac{1}{2}$. Then she said she would like to draw: 'My favourite hobby.'

(This was not an interview in which the squiggle game was needed.)

(1) Flowers in a vase.

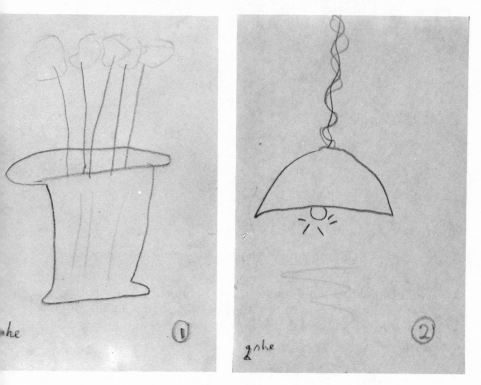

(2) A lamp, which hung from the ceiling in front of her.

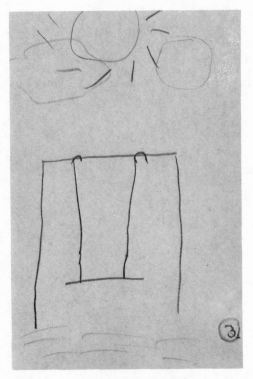

(3) The swings in the playground, sun out and some clouds.

These three drawings were poor as drawings, and they were unimaginative. They were representational. Nevertheless the conventional clouds in the third drawing had a significance, as will appear towards the end of the series. I had no idea of their significance at this stage.

Ada now drew:

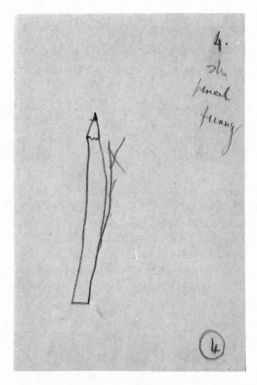

(4) A pencil. 'Oh dear! Have you a rubber? It's funny, there's something wrong with it.'

I had no rubber and I said she could alter it if it was wrong, and she did, and said: 'It's too fat.'

Comment

Any analyst reading this will already have thought of various kinds of symbolism, and of various interpretations that might have been made. In this work interpretations are sparse and are reserved for the significant moments, as will be illustrated. Naturally one had in mind three ideas: (1) erect penis; (2) pregnant belly; (3) podgy self.

I made comments, but no interpretations. For instance, while she was drawing

(5) A house, with sun, clouds (again) and a flowering plant, I asked if she could draw a person.

Ada replied that she would draw

(6) her cousin, but as she drew her cousin she said: '*I can't draw hands.*'

I was now growing confident that the theme of stealing would appear, and so I was able to lean back on the child's own 'process'. *From now on it did not exactly matter what I said or did not say, except that I must be adapted to the child's needs and not requiring the child to adapt to my own.*

The hiding of the hands could be related either to the theme of stealing or to that of masturbation—and these themes are inter-related in that the stealing would be a compulsive acting out of repressed masturbation or drive-fantasies.

(There was a further indication of pregnancy in this drawing of the cousin, but the pregnancy theme did not develop significance in this session. It would no doubt have taken us to the mother's pregnancy when Ada was 3 years old.)

Ada rationalised. She said: 'She's hiding a present.' I asked: 'Can you draw the present?'

(7) The present—a box of handkerchiefs.

Ada said: 'The box is crooked.'

I asked: 'Where did she buy the present?' And she drew

(8) The counter of John Lewis (a leading London store).

Note: The curtain down the middle of the drawing. (see No. 21.)

I now asked: 'What about drawing the lady buying the present?' Undoubtedly I was wanting to test Ada's ability to draw hands. So she drew

(9) Which again shows a lady with her hands hidden because the view is from behind the counter.

It will be observed that the pictures are drawn with a stronger line now that the imagination has entered into their conception.

The theme of buying and giving presents had entered into the child's presentation of herself, but neither she nor I knew that these themes would eventually become significant. I did know, however, that the idea of buying is regularly employed to cover the compulsion to steal, and that the giving of presents is often a rationalisation to cover the same compulsion.

> I said: 'I would very much like to see what the lady looks like from behind.' So Ada drew
>
> (10) This picture *surprised* Ada. She said: 'Oh! She has long arms like mine; she is feeling for something. She has on a black dress with long sleeves; that's the dress I have on now, it was Mummy's once.'

So now the person in the drawings stood for Ada herself. In this drawing the hands are drawn in a way that is special. The fingers reminded me of the pencil that was too fat. I made no interpretation.

Stock-taking

It was not certain how things would develop; perhaps this was all that I would get. In a pause I asked about techniques for getting to sleep, that is, for dealing with the change from waking to sleeping, and the time that is difficult for children who are having conflicting feelings about masturbation. Ada said:

> 'I have a very big bear.' And while lovingly drawing it
>
> (11) she told me its history. She also had a live kitten in bed with her in the mornings when she woke. Here Ada told me about her brother who sucks his thumb and she drew the next:
>
> (12) In this drawing is shown the brother's hand with a supernumerary thumb for sucking.

Observe the two breast-like objects where there were clouds in earlier drawings. It could be that this picture includes memories of seeing her baby brother on her mother's body, and near the breasts. I made no interpretation.

Our work together was now hanging fire. One could say that the child was (without knowing it) wondering whether it would be safe (i.e. profitable) to go deeper. While she was thus engaged she drew

(13) 'A proud climber.'

This was the time of the climbing of Everest by Hilary and Tensing. This idea gave me a measure of Ada's capacity to experience an achievement, and in the sexual field to reach a climax. I was able to use this as an indication that Ada would be able to bring me her main problem and give me the chance to help her with it. This gave me confidence while I was waiting, waiting for what?

I made no interpretation. I did, however, deliberately make a link with dreaming. I said:

> 'When you dream, do you dream of mountaineering, and all that?'

Dreams

There followed a verbal account of a very muddled dream. What she said, talking very fast, was something like this:

> 'I go to the U.S.A. I am with the Indians and I get three bears. The boy next door is in the dream. He is rich. I was lost in London. There was a flood. The sea came in at the front door. We all ran away in a car. We left something behind. I think–I don't know what it was. I don't think it was Teddy. I think it was the gas stove.'

She told me that this was *a very bad nightmare* that she once had. When she woke she ran into the parents' room and got into her mother's bed, where she spent the rest of the night. She was evidently reporting an acute confusional state. This was perhaps the centre point of the interview, or *the essential reaching to the bottom of her experience of mental illness*. If this be true, then the rest of the session could be looked upon as a picture of recovery from the confusional state.

After this Ada drew

(14) Paint brush and box,

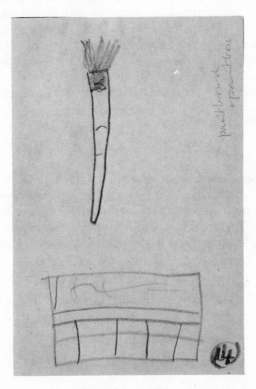

(15) An aspidistra which she thought of while talking of spiders and other dreams of stinging scorpions 'walking down in armies, and one big one in my bed', and

(16) A muddled picture indicating a mixture of house (fixed abode) and caravan (movable home, reminding her of the family holiday); and then

(17) A poisonous spider.

The spider had characteristics that link it with the hand; it is likely that the spider here symbolises both the masturbation hand and also the female genital and orgasm. I made no interpretations.

> I asked what a sad dream would be and Ada said: 'Someone was killed, mother and father. They came all right again though.'
>
> Then she said: 'I've got a box with thirty-six coloured pencils.' (Reference to the small number supplied by me, and, I suppose, my meanness.)

Here we had reached the end of a middle phase. It must be remembered that I did not know whether anything more would happen, but I made no interpretations and waited for the working of the process which had been set up in the child. I might have taken the reference to my meanness (pencils) as a sign that her own stealing impulse would be appropriate at this point in the interview. However, I continued to make no interpretations and to be waiting in case Ada should wish to go further.

The Last Phase

> After a while Ada spontaneously said: 'I had a burglar dream.'

Now the final stage of the interview started. It will be observed that Ada's drawings became much more bold at this point, and to anyone watching her draw it would have been clear that she was actuated from deep impulse and need. One felt almost in touch with Ada's unconscious drives and source of fantasy.

> Ada drew

(18) A black man is killing a woman. There is some kind of thing behind him, with fingers or something.

Ada then drew

(19) The burglar, his hair sticking up, rather funny, like a clown. She said: 'My sister's hands are bigger than mine.'

The burglar is stealing jewels from a rich lady because he wants to give a nice present to his wife. He could not wait to save up.

Here, at a deeper level, appears the theme represented earlier by the woman or girl buying handkerchiefs from a store to give as a present to someone. It will be seen that there are shapes like the clouds of the earlier drawings, and these are now like a curtain, and *there is a bow.*

I made no interpretation, but I found myself interested in the bow, which, if untied, would reveal something. This could be a pictorial representation of nascent consciousness, or release from repression. These curtains and the bow reappear in

(20) which is a drawing of the present. Ada added, looking at what she had drawn: 'The burglar has a cloak. His hair looks like carrots or a tree or a bush. He is really very kind.'

Now I intervened. I asked about the bow. Ada said that it belonged to a circus. (She had not been to one.)

She drew

(21) which shows a juggler. This could be thought of as an attempt to make a career out of the unresolved problem. Here again were the curtains and the bow. The dissociation is represented by the fact that the picture is in two halves in that the curtain is down, but also it is up, and the juggler's act is on.

Active Intervention

I now saw the bow as symbolical of repression, and it seemed to me that Ada was ready to have the bow untied. I therefore said to her:

'Do you ever pinch [steal] things yourself?'

This is the place where the subject of my study of the antisocial tendency appears in this description of a therapeutic interview. It is for this detail that the reader has been invited to follow the development of the process in the child who has used the opportunity for contact with myself. There was a double reaction to my question, and here is represented the dissociation.

Ada (1) said 'No!' and at the same time she (2) took another piece of paper and drew

(22) An apple tree with two apples; and to this she added grass, a rabbit and a flower.

This showed what was behind the curtain. It represented the discovery of the mother's breasts which had been hidden, as it were, by the mother's clothes. In this way a deprivation had been symbolised. This symbolism is to be compared and contrasted with the direct view depicted in drawing 12 which contains a memory of the baby brother in contact with the mother's body. Drawing 12 had no therapeutic significance for her.

I made a comment here. I said: 'Oh, I see, the curtains were mother's blouse, and you have now reached through to her breasts.'

Ada did not answer, but instead she drew with obvious pleasure

(23) 'This is mother's dress, that I love best. She still has it.'

The dress dates from the time when Ada was a little girl and indeed it is so drawn that the child's eyes are about at the level of the mother's mid-thigh region. The theme of breasts is continued in the puff sleeves. The fertility symbols are the same as in the early drawing of a house, and are also changing over into numbers.

The work of the interview was now over, and Ada wasted a little time 'coming to the surface', playing a game which continued the theme of numbers as fertility symbols:

(24), (25), (26).

Ada was now ready to go, and as she was in a happy and contented state I was able to have ten minutes with the mother who had been waiting an hour and a quarter.

Early History in Brief

In this brief interview I was able to learn that Ada had made satisfactory development until she was 4 years 9 months old. She had taken the birth of her brother in her stride when she was $3\frac{1}{2}$, with some exaggerated concern for him. At 4 years 9 months, the brother (then 20 months old) became seriously ill, and remained ill.

Ada had been very much mothered by her older sister, but now (when the brother became ill) this older sister transferred her attention absolutely to the small brother, and so Ada became seriously deprived. It was some time before the parents realised that Ada had in this way been seriously affected by the loss of her sister's concern. They did all they could to mend matters, but it was two years or so before Ada seemed to be recovering from a setback caused by this loss of the sister-mother.

At about this time Ada (7 years old) started to steal, at first from the mother and later from the school. Recently, stealing had become a serious matter, but Ada could never own up to it. She even took stolen money to her teacher and asked her to give it out to her slowly, thereby showing that she had not dealt with the full implication of her stealing acts.

Along with this compulsive stealing Ada's schooling had become affected by a lack of ability to concentrate when working. She was always blowing her nose, and she had become fat and ungainly (see drawing 4–'pencil too fat–something wrong with it').

In short : Ada had suffered a relative deprivation at 4·9 years, though living in her own good home. As a result she had become confused, but as she started to rediscover a sense of security she had developed stealing as a dissociated compulsion. She could not acknowledge her thefts because of the dissociation.

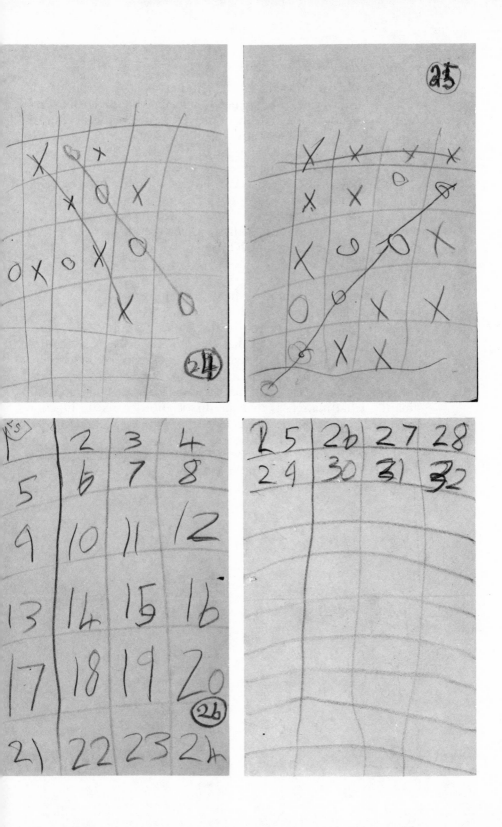

Result of this Psychotherapeutic Interview

The interview produced a result. Although Ada was stealing right up to the interview she has not stolen since, that is in six years. Also her school work quickly improved. (The nocturnal enuresis did not clear up till a year after the interview, however.)

The mother reported that Ada came out of the clinic *with a new relationship to her*, one of ease and intimacy, as if a block had been removed. This recovery of an old intimacy has persisted, and it seems to show that the work done in the interview was a genuine re-establishment of infant-mother contact which had been lost at the time when the big sister suddenly switched her mothering from Ada to the ill brother.

The Dissociation

Here then is an example of the dissociation to which I am referring. Ada could not own up to stealing. When in the interview she was asked: 'Do you ever steal?' she said firmly: 'No!' but at the same time she showed that she now need not steal because she had found what she had lost—contact with her mother's breasts in her own inner psychic reality, or in terms of mental representations, or of internal objects. The language does not matter, what matters is that the dissociation ceased to function as it had become suddenly a defence that was no longer needed.

The details of the case illustrate well the theory that is needed in work of any kind, whether therapeutic or custodial, with anti-social and delinquent children.

CASE XIV 'Cecil' *aet* 21 months at first consultation

These case notes concern a boy, a characteristic of whose emotional development was a capacity to regress to dependence in his home setting. The parents met these regressions adequately, and in this way turned them into positive therapeutic experiences.

The case has special interest in that the process links very closely with the regressive episodes that characterise the life of any child in a reliable home setting, that is, apart from the question of psychiatric illness either in the child or in the family.

The management of this case was based on six consultation hours spaced as follows:

Date	Age of boy (b. Oct. 1953)
12th July 1955	21 months
12th Oct. 1955	24 months
8th Feb. 1956	28 months
6th Feb. 1957	$3\frac{1}{2}$ years
GAP	
17th Oct. 1961	8 years
1st Feb. 1962	8 years

Cecil was referred to me by the teacher at his nursery school in a district outside London.

Consultation with the Father, 12th July 1955

I first interviewed the father, who was genuinely concerned about his child and had a good grip on the total situation. In an hour's interview he told me the details of Cecil's life.

FAMILY

There were two children of the marriage, Cecil, 21 months, and Kenneth, 1 month, who was at that time being breast fed. The father described the mother as 'intelligent but not always easy'. Cecil was born normally (7 lb.) and had been breast-fed for eight months. He was eager and had been fed 'on demand'. He had been in fact rather greedy, and

239

would tend to wake after one hour, so that from 6 weeks old he was not a good sleeper. For this he was taken to a hospital clinic and given chloral. On the whole he was happy as a baby and started early to play. He became easy to manage, and weaning at 8 months presented no difficulty.

The father said that his wife had been more competent with Kenneth who did very well from the start than she had been with Cecil, implying that there was real difficulty with Cecil in the early weeks. At 10 months Cecil was piling bricks one on top of another. He sat and walked in good time. At 21 months he was not using words.

The father then tried to describe the difficulty about which he was consulting me. He said that Cecil changed in *November 1954* at the age of 13 months. He related this to the fact that his wife had become pregnant in the previous month and she was *liable to be anxious when starting a new pregnancy*. At 13 months, therefore, Cecil began to go back. He displayed again what the father described as 'his baby difficulties', the sleeplessness in particular and in general a lack of confidence in the mother, so that it became necessary for either the father or the mother to be actually with him. At the same time he began to lose his interest in toys. Each night he would wake several times and either the father or the mother would go to him. When he woke, he woke screaming. On the credit side, he was feeding well and growing at the proper rate, and an interest in music had appeared.

Cecil had become able to use the pot if wanting to do so, but in this phase (which started when he was 13 months old) Cecil had given up using it altogether. He was not having nappies but was wetting when he felt like it on the ground. The parents were not strict about this.

The second child was born at home five weeks before this consultation with the father. Cecil was 20 months old when the baby was born. During the three weeks prior to the baby's birth Cecil's symptomatology had got worse, especially in the matter of his difficulty in going to sleep and his waking screaming, and he had started to resist going to bed. The night before the consultation he had cried for three-quarters of an hour, pushing everything away, stamping his feet and striking himself. He would have attacks of this kind every day or so, and perhaps two a day.

Before the baby came the parents tried to tell Cecil what to expect, but he did not understand as far as they could tell. When the baby came, he was 'not interested in him', or he would look at him and poke his nose or ears, and lead his parents off to look at something else. At the same time he himself wanted to get into a pram or a cot.

TRANSITIONAL PHENOMENA

The father told me, when I made routine enquiries, that Cecil had first sucked his fist and then one thumb, but only on going to sleep. He never liked to have any special object. During the past month, however, that is to say since the birth of the baby, he had been sucking his thumb all day and especially if the baby was being fed. Cecil had not actually tried to get to the breast but he had been very pleased to take food at the same time that the baby was being fed at the breast. The father reported that play had now (at 21 months) almost ceased. Water and sand were neglected, and toys had become unimportant. At times he would mope and sit sucking his thumb. On the other hand, he had developed his new and very positive interest in music. He liked to do housework, pretending to wash-up and to use the Hoover.

The general practitioner was helpful in the management of Cecil, but the time had come when drugs no longer made a difference to Cecil's state.

At this stage in the consultation I realised that I had been consulted over the telephone by a colleague in regard to the management of this very case. The father told me that this doctor had advised him and his wife to employ a nurse for Cecil. It amused me to find that when I strongly contradicted this advice I was contradicting myself, and this showed me how different is the advice that one can give at a distance from the way one acts when

241

one is in actual contact with a case. The parents had tried using a nurse, but very soon Cecil had refused to let her supplant the parents, although he seemed to be fond of her.

Comment

Now that instead of talking about the case with a colleague over the telephone I was in direct contact with the case, far from advising the use of a nurse I found myself entirely caught up in the idea of enabling these parents themselves to deal with their child's illness. I took into account the fact that along with all these troubles Cecil was affectionate and rather sweet-natured, and he was even becoming loving towards the baby boy. He was able to make positive use of sleeping in the parents' bed, except when he had one of these bouts of crying, at which times nothing was of any use.

I was forced to agree with the father's suggestion that the pattern of the very early infantile disturbance of the first few weeks had seemed to be reactivated in detail in this new period which started in November along with the beginning of the mother's anxiety about her pregnancy.

After this consultation I wrote the following letter to my colleague:

> This is an official note on the subject of Cecil. I find myself in a very difficult position, interviewing a man and discovering half-way through that he had already consulted yourself. Moreover, setting aside all matter of etiquette, I was in the ludicrous position of countermanding advice that I myself had given you, and which you had passed on to these parents. I told the father that sometimes you and I discussed cases and that I remembered your speaking about the advice you proposed to give in this case, and that this seemed to me at the time to be eminently sensible. For some reason or other I found the picture of the home situation different from what I had expected from second-hand report.
>
> This child, who started to change last October at the moment when the mother realised she was pregnant (she always becomes pathologically (hypochondriacally) anxious when pregnant), is in

a rather seriously regressed state, but his appetite and general health are not very much affected, and the father, at present, seems to be able to meet the child's needs. I am sure that you would agree with me that handing the child over to a nurse would be a good thing only if the two parents were actually failing. It must be a matter of opinion whether one can say that there is a failure now in the meeting of the child's special needs. I am guessing that the parents are not failing the child at present, and that they may be able to bring the child through the present illness.

I have no doubt whatever that the child, who does not seem to mind the birth of the baby, and who is fond of the baby, was nevertheless seriously affected by the mother's change of attitude last October when she became pregnant and anxious.

These parents would consider psychotherapy for the boy even though this would mean a considerable disturbance of the household routine. I have suggested that the whole matter shall hang over until after the holiday.

On 14th July 1955 I received the following letter from the father:

> Your advice about Cecil has helped us to feel more confident that we may be able to help him ourselves, as we want to do. We will write again about 20th August as you suggested.

This letter confirmed the idea that I had formed that he and the mother wished to deal with Cecil themselves if I would help them to do so. I replied in the following letter on 15th July:

> I feel sure now that if you yourselves are able to see Cecil through this will be much more satisfactory all round than getting outside help. On the other hand we must not be afraid to take the other line if it should become necessary. It is since speaking to you that I have felt like encouraging you to try to do it yourselves.

In the father's letter of August he reported progress, giving just the kind of detail that I wished to know:

243

You will remember you asked me to write to tell you how our son Cecil was getting on since I saw you in July.

For the last 3–4 weeks he has been happier much of the time—but with some days when he is miserable. Eating, playing, sleeping and generally co-operating, these all improve or deteriorate together. I sleep in bed with him. He only wakes up in the night once or twice now, sometimes getting out of bed and crying, but for a shorter time than previously. In the morning and after a mid-day sleep with my wife he now wakes nearly always without crying. But he does not use his bed normally, but likes to get in and out of bed several times, often going to sleep on the floor.

He plays more than he did; he is still passionately fond of music and dances to it; he is very keen on looking at picture books. He still does not talk but makes a wider range of sounds (22 months).

He is sometimes very noisy and laughing and at other times he is very quiet and sad looking, and then he sucks his thumb. He often looks pale and tired.

I should be very glad if you could see Cecil and my wife. We are anxious to know if he should have treatment—or whether you think he may grow up happily without it. I am very keen that my wife should see you as I think she has unnecessarily lost confidence, and I think it would be of great help if you could give her a general picture of the situation.

After this I arranged to see Cecil's mother. I was beginning to realise that she was liable to depressive moods and hypochondriacal fears.

Consultation with the Mother, 12th October 1955

The mother brought Cecil. Cecil slept almost throughout the consultation on her lap. At this time he was 2 years old and his brother was 4 months old.

The mother gradually told me her version of the story, which was very similar to that given by her husband. She said that Cecil was now happier and sleeping better than he was when her husband brought him at 21 months. Occasionally he would scream, or fuss in some other way, usually at the time of the feeding of the baby who was still on the breast.

244

She then spoke of the changes in Cecil for which they were consulting me. He had played in a normal sort of a way before he was a year old, but then he lost the capacity to play.

> At this point in the consultation Cecil woke enough to stretch his hand so that a finger was in his mother's mouth while he was sucking his own thumb.

The mother went over the details of what happened in November, two months after her conception of Kenneth, when she was not really feeling well, and when Cecil (about 13 months old) began to alter. Cecil gave up using the pot and he wanted to be like a baby, lying in the pram, and insisting on being bathed in the way that babies are bathed. In his playing he wanted to be making the cot up in the way that his mother has to make it up for a baby, and now (at 2 years) he does this with a doll. Sometimes recently (the mother said) he has become angry, hitting the baby and the mother. She recognised this as an improvement on the other technique whereby he became a baby himself. The mother said that she was very much occupied or preoccupied with the new baby, and Cecil had resented this at first. Cecil had been able to use his father in an affectionate way when in a state of strained relationships with herself. Now (at 2 years) Cecil was enjoying himself but was playing on his own, that is to say, *not using toys* in the way that he used to do before he became ill. He had become 'almost obsessionally' clean, and very pleased to be allowed to help in housework and cooking. He could dress himself with a little help and he was eating normally.[1]

In answer to my enquiry the mother told me that Cecil had had a teddy from early infancy but that this had never meant very much to him. He now had a gollywog which had become important to him in a special way. 'He talks to it,' she said, 'making noises for it, putting it to bed and feeding it at the navel.'

Her chief complaint about Cecil now was that he was not talking. He made himself understood, however, and understood everything. There were no children available for him to play with.

Cecil had good muscle tone and had now begun to like having a bath again, playing with the taps, and playing with water in the sink.

[1] Looking back one can see that the loss of use of toys indicated a loss of symbolism due to the loss of the object symbolised. This eventually became the basis for the stealing.

Strangers in the house made him anxious and he would stand by his mother sucking his thumb, not making contact with the strangers. The mother said that the father had never been angry with Cecil; he was indeed very long-suffering. All the week when the father had to be away from home Cecil tended to whine, and the mother interpreted this as a longing for the father, and this fact made her annoyed sometimes. She might prefer it if the father were more firm, because she felt that troubles tended to appear when the father was away, and when the father was present Cecil went to him instead of to the mother. When Cecil woke crying at night he would tend to cling to his father rather than to her.[1]

I followed up this consultation with a letter to my colleague on 13th October:

> A further note about this child. At 24 months he is not yet talking. On the other hand there are many signs of improvement, and I think that the mother is coping satisfactorily with the difficult problem of bringing the older child round while bringing the baby up. Cecil is gradually emerging from his need to be like the baby and has even been able to express anger with the baby and the mother when they were together. Partly he is solving his problem along the lines of identification with the mother, being preoccupied with housework, which he does quite well, and treating his dolls exactly as the baby is treated. One good sign is that he has now for the first time adopted an object, a gollywog, and he is also becoming interested in his teddy which he has had from early times but which he has previously more or less ignored. He still sucks his thumb at appropriate moments.
>
> He seems happy and able to enjoy the company of a temporary nurse. He is obsessed with cleaning and playing with water. He dresses himself, nearly. He is eating well. There is an almost complete absence of play with toys, and this remains as a major symptom, and it is quite clear that he was playing with toys up till last November when he became ill in reaction to changes in his mother.
>
> He came to me asleep and stayed asleep during most of the consultation. Without quite waking he did put his finger in his mother's mouth while he had his thumb in his own. In the end he

[1] This would now appear to us all to be wrong in that Cecil needed the father at this stage as a mother, to supplant the mother when she failed.

246

woke and behaved like an intelligent child. He was still sleepy but he played with a toy I gave him and took it away. He has never yet spoken a recognisable word, but he talks to his dolls in his own language and he understands everything and makes himself understood.

He is fairly well established in his body and I think his muscle tone is not flabby.

I think it will be seen from these notes that the risk I took in advising the mother to look after this child may prove to be justified. There is still a sleep disturbance but usually this amounts to his waking once, which is not too bad. He goes to sleep happily and wakes happily in the morning.

A major factor, one corresponding to the mother's nerviness, is the father's gentle nature. It is difficult for the father to give directions or to be angry. The mother says that if anyone ever has to be angry it has to be herself. In this way weekends are the worst time, with father at home and the child whining all the time, clinging to his father and pushing mother away. During the week, with father away, he is not difficult and he is usually not whining but appears to be happy.[1]

There is a long way for this child to go yet, but I think he might become normal if we use the word normal in rather a broad way.

Interval. October 1955 to February 1956

I next saw the mother on 8th February 1956 and she again brought Cecil. The father came too.

It was reported that the baby (8 months old) had had eczema, but was otherwise well and still being breast fed. Cecil (now 2 years 4 months) was on the whole happy. He had started using words of one syllable.

> While I was talking to the parents Cecil was sucking his thumb and keeping his other hand in his mother's bag.

Compare this with Cecil's behaviour during the consultation on 12th October. The mother's bag had now taken the place of her mouth.

It was reported that Cecil was playing more, but all the time

---

[1] This seems to contradict a previous statement, but there was a change taking place belonging to Cecil's uncertainty as to whether his father was a mother substitute or a father. This was at an intermediate stage.

watching to make sure his mother was there and ready to be attentive to him. He had evinced a slight interest in the baby, occasionally even being affectionate towards him, but at other times showing that the baby was a nuisance to him. Meals had become peaceful. He was no longer insisting on having his meals with the parents. An affectionate relationship to the mother had returned, but the very positive relationship to the father (which sometimes upset the mother) remained. But he was now able to be happy with father and mother together, and had become able to allow the father to leave him without becoming distressed. He had now been using the pot again for defaecation.

In regard to language, Cecil had become able to communicate complex ideas or orders. For example, he would show his undone shoelaces; if the mother did not do them up he would say: 'Undone!'

> At this point in the consultation Cecil was discovering the toys in the room while sucking his thumb. His mother's keys had dropped on the floor and he put a key to the lock in his mother's bag. A new version of his finger in her mouth. Key now represents finger. One can see here the root of the compulsive thief's interest in keys and locks.

Cecil had wanted to bring his gollywog, although the mother said: 'He is not really all that interested in it.' Lately he had been sucking his thumb much less.

> While we were talking he had taken all the money out of his mother's bag.

Compare with earlier behaviour:

(a) Finger in mother's mouth
(b) Finger in her bag
(c) Key in the bag's lock, and now
(d) Taking the money out of her bag

All this related to an improving interpersonal relationship. All the time his interest in the toys that belong to my room was in abeyance. It was obvious that he had a potential interest in them, but he could not get to them. He picked a button out of the mother's purse and gave it to his mother. The mother said: 'Off

248

my coat', but she did not take it, and this detail illustrates the very subtle something in the mother which constitutes a difficulty in her capacity to communicate and to be communicated with at a most primitive level. To just this extent she failed to accept; but it has to be remembered that she was concerned with her relationship to me in the consultation.

The mother reported that Cecil continues to use the parental bed. Waiting for him is a cot in the parents' room. It appears that there is still some difficulty about the parents' going out together because Cecil is liable to wake from 9 o'clock onwards, and then he expects to find them at home.

I wrote again to my colleague on 9th February 1956:

> This is to keep you in touch with the progress of Cecil. He now looks like a normal child. He uses many words and communicates freely although without sentences, plays on his own and is not all the time obsessed with putting himself into the infant position in relation to his mother. He would pass for normal but there are residual symptoms. The main trouble is at night, although the nights are very much better than they were. He can now stand the parents' being together and he has no trouble about his father going off to work. On the other hand he needs to sleep in his parents' bed with his father turned towards him all the time. This means that the parents can never get together and the mother finds this is a terrible frustration. They are willing to put up with this for another few months if assured that the sacrifice is worth while.
>
> The overall technique, which indeed could be called 'spoiling', seems to have had good effect; moreover the mother says that she is gradually coming round to being able to make a more direct contact of give and take, and this is showing in her relation to the next child who, by the way, has eczema but is otherwise normal.

My next contact with the parents was by a letter, this time from the mother (2nd July 1956). In this letter the mother discussed the complication of Cecil's aggressive behaviour towards his brother. She could see that this aggressiveness had two sides to it, the evidence it gave of healthy development in Cecil, and at the same time the disadvantage from the point of view of the brother. I replied to the parents (4th July 1956):

249

Your idea of keeping the boy at home seems to have been justified. I don't think I can do very much about the remaining symptoms. It must be very difficult coming to recognise the fact that
Cecil has reason to hate his brother. I expect he is fond of him as
well and would not like it if he were not there to be hated. You
are quite right that he does not have to be made to feel guilty,
your job being simply to prevent damage to the brother. There is
no reason why he should not know, however, that through his
behaviour you get driven into taking the brother's side. It must
be very disturbing to you that you still have Cecil coming into
your bed at night. All I can say is that if you can hang on, that
may be the best way of treating the condition, waiting for
developments.

The next contact was a visit from the mother (6th February
1957). Cecil was now $3\frac{1}{2}$ years old.

When the mother saw me alone for half an hour she reported
an immense change. Not only had Cecil grown, but also he was
happier. Nevertheless he would not stay in his own bed. She and
her husband had not had a single night without him. They had
to make the best of the fact that Cecil is now in his own cot from
bedtime till 2 a.m. in order to have a sexual life at all. 'Cecil feels
he has a right to be in his parents' bed and he talks about it. We
tell him,' she said, 'that we are fed up, and he says: "When I
grow bigger".'[1] He was sleeping next to his father or across the
bottom of the bed. The mother said that she loved him very much
but she occasionally got exasperated. 'Things are altogether
easier with Kenneth.'

The family had now moved house and there were more children in the new neighbourhood than in the old, including a girl of
5. Nevertheless Cecil had not made any steady friendship. The
mother reported that his play capacity was variable; she said:
'He looks forward to children's visits but when the children come
he is likely to be impossible.' In the same way his relationship to
his brother was unpredictable. 'In short, Cecil has two sides to
his nature,' she said; 'one is happy and merry and the other is
possessive and jealous. In the latter state he tends to play on his
own, imagining that he is a workman or something.'

In dressing up he was choosing to dress rather more as a girl

[1] Compare with sophisticated phase (p. 260).

250

than as a boy, and he evidently envied the woman her rôle. He continued thumbsucking and had not a regular object of the kind I call 'transitional', but adopted many teddies and kept them in a pram. They were children. He was still very fond of his father. He had developed a phobia of doctors, but this resulted from seeing his brother inoculated and hearing him scream. He would scratch himself all over as if remembering Kenneth's eczema, but without producing a rash. If with his parents he went easily to sleep, but if alone he would lie awake, cheerfully sitting scratching himself till he bled. No genital masturbation had been noticed. He talked a great deal and was very fond of stories. The mother was now looking after the children herself without any help. A new feature was a much more deliberate hitting of the mother when he was angry with her, and the mother felt that she could now allow herself the relief of getting angry herself sometimes. He had remorse after hitting her.

After discussion we decided that Cecil must continue to receive this special indulgence at night if the parents could stand it. The strain on the mother was quite great, and I took the trouble to make it clear that I understood this.

After this consultation I wrote the following letter to my colleague (7th February 1957):

> I have had a visit from Cecil's mother. Apparently the boy has made a very good recovery as he has nearly emerged from his state of dependence. This regression has been beautifully met by the mother and father, who have allowed themselves to 'spoil' him. The residual symptom is his continued need to be in his parents' bed, which provides a very serious strain on his mother but one that she is willing to take for a further limited period.
>
> There is still, of course, a good deal of evidence of emotional disturbance, especially if the parents attempt to deal with the main symptom in any way other than by allowing it. Much of the day Cecil is happy and playing.

Next came a letter from the mother (9th March 1957) in which she took up the idea of a nursery school:

> When I saw you a few weeks ago about our son Cecil (3½ years) you agreed that it would be good for him to go to a nursery school. Only when I came to arrange for him to go to one of the

251

local nursery schools did I realise that there are long waiting lists everywhere (one is advised to 'book' a child at 6 months). I have tried both private and public ones. At the public one I have been told that if I write to the education authority telling them that Cecil has been difficult, and if I have a letter from you to say he would greatly benefit from going to the nursery school, he would then probably be able to go. I am wondering whether you think it is worth while doing this—or whether this should be left for more deserving cases.

As a result of this letter I wrote to the Education Officer (13th March 1957):

> I understand that Mrs. X., acting on my advice, has applied for a vacancy for Cecil in a nursery school. I would like to support this application on the grounds that Cecil has been through a long period of strain, and I consider that now that he has improved he is in great need of the sort of help that a nursery school can provide.
>
> Cecil first came to see me at 21 months. The boy was seriously disturbed following his recognition that his mother was pregnant.[1] One of the main symptoms was a sleep difficulty.
>
> I know that there is a waiting list for children for the school and all I wish to do is to refer to Cecil's difficulties and to give my opinion that as soon as he can make use of a nursery school it will be important for him to go there.

In response to this the county education committee gave permission for Cecil's 'exceptional admission to the local nursery school'.

AT 8 YEARS

Interval. March 1957 to October 1961
The next contact came in October 1961, when the junior school asked me to see Cecil, now aged 8 years, because he had been stealing. The mother came with Cecil, and I saw her before I saw

---

[1] It would not have been prudent to have described in this letter the way in which the boy was affected by the mother's pathological reaction to the idea of having conceived.

the boy. Cecil was now just 8 years and his brother was 6, attending the same school.

The mother reported that Cecil had got better but he had never become an easy child to manage. There had always been phases of difficulty. When he went from the nursery to the junior school he had started stealing, that is to say, when for the first time he met difficulties in his environment, and outside his own home.[2] There continued in Cecil the state of conflict between his wanting to be big and his wanting to be small. There had been some stealing at home; money had been taken from the mother's bag, and also recently there had been stealing from friends. He had also 'found' a watch. At school he was behaving well, apart from the stealing. He had not seemed to be worried about school until a week before the consultation, and then worry had begun to show in the symptom of his waking with stomach-ache. 'There is rather a chip on his shoulder,' the mother said, 'bound up with a jealousy of his brother.'

I made a note that the mother was in a depressed state. The father continued to be very patient in his dealings with his family, and the mother continued to be anxious in a general way.

After seeing the mother, I gave Cecil (8 years old) a long personal interview. I put the low child-table between us, and established a contact on the basis of squiggles.

Naturally, it was very interesting to me to be in contact with this 8-year-old boy, when I was still clearly remembering my contact with him at 21 months and at 2 years 4 months.

[2] Reality principle contrasted with therapeutic 'spoiling', or adaptation to special needs associated with regression to dependence.

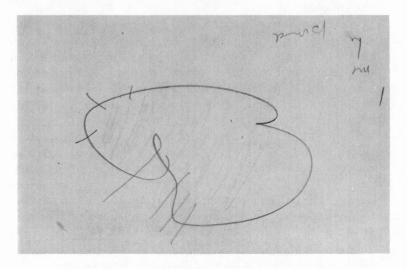

(1) My first squiggle he made into a pond.

(2) His, which I used to indicate a man or boy.

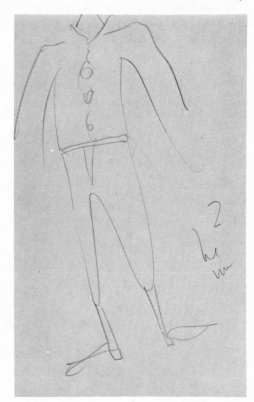

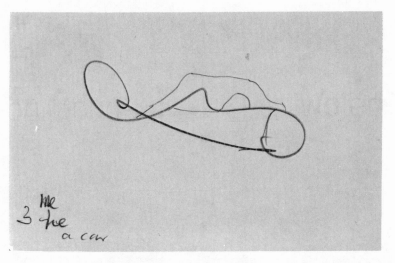

(3) Then he made my squiggle into a car. Each of his showed considerable imagination.

(4) His, which I made into some kind of animal.

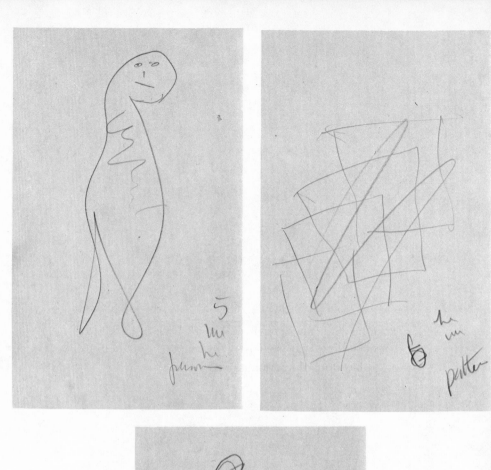

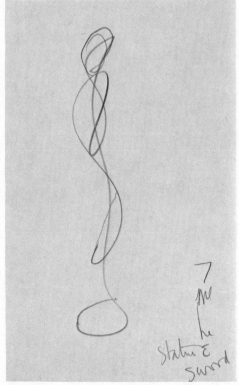

(5) He turned mine into a person.

(6) His, which I could only use by making what we called a pattern.

(7) He turned mine into a statue with a sword, again displaying ingenuity and creative imagination.

(8) His, which I turned into a crocodile.

(9) He turned into two apples joined together.

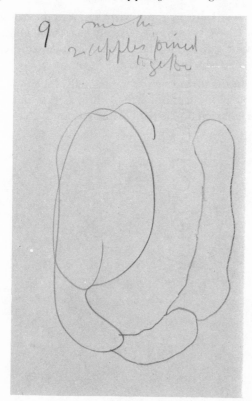

I was reminded of the way, when he was 24 months old, he had one finger in his mother's mouth while sucking his thumb. Something here is reduplicated that could be a unit.

(10) He then did a squiggle which I said was three apples and I said: 'Do you ever dream about apples?'

He said: 'I dream about what happens the day before and what I have been doing; usually nice.' When I asked about nasty or sad dreams he said he had one sad dream about his friend who broke his arm.

(11) His. In the dream he was in hospital a long time. He really did break his arm but actually he was only in hospital two hours. He fell on the path by the school.

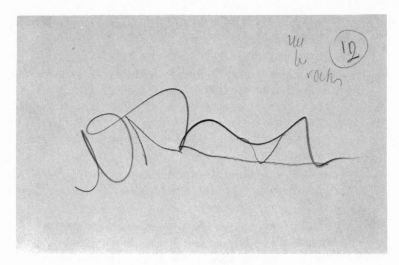

(12) He turned mine into rocks. This had to do with a holiday in France, and represented cliffs.

(13) He then turned his own squiggle into a G which he said could have to do with garters because he is just going to join the Cubs.

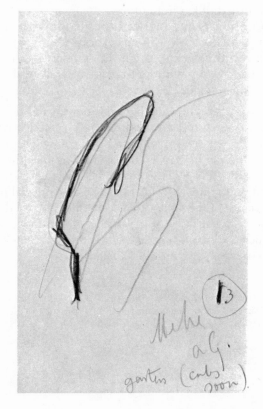

(14) His, which I turned into a squirrel, as he called it.

(15) Mine. He made it into a vase with a flower.

(16) His, which I turned into a flower in a pot. While we were doing this he was talking about loneliness and sadness. He knew, he said, what being lonely was. The first few days at school as a day-boy he was not sure what to do. The first day he got all muddled up after prayers and so he got late.

I asked him about the advantages of growing up and so knowing more about things. He said: '*I don't want to grow up ; it's a pity to leave the younger ages.*'[1]

At this point I weighed in with an interpretation. I referred here to the apples and said they could stand for breasts and for his need to keep in touch with his own infancy and breast-feeding.

I now (1970) think of the three apples of his squiggle No. 10, which I said might be three breasts, in terms of the exaggeration of the maternal form that appears in mythology as a goddess with three breasts. The three breasts of Artemis could be thought of as a denial of the threat of harvest failure.

It is a main point in my presentation that this interpretation seemed natural to this boy who had been kept in touch with infancy object relationships through the operation of the regressive tendency which was met more than adequately by the parents' technique of management.

I asked here about father and mother and how he used them when wanting to be held and treated like a baby. He said that he used mother mostly because 'father is always showing me how to do things, how to mow the lawn and everything'. In other words he felt his father to be pushing him on towards growing up. Here was a denial of the importance of the father in his early life. He said that he was good at digging. 'I am worst at doing things at school which I know already, like sums ; doing them for nothing ; it's so boring. Exciting new things I can do.'

[1] It was interesting to get this 8-year-old sophisticated version of his 3-year-old comment: 'When I grow bigger', in relation to the idea of sleeping apart from the parents (p. 250).

I then asked him a direct question about stealing, and he told me about a petty theft and also about a dream in which a car is stolen. The dream

(17) followed a real incident. In the real incident the car had in it the suitcases all packed for travelling abroad so the family had to go somewhere nearer home. In this drawing and the boy's association to it there is a mixture of fact and dream. He also told how he had borrowed a friend's pen to use it, which amounted to stealing. Then he said, as if he had come across something important: 'When my brother was 2 years old he stole 1s. from me.'

I assume that it was very important to him to express his sense of his brother's usurpation of his rights in this concrete way.

Here the consultation ended, and the boy parted on good terms with me, and quite contented to leave.

In this interview I was able to get a new version of the earlier contacts in which Cecil saw me with his parents present. The sequence was: first, he linked his thumb-sucking with claiming a right to his mother's mouth, then he used his mother's bag and its contents (including money) instead of the mother's mouth. Now he told me about stealing and about being stolen from.

The main detail of this consultation hour relative to the present theme is that the drawing of the apples and my interpretation had meaning for him because of the bridge into the past and into the unconscious kept open by this boy's regressive tendencies. Parental management had accepted these tendencies and had met the dependence and had thus turned them into a therapeutic procedure.[1] Behind all this was a 'deprivation' related to the mother's reaction to becoming pregnant.

I then wrote the following letter to the headmaster of the junior school (20th October 1961):

> I saw Cecil, as you probably know, and I also saw him in 1955. The mother has told me about certain difficulties which have been giving trouble at school, and I have had an opportunity to form an opinion of Cecil and of placing his symptoms in relation to the whole of his development.
>
> In his case, the recent stealing is related to a certain degree of a tendency in the boy to recapture very early infantile dependence. As you probably know, this sort of tendency goes along with the opposite tendency to be very independent. I was able to see when he first came to me in 1955 that Cecil had been adversely affected at the time of his mother's pregnancy and her rather exaggerated reaction to becoming pregnant. This happened when he was about $1\frac{1}{2}$ years old (October 1954).
>
> I realise that the management of a boy at school must be related to the management of all the other boys and cannot be exactly related to the boy's total development and to his difficulties that may date from infancy and early childhood. Nevertheless I let you know this detail because it may be possible for the school to adopt the principle of seeing Cecil through a phase in which these awkward symptoms may be expected. Sometimes it

[1] Cf. 'Withdrawal and Regression' (1954), in *Collected Papers: Through Paediatrics to Psycho-analysis*, Tavistock Publications, 1958.

helps masters who are in charge of a child if they can see that there is some sense in symptoms that have no logical meaning in the present day and in relation to the conscious life of the child.

This produced the following reply:

> Thank you for your letter about Cecil, which was very reassuring.
>
> We seem to have got over the difficult phase of stealing without other boys becoming conscious that the disappearance of their belongings had anything to do with Cecil. This has been very largely due to the most helpful co-operation of his parents.
>
> I am glad to be able to report that the boy seems to be settling down very satisfactorily.

In reply to a further enquiry I received a letter from the father (4th December 1961):

> Cecil is certainly easier in himself than when my wife last brought him to see you. He still has the same general symptoms but much less so. He sleeps better and does not often complain of stomach-ache. He is not miserable and distressed as he was.
>
> He still has times of being very babyish and easily jealous of his brother but these are interspersed with easier and more contented times. He seems very interested in his school and is less anxious about it.
>
> As far as we know he has not stolen since we saw you with him.
>
> When I last spoke to the headmaster, he too seemed to think he was getting on better. I hope he was able to say the same in his letter to you.

The other symptoms remained, although lessened in degree, and they included bouts of babyishness, but there had apparently been no stealing.

Next I saw the mother and the boy again on 1st February 1962.

First I saw the mother, who reported that there had been no stealing. Cecil had been more positive in his relationship to herself and to others, and more happy, and he was pleased to be coming to see me again. There were still babyish traces which the mother continued to meet as and when they appeared. The brother had now become rather a nuisance and was teasing Cecil.

264

Cecil was standing up to this new complication. The Christmas holiday had gone well. At school Cecil had worked hard and come out top of the form, and he had received a good report. Although he was not stealing he had a certain tendency to make up stories at school. An example: 'I have nine brothers and sisters', etc. etc.

Some degree of pseudologia fantastica regularly goes with the antisocial tendency and with stealing, and often remains when actual stealing has disappeared. It is a manifestation of dissociation.

The mother seemed to me to be less tired and not depressed. Cecil cannot be said yet to have made a definite friend of his own, and this (from the psychiatric angle) is his main residual symptom. Second to this would be his tiredness. The mother knows that she must meet the tiredness and let him go to bed at 5 o'clock if necessary.

Contained in this tiredness and early going to bed is depression and the residuum of the regressive tendency; also his sense of carrying his mother's depressive tendency.

At the end the mother reminded me, or told me for the first time: 'You do understand, Doctor, don't you, that with Cecil I was never outgoing; not even at the beginning. I realise this through my relationship with his brother with whom I have been easy from the start, and he has been easy with me.'

It seemed to me that the mother had come to be able to make this clear statement of the aetiology of Cecil's illness because of the fact that Cecil had now become so much improved, so that she felt less guilty; also because it is she and her husband who have produced this improvement by meeting Cecil's special needs consistently, over a long period of time.

After seeing the mother I had an interview with Cecil. He was positive in his relationship to me and very easy. He first chose to draw, and in fact drew a synagogue. We talked about his possibly being an architect. He often draws houses. He then asked me to do a squiggle[1]

    (1) and he turned it into a teapot.

---

[1] I feel that these drawings need not be shown.

(3) A crocodile's mouth made by him out of his own squiggle. (There had been a crocodile introduced by me in the first series).

I asked him whether he remembered the man with the sword in the first series and he said: 'Oh yes', and he became interested in the numbering of the drawings.

(5) He turned my squiggle into a kingfisher.

(7) He made mine into a mermaid.

(8) I made his messy squiggle into something by putting a plate round it and a knife and fork, implying that there was some eating associated with this, and in this I was influenced by his drawing of the crocodile which might eat me, or which might represent one aspect of myself in the professional relationship.

(9) He made mine into a rocket, a jet aeroplane.

(11) He made mine into a witch and broomstick. This had to do with a story that he knew, and the working of spells. Frightening dreams therefore came into the subject matter of our conversation.

(12) This he said is like a witch dream. It is his drawing (not based on a squiggle). The witch came to the house and he woke. He said: 'Sleeping is all right, but it is when you wake you forget where you are.' So I said: 'You dream nice dreams?' and he said: 'Yes', and drew the next—

(13) He was excited drawing a diesel engine with himself driving.

(14) A funny dream has to do with a clown and a circus with children watching. 'I might be a clown,' he said.

I asked if he dreamed about school and he said: 'No.'

'Have you any friends?'

'Yes, many, but not really a friend of my own.'

'Have you got one that you would like to be friends with?'

'No, not really.'

We then talked about a lot of odd details; his gollywog which is now in the cupboard, etc. He might be a teacher when he is 20, or dig up roads, or be a farmer, or drive diesel engines which he likes very much.

I said: 'Shall we draw any more?' and he said: 'Yes, one more.'

(15) He made my squiggle into a hole with snow in it. 'Yesterday's snow has gone but we played with the snow at Christmas time and made snowballs and a snow man', and somehow or other we came on to discuss the difference between the young and the old and the great age of his grandfather who is 87.

There was no special feature in this contact that would draw my attention to persistence of illness, character disturbance, or personality disorder. I felt that the boy was displaying freedom and a sense of humour, each indicative of health. There was no evidence of a regressive tendency or of a flight from it, in the material of the consultation.

Summary

(1) A case is given in detail. All that I know of the case is reported in illustration of the economical aspect of this type of case management in child psychiatry. The work of the case was done through six interviews spread over a period of six years, and by letters.

(2) The boy developed and maintained a capacity to regress to dependence, and the parents met this tendency. In this way the regressions had therapeutic value, and kept open a path to the feelings of infancy.

(3) Behind the need for this therapy was a relative deprivation, which was related to the mother's pathological reaction to the fact of her second pregnancy.

(4) This tendency to regression in the boy along with the parents' willingness and ability to meet the boy's dependence is closely allied to the periods of 'spoiling' that can be shown to occur in the case of almost any child brought up in a reliable setting.

(5) The parents, in this case, wished to play their part, and were eager to carry out the boy's 'treatment' themselves. They did, however, need to be told what they were doing and to be helped from time to time by myself as the psychiatrist who took responsibility throughout.

(6) The case was eventually helped forward by a psychotherapeutic interview in which the boy at the age of 8 years used me in respect of his antisocial tendency (stealing). At 8 years,

in the drawing game, we reached back to breast contact at a deep level, so that the stealing disappeared from the clinical picture.

(7) There are residual symptoms, including a difficulty in making and keeping a firm friendship. The outcome of the case was favourable, however, in terms of the personal health of the boy in relation to his family and social setting.

Further Note written Fourteen Years after the First Consultation

During the intervening period I have had interviews with the child or the parents in the course of most of the years. It turned out that the over-riding factor was the mother's tendency towards depression, for which she has been having psychotherapy which has helped her considerably. She has turned out to be a parent who has worked very hard at giving the children the setting that they need, this often being difficult because of her mood disorder. The father has been an absolutely essential stabilising factor in the whole situation.

Naturally in the course of these years there has been a great deal of management, which has been of vital importance, especially the choice of the right school. Cecil has used me as a stable factor in his life ever since the first interview and I can count on these parents to call on me for help as soon as things begin to get difficult.

It would have to be said in this case that I have continued this first interview in a dozen subsequent interviews spaced over the years. As I look back over the file I find that the ill person in this case has always been the mother, and I have been used by her to help with the effects of her depression on this one boy, while in her own analysis she has been dealing with her tendency to depression in a more general way. As will be obvious, the mother's analyst can deal with her hypochondriacal anxieties relative to her objects, but when one of the objects is a child who is being affected adversely, then it is necessary for someone else to be giving help to the child. It is necessary, however, to retain a clear sense of the case as one dominated by the mother's illness and not by the symptomatology as it appears in the child's personality, character, and behaviour.

The boy is now at grammar school. He has done well academically, and seems to be growing up in a way that is appropriate to the age of 17 years. There are residual regressive features including thumb-sucking and a paucity of special friends. His independence of his mother is becoming more and more evident and he has passed through a rather natural period in which he seemed antagonistic to his father. As the boy grows up and seems to be able to develop into a healthy young man the mother's depressive symptomatology is perhaps becoming more evident as such, as it cannot now take the special form of worry about Cecil.

CASE XV 'Mark' *aet* 12 years

In this next case there was a marked clinical change following the therapeutic consultation, and it would appear that this change was more the result of the communication between the boy and myself than of a change of attitude towards the boy in his family. It will be observed that this boy had a preoccupation with water and that eventually he established his identity by going to sea.

I propose to give as far as possible all I know about this case[1] in illustration of the way in which one can work in a limited area and in this way avoid the infinite amount of detail which inevitably clutters up a psychotherapeutic treatment. It is this delimitation of the area of operation that makes it possible for a child psychiatrist doing this work to carry a very heavy caseload, whereas the psychotherapist, and in particular the psychoanalyst, works with only a few cases at any one time. It is possible for the child psychiatrist doing this work to be involved in 100 or even 200 on-going cases, and this brings the work into a relationship with social pressure.

It will be understood, as I have repeatedly stated, that in my opinion the basis for the training to do this work is a thorough grounding in long-term psychotherapy of individuals, even psycho-analysis involving daily sessions over a number of years.

Family History

Girl	16 years.
Mark	12 years.
Boy	8 years.
Boy	7 years.

Mark was brought to me at the age of 12 years by his parents. The father was a colleague, a member of the university staff. In this case I first saw the two parents together as they wished to get my help in orientating to the problem. Much detail emerged in the usual way of an interview that takes its natural course.

The family was intact. The following significant landmarks in Mark's emotional development were reported:

[1] Except where it is necessary to distort or omit in disguising the case.

> Mark was breast-fed and *difficult to wean*. 'He resisted weaning very strongly.'

This is a matter of considerable theoretical interest. In my experience when a baby is 'difficult to wean' there is not infrequently a disturbance in the mother, either a difficulty in the area of ambivalent feelings, or else a depressive tendency. These two states are of course related, but in depression there is a more massive repression of the conflict.

The parents continued with what they wanted to say about the boy:

> Mark *had never been truthful*. (Later the parents said that this had been a fixed characteristic from 2 years.)
>
> Mark became at 7 (or earlier) a boy who '*if he wants must have*'.
>
> Mark started *to steal at 8 years*. (See below for minor correction of this detail.) This happened when he was away staying with friends. At 10 years he was taking money from his mother's bag and telling lies. There was the usual story of refusal to confess. Recently (12 years) serious stealing had taken place. This was associated with his passion for fishing. Stealing was from father's wallet and elder sister's bag, and in amounts of £5 and £10. He swore he had not stolen, and by doing so he incriminated his brother to whom he was devoted. He confessed only when confronted with finger-print evidence. Then he bought a fishing rod and elaborate tackle. He spoke of 'my dealer' and claimed he would be given a special fishing rod on his birthday by this dealer. He had in fact bought two rods and had hidden them. He had taken elaborate precautions against detection.

The family's attitude was reasonable, which was possible since the general relationships in the family were good. If Mark confessed he was never punished, but the parents were especially puzzled by the compulsive lying. Also they marvelled that all these troubles produced no unhappiness in the boy.

At last, after further incidents, the father, who was at a loss to know what to do, put Mark in disgrace; he must have his meals in the kitchen, and fishing was stopped. Mark remained without a sense of guilt, and continued to say his prayers.

The parents went on in the interview with me to build up a history of Mark's early life.

> He was happy. In fact at 2 years he said: '*I'm so happy to be alive*', conscious of a love of living.

There is probably a tie-up here with the parents' philosophy of life, which includes a 'cultivated joy of life'.

> Mark chose to live at home, rather than to continue at his preparatory boarding school. School reports said: 'Mark could do better if he tried.' He was good at games and was thought to have average ability. Eventually he went to a grammar school as a day-boy and there he made an attempt to 'redeem himself by hard work'. Mark was very fond of nature study and had an incredible knowledge in this speciality, using books intelligently.
>
> When I asked about sleep techniques, the parents reported: '*Mark adopts incredible postures* in his sleep. He is like a log. On going to bed he sleeps immediately and he has never told his dreams.' Also Mark had a twitching face recently, including blinking.
>
> Mark had many friends, they said, but no bosom friend; also he was attractive to older people. He had been sensibly informed in regard to sex by his father. When excited Mark would sweat and work his face, and in this way he became thought of as nervous. Mark liked handwork but showed no special artistic ability. He had taste, however, and could be moved by beauty. A feature in his life was the brilliance of his older sister. He was well aware of this, and possibly associated with this feature was a fear of his father which developed over a phase in which he was doing badly at school.
>
> Mark was courageous physically, swimming being his favourite sport. In fact, *Mark's main interests concerned water*. He was set on going into the Navy from 3 years to 8 years, but he temporarily lost this (at 9 and 10 years) when he was told he would have to work to get accepted.
>
> The parents brought out the point that he was affected by the new baby boy, born when Mark was 5. He called him 'our baby', and he had always been especially fond of him. They now said that it was *when he shared a room with this boy*

(*at 6 or 7*) *that he first stole from his mother.* (Previously the mother had dated the first theft at 8 years.)

The day after the consultation with the parents I had the first of three significant interviews followed by one (not described here) subsidiary interview with Mark. Although I knew a good deal about him it would have been valueless to have worked on the basis of this knowledge. What was needed was a history-taking of a different kind, a history revealing itself in terms of the boy's communication with me. A great deal happened during this first session, but that which can be reported here centres round the 'squiggle game' which we played together.

The First Interview

In my first personal contact with Mark, I adopted the squiggle-game technique. He was pleased to play this game, a game with no rules.

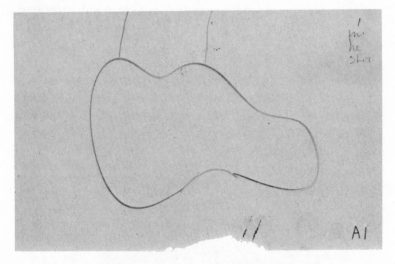

(1) My squiggle which he turned into a shoe.

(2) His squiggle which I turned into a jug.

(3) My squiggle which he turned into a man with a moustache (rather fantastic).

(4) His squiggle which I turned into a kind of animal.

(5) My squiggle which he turned into a face.

(6) His squiggle which I turned into two worms close to each other. There was a good deal of conversation about this, including a discussion on his part of the function of the 'saddle'. He indicated on the drawing the way in which worms copulate.

(7) My squiggle which he turned into a curious kind of a man's face.

Here I was already aware of the boy's tendency to undervalue fantasy. This corresponds to the parents' statement that 'he sleeps like a log and has no dreams'.

(8) His squiggle which I turned into a schoolmaster.

(9) A drawing of his of a man. This resulted from my talking about my using the imaginative part of the drawings to introduce the subject of dreams. He seemed surprised that I should talk about dreams and the drawing of the man indicated a dream figure which gradually lost definition from the waist down. I spoke about the stealing at this point, using a word that he supplied: *impulse*. I said that in stealing he was acting out ideas which were in his mind, like dreams. He had spoken about forgotten dreams, and I had said that when dreams become unavailable there may be a need to recapture them through acting on impulse so that the dream dominates what happens, and in this way reappears in the person's own life and conduct.

I now knew of Mark's ability to make use of my approach to the unconscious and to dream material; this approach was somewhat new to him, partly because of his own defence organisation and partly because of the family pattern. Nevertheless we could communicate in this way.

After this first consultation the mother wrote: ·

> After leaving your house with Mark last week my husband made only casual inquiries, avoiding direct questions. The boy showed no reaction of disturbance or pleasure. Later on in the evening he spoke to me at some length about his visit to you, and quite spontaneously. He was particularly struck by your questions about dreams and their meaning. He seemed puzzled by the importance of dreams and by your insistence on this point. I hope all this will be of some use. His comment about the toys was that it would be a 'paradise for his young brother'.[1]

[1] In this oblique way he referred to his own need to make a link with himself at a younger age.

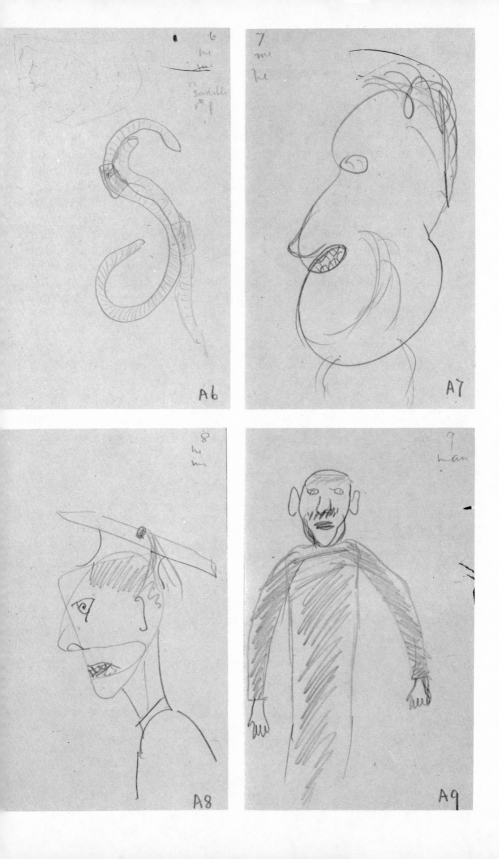

(There were toys in the room which are used by younger patients.)

A fortnight after the first interview with the boy and the day before the second interview the father rang me up to report. After the first visit to me Mark was not allowed to go fishing. He wanted to take a particular boat to the pond with his brother and he said to his mother that it was a present for his birthday. Could he have £1 to get it? He was so obsessed by the boat that he had only one idea, which was to get this particular one immediately. The mother was firm in refusing. He had already told the brother about the boat. The parents were struck by the way in which eventually he gave in and so accepted the frustration and did not buy the boat. This seemed worth noting by them because of its newness, which they attributed to the fact of the first interview with me. It will be seen that water is again involved in this incident.

The Second Interview

On the second occasion that I saw Mark, he was ready to play the squiggle game again.

(1) My squiggle which he rather skilfully turned into a human head.

(2) His squiggle which I made into a tortoise.

B1

B2

279

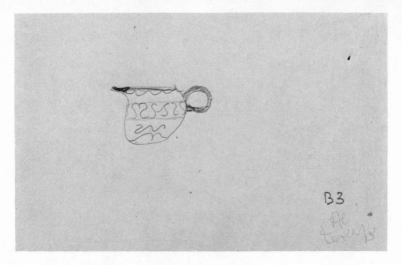

(3) He turned his own squiggle into a teacup, appropriately decorated.

Here appeared his wish to take full responsibility for a drawing and for the ideas that lie latent in it. Rather naturally, this was not markedly imaginative.

(4) My squiggle which he turned into a man very precariously climbing a rock surface with a pack on his back.

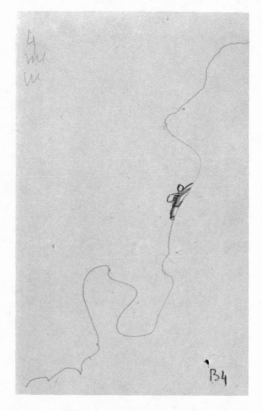

(5) His squiggle which I turned into the drawing of a girl.

(6) My squiggle which he turned into a surprising drawing of a pond with bulrushes and reeds, and a water-fowl enjoying the scene and just about to dive its head down for food.

Here was a picture. This showed me Mark's integrative capacity and also his capacity to love. The whole symbolised the persisting love relationship (both instinctual and dependent) with his mother, his fondness for water, and his concern with nature

generally and fertility.[1] It also gave me a glimpse of his special knowledge. The strength of Mark's ego organisation being evident, I knew I had the right to go ahead with interpretation of material presented.

(7) His squiggle which I turned into a lady's foot and shoe.

(8) My squiggle which he turned into a most extraordinary and fantastic face.

Here fantasy was appearing again in the form of the fantastic, which is not free dream material. Along with all this there was a good deal of talk, not particularly about anything. Mark could feel, however, from what happened, that I was interested equally

[1] One could guess here that he was able through water to make positive use of his mother's depression (sad tears).

in fact and in fantasy, whichever should turn up. Also he could understand my appreciation of the picture.

The Third Interview

At the third interview we again played the squiggle game.

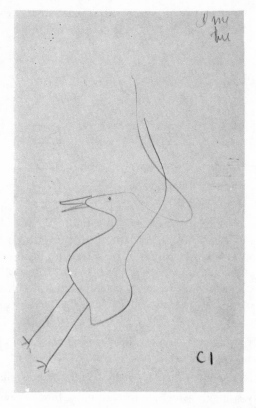

(1) My squiggle which he turned into a bird with long legs.

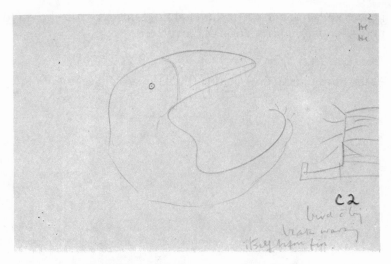

(2) His squiggle which he turned into a bird with a big beak warming itself before a fire.

The game had led Mark to express fantasy without feeling foolish about it. The picture which he had in front of him was entirely his and the whole idea came unexpectedly to him from his own unconscious. My function here was not to interpret. The main therapeutic factor was that the boy had found a bridge to the inner world in a way which was quite natural. This drawing was like a dream that has value because it has been dreamed and remembered.

(3) My squiggle which he turned into the man in the moon. Fantasy continues.

(4) His squiggle which I turned into a head and shoulders.

(5) My squiggle which he turned into a bird rather effectively flying upwards. He did this with a minimum of additions and got a good deal of satisfaction from the movement portrayed.

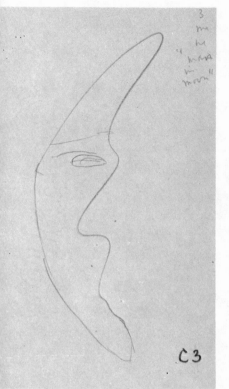

C3

C4

C5

(6) His squiggle which I made into a face and he named it 'Mr. Facing-Both-Ways'. He justified this by a quick drawing of what would be eyebrows from my point of view. From his point of view this was a mouth, the mouth that I had drawn being eyebrows from his point of view. This was all done in a flash.

Here was indicated the dissociation in Mark's personality, relative to stealing. At this point Mark reached a stage at which he was nearly aware of the split in himself which enabled him to steal without shame or guilt or anxiety. I made no interpretation of this.

(7) My squiggle which he turned into a most extraordinary
     being with arms and one leg, a floppy sort of individual,
     rather bird-like, and the drawing was certainly humorous.

Here came, among other things, a sense of humour, always a
sign of freedom affording elbow room, so to speak, and in this
way assisting the therapist.

(8) His squiggle which I made into a face and which he called
     an Eskimo.

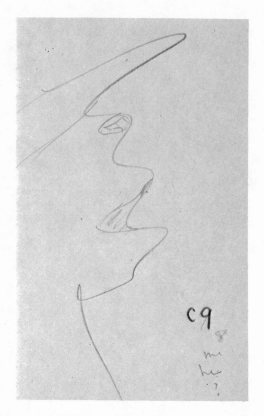

(9) My squiggle which he turned into a weird face of a man. At this point it was easy for me to ask him about dreams. He said: 'I forget them. In any case they are only ridiculous', and he was obviously afraid of being laughed at, if he should remember them. He did, however, start to draw the next, which was not based on a squiggle.

(10) Here he is kneeling in the road making squiggles in the dust. This was a dream.

This was a significant moment. The drawing led to the subject of depression. He called this 'feeling bored'.

> He said: 'I only feel it for a few seconds just when I am waking up. I often think it is a strange life; perhaps life *is* a dream.'

Here he was a very serious person. Instead of being in a state of dissociation he had here become a unit, and a depressed person.

> In answer to a question as to whether he had ever felt really down, he referred to a time when he had stayed away from home because his sister had measles. *He was perhaps 8.* He said he was homesick, sad and lonely.

Here, as is commonly found in this work, the patient takes the therapist to the date of the period of maximum strain. At 8 years Mark had intolerable dreams and a nightmare that indicated a severe depressive mood. The mood indicates ego organisation and maturity, and some capacity to cope with the threat of disintegration of the personality.

> I referred to *the love of his mother* which was at the back of his sadness at parting from her, remembering the history of difficult weaning. His comment on this was: '*If mother's away things are different.*'

289

We then talked about fishing. The love of his mother was the thing that he clearly expressed and in a deep way as it came out of his remembering feeling depressed. Hence the extent of his hopelessness at being parted from her.

(11) Finally I made a squiggle which he turned into a weird kind of human being.

He was now ready to go.

General Comment

In this series of three psychotherapeutic consultations there came about a natural development of a bridge between Mark's conscious and unconscious, or a bridge between inner and outer realities. If asked about dreams at the beginning he would not have been able to remember any. ('He sleeps like a log and never reports dreams.') By the end of the third interview Mark was able to tell me about his period of maximum strain, which he remembered because of a dream that brought him right into the depression that was reactive to his separation from his mother. This was at the age at which he started stealing (except that he had stolen once before, from his mother, at the time when he first shared a bedroom with the baby brother).

Naturally, there are precursors to all this. In Mark's case the antisocial tendency indicating a continuing reaction to a deprivation reaches back to the actual weaning from the breast. (No doubt the mother's psychology needs to be taken into consideration here, since it is almost always true that the mother of a baby that is difficult to wean is herself somewhat depressed at the time, or somewhat depressive by nature.)

The antisocial tendency was represented by:

(a) Pseudologia fantastica (from 2 years).
(b) 'What I want I must have' (from 7 years).
(c) Stealing from the mother (8 years).

Discussion

This case illustrates three main themes:

(1) The first interview with the parents gave a clear picture of the case, which enabled the parents to re-orientate to the problem. It was not for use by me in therapy.

(2) The three interviews with Mark gave me a new view of the same problem, and gave me opportunity for doing fairly deep psychotherapy. All the essentials were in the material, and in usable form:

A mother-fixation, first evident at weaning.

A significant separation at 8 years.

Stealing as a reaching across the 'weaning' gap and between the dissociated personality structures, and from external to internal psychic reality, to and fro.

An undervaluation of fantasy.

The splitting defence, pseudologia, which cleared up as a result of the consultation.

Rediscovery of the fantastic, and then of fantasy.

Unification in the personality, bringing with it a depressive dream and a sense of concern.

A sea-fixation, which alternated with a water obsession and which proved to be a satisfactory sublimation of the mother-fixation.

291

(3) The case also illustrates the theory of the antisocial tendency as a reaction to deprivation (not privation), and appearing clinically along with hope in regard to object relationships. In this case the stealing was related to a manic defence against the depression felt as such at 8 years, and was also related to a split in Mark's personality which made him clinically two people, one who had a compulsion to steal and the other who had strong moral principles and a wish to be like his parents and to do well in the world (in Mr. Facing-Both-Ways).

According to the theory on which all this work is based, the boy in stealing was unconsciously looking for the mother from whom he had the right to steal; in fact from whom he could take because she was his own mother, *the mother that he created out of his own capacity to love.* In other words, he was looking for the breast-feeding from which he had been weaned and yet not weaned. His difficulty in weaning was turning up again in the present in the form of impatience at frustrations and the need to steal in order to circumvent frustrations by claiming rights.

Result

There was a clinical improvement following the first interview, which showed as a new acceptance of reality. After a month the father wrote:

> Mark is in very good condition in every way, so far as we can see. In particular, he is far more interested in his work at school than ever before and he is taking it much more seriously, with improved results. He has started to learn a wind instrument, which was his own idea; and he is very keen on it indeed. He formerly learned the piano, but was indifferent to it and had to be pressed to practise whereas he is eager to practise the wind instrument.
>
> We took him away for a couple of weeks at Easter to stay with a relative by the sea. He did not ask to fish, which he knows is still forbidden, but was nevertheless exceedingly happy by the sea-shore. He has transferred his interest in fishing to sailing model boats. He makes these boats quite skilfully, but he shows signs sometimes of becoming obsessed by them, and this makes us a little anxious, as the previous trouble arose (it seemed to us) from

an obsession with fishing. He wants to talk incessantly about them and about his expeditions to the pond.

After a further three months the father wrote:

> We have been very pleased with Mark's progress this term. He has done very well at school, came out top of his form, and had an excellent report in all respects. He seems stronger morally and appears to derive strength from a habit I have got him to adopt of saying to me each morning that he will put honesty and truthfulness first today.
>
> We are just about to send him off for a long summer holiday at a boys' camp under suitable supervision. He is greatly looking forward to it. After that he will go to stay for a week with an old friend of mine and I have told him that–for the first time–he can resume fishing while he is there if he feels strong enough to be sensible about it. He says he does. We shall see how it works out. He has been very happy again.

Here the father shows that he has continued his active technique for instilling moral strength, which is part of the family pattern, and which I made no attempt to alter. Also he has played a more vital rôle in Mark's life, and corresponding with this the boy's mother has stepped somewhat into the background since the time of the first consultation. I found that there had been a complete cessation of the stealing, and lying was no longer part of his way of life.

The father wrote again eight years after the first series of therapeutic consultations, Mark being now 20 years old.

> Thank you for your letter. I am very glad to give you an account of Mark's progress during the past four or five years.
>
> He has pursued unswervingly his chosen vocation as a sailor, and this very week he has completed his four years' apprenticeship as a midshipman in the —— Line. He always goes to the Far East and is usually away for several months on a voyage. He has a deep satisfaction in the life at sea, although he found it involved great physical and emotional hardship, especially in the early years. He faced it with great fortitude.
>
> He has of course developed in every way and is much more mature. He has great pride in the line in which he serves and also a sense of duty and of responsibility.

Our home means a great deal to him, and he spends the whole of his leave here. He obviously feels this to be the stable element in his life at present. He appreciates frequent letters from the family more than anything else and he writes to us and to his brother and sister from every port. This is a notable fact considering that he is not a literary type in any way. He is very affectionate in his letters; but he appears rather casual outwardly when he is at home. He has one great friend whom he knew at school and they are inseparable when he is at home.

Mark is much attracted by girls and enjoys going to dances with them when ashore. He talks freely to myself and my wife about his girl friends and brings them to the house. He talks openly about wishing to get married when he has qualified as an officer, though I don't think he has found a girl he wants to marry.

The timeless quality of life at sea seems to appeal to him. He often writes in his letters about the days slipping past, and of time moving past him in an effortless passage. At sea there is a fixed routine, but no pressure of time, no sense of the day of the week or of the date, all of which he finds very irksome on land.

He has become much more sensible about money. He sends me an allotment of his pay every month and I accumulate this for him. He brings home from the East very generous presents and to do this means a great deal to him.

When he is at home, he needs an unplanned life without obligations or engagements, except for dates with girls. His room is always in great disorder, in contrast with the strict neatness imposed on midshipmen in regard to their cabins. But he is very careful about his personal appearance and always wears smart clothes, whereas as a boy he was particularly neglectful of his clothes and appearance.

We are expecting Mark home next month after a very long absence of ten months and he will then be at home attending a navigation college for about three months. It will be interesting to see how he reacts to a very different kind of life from the one he has been leading.

If there is anything else you would like to know, please do not hesitate to mention it. So far as we can see, the lad is getting on satisfactorily. If you have any advice or warnings to give us, we should naturally appreciate your giving them to us.

In a final follow-up, in 1962, the father reported that Mark had continued to follow his calling, and to be successful in it. He was then 26 years old.

This is a satisfactory child-psychiatry result; the treatment did not over-tax the parents' resources, and it put but little strain on the psychiatrist. The parents did the bulk of the work and provided the continuity of management that was essential.

Essential, however, were the three significant psychotherapeutic interviews which I have described here, and which gave Mark the opportunity to get rid of the dissociation in his personality which made him lie and which led to his being antisocial without sense of guilt.

CASE XVI 'Peter' *aet* 13 years

The following case is intended to illustrate the fact that often the main part of the work is done by the parents. My personal interview with the boy was a relatively insignificant part of the total procedure. It did, however, enable me to get the kind of history of the case that I need, which is the history taken through the patient. On the basis of this I was able to give support to the parents for the immense upheaval which was needed in order to manage the case. The parents saw their son through successfully, so that after a regressive episode he began to make new growth based on a firmer foundation.

Drawing sequences are not necessary in this case.

Peter was sent to me by his private boarding school. He came with a letter from the school doctor:

> Peter came to this school in January of this year, entering School House where his housemaster is the headmaster. Official opinion there has been that although intellectually dull he is 'such a very nice boy'. He has twice been a patient for a few days in the Sanatorium and the other members of the staff concur in my view that he was most unlikeable during these two phases of illness, being aggressive and insolent in a strangely impersonal way. He certainly gave the impression at that time of considering himself superior in all respects, at least so far as all the members of the staff were concerned. He seemed to be accepted by his contemporaries. I was inclined to ascribe the aggressiveness to an excess of 'inflation' not uncommonly found in the new boy.
>
> Yesterday, the headmaster told me that Peter was responsible for a long series of misdemeanours which had disturbed School House since early in March. The first known instance was when a senior boy returned from a period in the sick room to find his pillow and sheets badly slashed. The next night it was found that all new boys' beds had been similarly treated and that ink had been wantonly splashed about on walls. Since then, there has been a series of thefts, of money, of wallets, of pens, shoes and gloves. Also, boys have repeatedly found in the lavatories letters from home, opened and disfigured. These must have been removed from the post-table before their owners could collect their mail.

The headmaster has kindly committed to typescript the summary of events, and this I enclose. There can be no doubt that Peter is responsible for almost all these antisocial acts. The issue of the missing fountain-pens was the only one with which he alone was confronted (the whole House had to face up to the sheet-slashing enquiry), and when weight of incriminating evidence led to admission of guilt in that regard he volunteered the truth about the stolen and opened letters, doing this in advance of any mention of them by the headmaster. He said he wanted the owners of the letters to find them so that they would know that someone had interfered with their property, and that was why he left the evidence in the lavatories.

I had a short talk with Peter yesterday and found him entirely composed and at ease. He said that it had been found out that he had been 'taking things', but showed no concern about possible official reaction. He had no ideas regarding his future but remarked: 'this [stealing] would be a difficult thing to get rid of after leaving school'.

Asked about the motive, he seemed at a loss and then said: 'To get my own back.' Subsequently he admitted that most of those who suffered at his hands had no prior acquaintance with himself. He could not say why he had taken the money, shoes and fives-gloves.

As regards the sheet-slashing, he had attacked the bed of the senior boy because this boy had been unpleasant to him. It appears that he sits next to him at orchestra practice, playing a similar instrument. Peter says that this boy does not finger correctly and that he told him about that and wanted to show him how it should be done. He considered that his verbal response to the offer was disagreeable, and consequently he took revenge upon his sheets. Despite a grave warning to the House, he slashed all the new boys' sheets the following night, including his own (which were the most damaged of all) in order to ventilate a grudge against one of these (five) boys. I suspect him of having inflicted an illness upon himself that same night by swallowing a quantity of some chlorophyll tooth-paste or some other substance containing chlorophyll. He vomited twelve times during the night and was admitted to the San. the following morning where he produced the final specimen of vomitus which was copious and consisted of brilliant green fluid. Unfortunately, we were then in the midst of a brisk epidemic of the Winter Vomiting disease, and five cases of vomiting were admitted from his House on that particular morning. Although puzzled by the unusual appearance in his case, I am sorry to say I did not follow the matter up.

Yesterday I asked him, quite suddenly, whether he had indeed taken such tooth-paste, and he immediately answered, 'That was when I was using Kolynos.'

It seems to me that the indications point to the emergence of a psychopathic personality and I have advised that he be taken home and that expert opinion be sought.

Today I met the boy's father and am greatly impressed by his courage and control in what must be for him a major crisis. He seems to be a man of sterling qualities.

Enclosed with this letter was a detailed statement by the headmaster, together with a typescript of a statement made by Peter and taken down in detail by the headmaster. These statements gave the facts of the previous term and the events leading up to the discovery of the thefts and the way in which Peter had been interviewed by the headmaster. There were a lot of details about some stolen pens, and Peter had written home asking: 'Have you sent me a box full of pens, etc. ?' The handwriting of this letter showed signs of disturbance and was quite unlike that of another letter written a few days earlier. The headmaster had received an anonymous letter which he felt confident was written by Peter and which ran as follows:

Peter did not steal those pens! I did! As I hate him I put the blame on him. He has been nice to me just lately so please do not punish him. Please punish me if you can find me. My house is E. house. I took all the pens. I think everyone in this school is horrible including you very much. In the near future I am going to commit suicide so mind out.

It was clear from these letters and statements that the headmaster and the school doctor considered this boy to be very ill in a psychiatric sense and on the basis of the information given the diagnosis would be: '*Psychopathic personality.*' They were decided that it was necessary for Peter to leave the school.

First Therapeutic Consultation

Family History
Girl   17 years.
Peter   13 years.
Boy   11 years.

Peter came to see me along with his father. I saw Peter first and gave him forty minutes before I had a brief talk with the father. Peter and I made a rather superficial contact, using the squiggle game as a convenient diversion from more direct contact. In this case the patient, Peter, plunged in with certain things he was wanting me to know. After telling me about his 17-year-old sister and 11-year-old brother he gave me an early memory. It was at 3 years. His sister had a bowl with fish in it. She was about 9. He threw it on the floor and it broke. There was another incident at about the same time when he climbed through the hatch with his sister and knocked over a salt cellar, breaking the glass. This was accidental but the other was deliberate. I thought it significant that in each of these two memories there was damage done, and that he was reporting a fear of violence in himself.

He said he was fond of his parents and of his sister and brother, but that he made very few contacts outside the family.

I asked him about ways of going to sleep, and he told me his brother sucked his thumb and used to kneel over and rock and move the bed across the room. He himself was a thumb-sucker. He had no memory of objects. At home he went to sleep quickly but at school lay awake an hour thinking things out. At school he got up with difficulty. Play seemed to be fairly ordinary at home. His sister was at a day school. His brother was away at a choir school. He himself was musical, playing the 'cello and singing. Music was his best experience. He would never have got to public school but for a man who coached him. He did not know what he wanted to be. He did some pinching at the prep school and now had been stealing a good deal at the public school.

I knew that I had not cut much ice with this consultation, but I had been there to be confided in.

Interview with the Father
The father first explored around the idea of physical disorders that could be treated by drugs or hormones, and as he himself

had benefited from such treatment he wondered whether the boy could have a need for something similar. He accepted my rejection of this possibility. The boy had had acidosis as a child and also a great deal of trouble with his ear, with discharge and pain. When at prep school he had had a fierce fever, thought to be polio, but there was no paralysis. He had had many minor illnesses and was never really well physically.

Describing the other children the father said that his elder daughter was quick and impatient, and that the younger son was very bright. They were all fond of each other but constantly bickering. The mother, it appeared, was a straightforward person, able to enjoy her position in the family. The boy seemed to be equally fond of each parent. He had always found teasing difficult to bear.

Peter had (the father said) felt less loved than the others. This was clear from the age of 5 and perhaps from 3, when the new baby was 6 months old. It was as if he lost position as the brother began to exist as a rival person, Peter then being neither the youngest nor the oldest.

Here was a correlation between the two stories, in that the age of 3 was important in each!

The symptoms as described by the father were vague, such as a compulsion to draw attention to himself when visitors came to the house, making faces, and so on. There were other minor evidences of a small degree of reaction to deprivation, and these became more real at the time when there were two or three instances of stealing at the preparatory school.

Peter had been happy at the junior school near home before the preparatory school, but the hours at this school were short. He had always loved the country. Once at this early stage he stole at home from his mother's house-keeping (£1), bought presents for friends and gave it all away.

The headmaster of the public school was willing to keep him; he said: 'That's what we are for.' But the antisocial behaviour must be changed. The matron seemed to be very well able to fit in with the boy's idea of a dragon; what she was really like I was unable to ascertain.

The boy was affectionate with all his family, more so in the last holidays after the psychiatric illness at school. He had a desire to be positively helpful, in the garden and in the house, and really carried tasks through. There had been no bed-wetting.

It is important to note the co-existence of personality growth and the phases of breakdown into illness phases.

Two days after this initial consultation I received the following letter from Peter's father:

> Since Tuesday morning Peter has seemed tired and lethargic. Except for remarking immediately: 'He played squiggles [which P. explained] with me and asked me questions all the time', and later after we were home: 'He knows how to cross-examine', he has not spoken to us of his time with you. We have purposely not asked him about it.
>
> We do occasionally sound him about his doings at school and he seems glad to bring them out.
>
> Other points that have occurred to us are: His speech has always had its slight lispiness. His eyes from infancy have often had a 'far away', strained look. (Recently tested: 'perfect'.) He fell from a tree to hard ground, at age 7+, with no apparent damage. Peter is coming by himself on Friday. My wife of course would much like to see you sometime.

Second Consultation (*Three Days Later*)

Peter came alone. It was obviously going to be a sticky interview. Once again the idea of our playing together was not going to work. I found myself asking questions and then (pulling myself together) I said: 'I sound like an inquisitor, but as nobody else is speaking there doesn't seem to be any other way.' So I switched over to noughts and crosses which he enjoyed and at which he beat me. I tried to get into conversation with him alongside drawing in a desultory sort of way, but the interview never became one in which he gave himself away. Perhaps the nearest we got to each other was when he said that he thought that if he went back to the public school the troubles would not end. What he partly meant was that the boys would always remember him as a thief and he would not be able to live down what he had done. But he also meant that he will not be able to avoid doing it again.

CENTRAL THEME

Then it emerged that he had a very big desire to live at home. He always had had this, and he had thought out how to get to a school as a day-boy, living at home, although his father had said that there were no suitable schools near. There was, however, some kind of a day school nearby, and Peter had not given up hope of finding a place somewhere.

I ended the interview, which lasted an hour. It is impossible to report this hour accurately because so little happened in it. It did cross my mind that perhaps the clue might be that the boy was of weak intelligence and I therefore asked for an I.Q. test. The result given by my psychologist colleague was I.Q. = 130.

I now arranged to see the mother. I was equipped with the knowledge of Peter's longing to live at home.

Consultation with the Mother

The mother and I discussed the idea that Peter might live at home, to rediscover his home and to enjoy it. Later he might go to a local day school. I described what would be expected, and said that I had no idea how long Peter would use his home as a mental hospital in which he could regress to dependence and to infantile behaviour, but I thought this phase would last a year. The main thing was that Peter should be told: *'Dr. Winnicott says you are ill, that you are to leave school, and that you are to live at home. Later, if you get well enough, a day school may perhaps be found.'*

I then sent the following letter to the school doctor:

> I have now seen Peter's mother. I find myself with a definite opinion, which is that this boy should not return to school at the present time in spite of all the advantages, such as the beautiful location of the school, the understanding attitude of the head-master, and the fact that the parents are known to the school, and also the high standard of scholarship. You can imagine that I have been diffident about giving this advice but if the boy returns there will be more trouble and eventually he will have to leave, probably in disgrace instead of as an ill person.
>
> The boy has had an illness which has been recognised by your-self as an illness in spite of its being a disturbance of emotional development without physical disease. In this case there is a treat-ment available which is that the boy should live at home. I find that this is acceptable to the mother although perhaps not very acceptable to the father.
>
> After seeing the mother I feel that I can put upon her the burden of dealing with this boy's convalescence from illness. I would not mind if he were to do nothing else for a year but help in the house and cut the grass and do all the things that he likes

doing, all of a constructive kind, including playing with trains like a boy who is much younger than 13. I am not yet able to predict how much this boy will need to regress to dependence in his home setting before he is able to go forward and take up the developments that belong to puberty. He is not yet ready for puberty, however.

I would be grateful if you would let the headmaster know that I have advised the parents in this way, and also if you would thank him for his very helpful notes. It is not absolutely impossible that this boy should recover from his illness and one day be in a position to return, but this need not be discussed at the present time. The problem of his readmission will not arise for a year or two. I think it more likely that the boy will go to a local day school.

It may interest you to know that I have had an Intelligence Test done by an educational psychologist, and his I.Q. is given as 130 or 'well above average'. It is clear I think from this that Peter's emotional difficulties are seriously interfering with his scholastic attainments.

I also wrote to the mother:

You have rather a big task in front of you with Peter, and I would like to invite you to send me a note, however brief, perhaps once a week, just to keep me in touch with tiny details. You may find this too much of a nuisance, in which case we can arrange to 'phone each other.

There is another point. After seeing you I rather took it for granted that we had made a plan for action. I am well aware, however, that I have not talked the matter over with your husband, and I am therefore taking for granted that everyone is agreed on the plan of action that I recommend. I hope you will let me know if I am taking too much for granted here.

In this case I was quite definite in advising the parents because I felt that they needed me to take total responsibility for interrupting the boy's school life in the way that appeared to be necessary.

Summary at this Stage

This boy, of good intelligence, living in a good family, presented serious symptoms of the kind that I call the antisocial tendency. When directly questioned he did not know why he was compelled to act in the way he must act. There is therefore a degree of dissociation. The degree of dissociation would not warrant the use of the term 'split'.

The history-taking that belongs to the psychotherapeutic consultation reached to the idea that the age of 3 was significant. At this age the boy suffered a relative deprivation. The father's story confirmed this. At the birth of the younger brother Peter lost his sense of having a place in the family.

Now the boy had a conscious wish to live at home, and it was necessary for me to extend my social diagnosis, and to ascertain the capacity of the parents to carry through a treatment of their own child. I therefore arranged to see the mother alone, and I gave her too an unhurried hour. It was not wise to take notes of what transpired during this hour, in which the mother was free to talk of herself if she wished to do so. I did, however, take notes of the details of Peter's early life.

> The family was a happy one. The older sister and the younger brother were both away at school, and the mother, who had a very full life, did all the time wish that she had the children at home.
>
> The father was very fully occupied during the war so that he scarcely saw Peter in his first three years, but when Peter was 3 and his younger brother was 6 months old, the father was able to give the latter his full attention. It was too late for him to do for Peter what Peter had needed. Here was the setting for the crisis belonging to Peter's 3-year-old childhood. In this sense he was father-deprived at 3.

EARLY HISTORY

> Birth: quick—baby large and well.
>
> Breast-feeding: 3–4 months.
>
> There was a nannie who came when Peter was 2 months old and stayed till he was 5 and his brother was 2. She was narrow-minded and possessive, but at this stage after the war there was no choice. Mother was always there; she did

304

the cooking and taught Peter at home. When the nannie
went he was glad but continued to visit her.

Feeding: he was slow at feeding himself, sloppy, and not
to be hurried or harried.

Defaecation: natural.

Bed-wetting till 3. Dry in day, early.

Peter went to day school at 5 and he went away to prep
school at $9\frac{1}{2}$ 'while he was loving, young and innocent'.

Sleep: recently Peter had been waking in the night. The
mother gave me her version of the children's techniques
for going to sleep: The older sister sucked her thumb,
using also a bit of a jersey with a long sleeve; Peter sucked
his thumb until he was 5; the brother used rocking.

The mother said she was a natural mother, and had always
enjoyed her infants and children. The father had worked very
hard: 'He gets tired, which in his case means depressed, and he
has derived benefit from taking thyroid.' (Hence his belief in a
physical drug for Peter.)

A further detail was that at 6 years Peter absconded for the day.
He said: 'I've been round the lake.' Looking back, it is possible
to see this as a symptom of unhappiness. He has never had ideas
as to what he would like to be when grown up.

Both his sister and brother were at boarding school over this
period.

The mother wrote me the following two letters:

Thank you for your letter. I think that the plan of action which
we arranged was that I should observe Peter for a time and let
you know his reaction to home-life and to the news that he would
not be returning to the school, and that we should meet again.
My husband and I would very much like to come together to see
you. There are some things we would like to ask you and some
further suggestions for Peter's schooling which we would like to
put before you.

The day after I saw you and told Peter that he would not be
going back, at any rate for some time, he had a very gloomy
morning and was rather surly when advised by his father to do a
small carpentering job differently. That blew over and since then
there has not been a cloud in the sky. He occupies himself hap-

pily with home affairs and in the garden. He plays about quite a bit but does not do babyish things. He comes shopping and walking with me and is sleeping better and eats well. He had a grand swim and sunbathe with his sister today and on Wednesday is going to London with his father to choose a fishing rod for his birthday.

I told him that he would not be going back this term and perhaps not for a year. We have talked quite a lot about day schools. I have explained to him, and to other people, that he has had a mental *illness*, and that he is to stay at home and get quite better.

And a fortnight later:

This is just another note to tell you how Peter is getting on. He continues to be very happy and interested in everything at home. Occasionally for a short time he is a little bored and wonders what to do but he soon finds something like gardening, reading, making fudge, etc., and yesterday he started an aeroplane and has been going ahead with energy. He has made friends with a young teacher who lives near, and his wife. They are very sympathetic and understanding and genuinely fond of him and I think their friendship is having a great influence on him.

He sometimes complains of not sleeping well but I do not think he lies awake for long. He eats well and looks wonderfully better. He is very affectionate and demonstrative and frequently puts his arms around me.

He swims quite often and can go to the swimming bath whenever he likes. He does not appear to be shy of going when boys he knows are there. He has occasionally been angry with inanimate objects and has gone into the garden and thrown things about and *bashed*. But this has not happened for the last week.

Would it be possible for us to come and see you?

Third Therapeutic Consultation

I next saw Peter six weeks after the first interview and he had a non-committal interview with me, with drawings. Afterwards I saw his parents, who reported the details of Peter's use of his home as a mental hospital, and they mentioned the toleration of his sister and brother who were of course somewhat jealous because they each go away to school. Peter kept himself fully

306

occupied at home, and *there had been no antisocial behaviour*. He had become constructive in his play and the parents were seeking a suitable day school, since Peter seemed to be nearly ready for a school, as they thought.

Next, I telephoned some weeks later and was told of Peter's continued improvement. It had now been almost arranged that Peter should go as a day-boy to a local school. I wrote the following letter to the mother:

> I am writing this letter to you so that you may have something in writing should you be applying to a school for the admission of Peter. Naturally I shall be very willing to give further details if asked.
>
> In general I would say that Peter is an intelligent boy with good potential but that he is going through an illness which is in fact a disturbance of the emotional development. This illness is likely to clear up in time but while it was at its height it produced certain compulsive behaviour which caused concern at his public school. He is not a delinquent and it is important for me to say this since stealing was one of the symptoms of distress.
>
> It is very important for this boy that he shall live at home especially during the next year, and if it were possible I would like him to go from home to an ordinary day school.
>
> At the moment I have asked you to put his recovery in a psychological sense above his education and I believe that in doing this you are in fact doing the best possible from the educational point of view. I feel sure from what you have been able to tell me that you have already brought about a marked improvement in this boy's health by having him home and I am not expecting him to present unusual difficulties should he go to a local day school.
>
> I hope that this information will help in the initial stage of your search for a suitable school.

I received the following letter from the father a month later:

> We have the chance of getting Peter into a nearby alternative school which is a public school (boarders only) straight away as a 'home boarder'.
>
> This has come about first through the interest of the head-master, and then equally strongly through the immediate intense

307

interest of the house master himself who, after hearing the whole story and reading your letters, declared himself and his wife ready to go all out to give Peter the right new start and the right constant help, provided (1) that my wife and I were absolutely convinced this would be the right course as far as we alone could judge, and (2) that you would not regard us as flying recklessly in the face of the cogent advice you gave us to find a real day school.

As to (1) my wife and I feel that here is a quite exceptional chance with an outstanding house master and his wife (they have done wonderfully for some 'difficult' and for some peculiarly gifted boys who in less able hands could easily have been unhappy 'misfits')—an exceptional chance to let Peter in many senses *continue* in a place that already he knows well; he lives in its swimming pool, knows well its playing fields, buildings, concerts, chapel services, he has actually been taught by the genius in its workshop, and he also knows a great many of the masters including the master who runs the farm, and he has friends amongst their children. The only accessible alternative is a day school, but here, apart from the headmaster who is a splendid person, we know no other master, and it happens that we don't yet know any of the parents or the boys; so that, in the sphere of human contacts, everything there for Peter would have to be begun from scratch.

As to (2) what my wife and I and the house master wish to ask you is this: You have given your clear advice that the answer is a real day school. In view of all the above circumstances (my wife and I of course regard them as wholly and a little unexpectedly favourable) do you feel able to approve of our taking this opportunity of Peter's becoming a home boarder at this boarding school in our locality, becoming one of only three or four day boys in a boarding school?

If this gives you a clear enough picture, we shall be most grateful to know whether we may go ahead.

Replying to this, I advised the parents *to ask Peter about it* and to go ahead if he responded favourably.

The father wrote again (three months after the first consultation, Peter now 14 years):

Thank you very much indeed for writing. We are glad that you think the risk would not be altogether unjustifiable.

Peter has been 'in' the project almost from its beginning. He came with us to the house master and got on well with both master and wife. He is now able to talk about it, and we think he is truly interested and likes the idea. We are all off tomorrow for a fortnight's holiday. It does look as if when we come back we shall be right to go ahead.

Two months later I telephoned to the mother, who told me that Peter was well and happy, that he was now in the lowest form at the local public school as a day-boarder, and that he was enjoying rugger.

I telephoned again three months later and the mother said: 'Peter is wonderful; he has not missed any school on account of colds or feverish attacks, and he plays better with his brother and sister during the holidays. He had a good report from school.' She said that the second term would be the test.

One month later the mother wrote me the following letter:

Thank you very much for your letter. It certainly is not a nuisance, we are indeed grateful for your continued interest.

Peter is very well, has put on weight and has grown a little, and has successfully *not* had a cold that looked like coming on. He has begun to work, I think, and has had good marks for French and an English essay and has been put in the top division for maths, in the lower school. I do not think he has really made a friend yet but he seems to get on well with everyone. He is always happy to come home and we have now got a dog for him to love and look after.

I think he has sharply contrasted moods of feeling happy or not, and he is becoming able to know how he feels and speak about it.

The next letter (two months later) from the mother was as follows:

Peter has had a good term. He was absent for one day with a cold. He was very tired at the end—I think nervously exhausted—and had two days in bed with a so-called sore throat. And for the first week of the holidays he had a slight nervous twitch of the face. Our younger son is at home now and they are playing more happily together than they have ever done—and the nervous twitch has gone, and all signs of tiredness. He came second in form, had a good report, and is going up next term. His face was radiant when he heard this news. Mathematics seems to be his best subject. He also goes a lot to the workshop and is making a canoe—the materials are a birthday present in advance. He does not appear to have made a special friend but seems to get on well with everybody.

Peter's brother leaves his boarding school next summer and we would very much like to have him at home afterwards. It's such a joy having Peter at home that we want to share this joy with our younger son. He can probably go into another house at Peter's school as a daily boarder like Peter, especially as he is scholarship standard. Do you think it would be bad for Peter if his brother joins him? He is very much quicker than Peter but they are wonderfully good friends now. If they are in different houses do you think any personal rivalry would be swallowed up in a 'house rivalry' which is ordinary, which everybody suffers from?

To this I replied:

I am glad Peter had a good term. The problem you raise concerns Peter's brother, and I should think that Peter would be able to deal with having him at home, although, as you suggest, it is a bit different from having him home in the holidays. Perhaps you will be able *to mention the idea to Peter* before the whole thing is settled up. I am glad they will not be in the same house.

It is very helpful to me that you keep me in touch.

The mother wrote again three months later, fourteen months after the first consultation:

Just another report about Peter. The news is not quite so good this time as he has had to miss five weeks of school because of a streptococcal throat. He ran a low temperature for two weeks before the doctor found out the cause. He even began to wonder whether some nervous trouble was the cause. Then two of Peter's friends at school had sore throats with high temperatures—easily recognised—so Peter's throat was swabbed and the trouble found. The doctor thinks he may have been a carrier.

All the time he was at home—not always in bed—he made aeroplanes. He is never idle and loves using his hands. He is quite well again now and doing exams after only half a term's work. I do not think this worries him exactly but I think he would like to be successful. He has finished his canoe—painted a beautiful blue and white—and we have launched it successfully on the river near Henley. This is a source of great joy to him and it is much admired by everyone. He has no real friend of his own age as he has been at home so much. But he is very happy and good-tempered. He is now 15 and his voice unbroken. He is going a long way away to stay with his uncle and family for two weeks—the first time to go away on his own since he left boarding school. After he comes back we are all going for a family holiday with friends. I hope all this will really set him up in health.

And again a month later:

Thank you very much for your wise letter. I am writing to ask you if you will again give me your advice. Peter did not do well in his exams. He could not and he was very sorry about it. I had been wondering whether I should suggest that he have some extra lessons to help him catch up. We talked about it together and I had begun to think it would be better not to worry him. Now his report has come. Will you be kind enough to look at it? This is from a young and inexperienced form master and I do not think Peter will be in his form again next term. But I feel sorry that he has suggested that Peter is lazy. He could not be energetic when he returned late in the term—partly because he was full of penicillin. I would like to go and see this master before the term starts to explain more about Peter but I do not know what line to take. Also I do not know the best way to help Peter. I can say that reports don't matter, but I know that *he* thinks they do. He lost touch with his own generation of course in the five weeks of sore throat but I think there are one or two possible budding friendships. Also he missed being in the house play which he would have loved to have been in.

My husband is away for six months,[1] so we cannot discuss all this together. I would be very grateful for your advice. Please do

[1] The mother perhaps could not see the special significance in this case of the father's absence.

311

not hurry. Peter is away and has not seen his report yet. Do you think extra lessons in one subject would be a help before term? I do not think I am anxious about his work *as work* but because I feel he could be so much happier if he were confident about it.

I replied to this by telephone and returned Peter's school reports.

The next letter from the mother came twenty-five months after the first contact.

I would like to write to you once again about Peter. The news is very good. He is wonderfully better and happier. You would hardly recognise him as he has grown so much and is now taller than my husband. He still has the same very young face. His school reports have been good and he has only missed a few odd days from school since September. He has not yet made a close friend at school and seems to lead rather a solitary but contented life. He is full of activity at home, gardening and cooking, and such things. He spends a good deal of time at the school work-shop where he can do carpentry with help.

There is something I would like to ask you. Last September he had a number of migraine headaches at short intervals from each other. He had had them before but not so frequently. They were not so bad that he had to go to bed but were enough to make him miserable. I have always had them myself from time to time and have discovered that if I take iron I do not have them. I was given iron tablets and have been taking them off and on ever since my daughter was born. I had the feeling that they would be good for Peter. So I have been giving him one every morning except during the holidays when he had one every other morning. I am sure they are supplying something he needs. But have I been doing a wise thing? Could they be doing him some harm that I do not know of?

My daughter (aged 19) has gone abroad au pair so Peter is enjoying being *the only one at home*. He has been very happy with his young brother during the holidays. Peter's matron seems very fond of him and he seems to be making his own niche in the house.

He had me upset last term when he was discovered cheating in form because he had forgotten his book and could not own up. We knew about it because the master told my husband and his

312

house master knew about it. He did not tell us and did not know that we knew. He seemed quite able to deal with it rationally himself and fortunately the master in question was very sensible.

Thank you again for your help.

I wrote to the mother again:

> It was good to get a letter from you just when I was going to write and ask you about Peter. The news seems to be good.
>
> I want to let you know that I can see no reason why Peter should not have iron tablets. You must not be too disappointed, however, if he does sometimes get migraine in spite of this. Also if he should get constipated I think you would feel that it was time to leave off the tablets, at any rate for a while.

Six or seven years after the first contact I wrote to the mother asking her to let me have news of Peter, and she replied (Peter now 22 years):

> I have thought of writing to you many times but have always decided to wait a little longer to be quite sure that all was well. I have only good things to tell you. Peter was at this school for five years—the first four as a day-boy, which meant breakfast and supper at home, and all the rest of the day at school. He was a boarder for the last year and a house monitor for the last term. He was well and happy all the time but did not make any real friends. He was in the Shooting 8 and played football for the house. He is 6' 4½" and broad! He took A-level in maths, physics and chemistry but only passed in chemistry, which was his chief interest. He set his heart on going to University in spite of getting no encouragement from his teachers. He took A-level physics and maths again, working with a coach in London and living at home. He passed both and was admitted to a distant University to study biochemistry. His letters are very happy. After he had passed his exams he got a temporary holiday job in the research department of a London firm. He went to the O.T.C. camp in the Highlands of Scotland and he also explored the Highlands on his own, hitch-hiking with a rucksack.
>
> It only remains to be seen whether he can cope with the work for his degree.
>
> Thank you again for all the help you gave us when we needed

it so badly. Although we have not needed to come again, it has been a great strength for us to feel that you were there.

Thank you very much for your kind enquiries. I am sure you will be pleased with what I have told you. We have never spoken to Peter about his visits to you or about his problems at that time. Do you think that some time we should?

I replied:

I am most grateful to you for your long and interesting letter. Naturally I am very pleased to hear about Peter. I see no particular reason why you should make a special effort to talk to him about his visits to me, but perhaps one day the subject will come up naturally.

Conclusion

Here then is the case of a boy whose antisocial symptomatology was severe. He was treated as ill, not naughty, and allowed to use his home as a mental hospital. In a year or so he had recovered from his abnormal psychiatric state, and the work had been done by his mother and by the whole family and by the capacity of a local boarding school to adapt to his special needs.

My main function was to say definitely: this boy is ill, he must be told he is ill, and he must be allowed time to make a natural recovery from his psychiatric illness.

It turned out that the main etiological factor was a relative deprivation at 3 years, which showed up the boy's father-deprivation throughout the first three years, due to the war.

CASE XVII 'Ruth' *aet* 8 years

The case of Ruth came to me in the following way. A man consulted me about himself; this was Ruth's father. In the course of the hour or so in which he said what he wanted to say about himself, he told me a great number of facts. Among these facts were two things that were significant in the description of Ruth's problems. The first of these was that his daughter, the middle one of three, had started to steal at school, and along with this she had changed in her personality and become secretive and furtive. Her school work had degenerated and the school had asked for her removal. The other fact was that this man, who was trying to keep his family together while doing his own job, had become confused in the management of his wife's illnesses. His wife had three illnesses and these had involved him in three sets of hospital situation and somehow or other there was a failure of communication between the social-work agencies in the three hospitals. He felt torn into three pieces and a great deal of his time was taken up with complying with the demands of the three hospitals and taking his wife first to one and then to another, and it seemed as if there really had been a failure of communication with him himself. At the end of the interview with me he said that because one person had listened to his various and varied complaints he had now for the first time become able to see them as a unit and he said he felt he could now manage them without further help.

He did feel, however, that he needed help for Ruth and I therefore arranged to see his daughter. It would be necessary for me in my interview with the daughter to reverse her tendency towards antisocial behaviour. If I could succeed, then I felt confident that this man could cope with the total family situation including the three illnesses of his wife, helped of course by the very positive qualities which she also displayed in spite of her illnesses.

It is necessary to enumerate the three illnesses because they affect the problem that Ruth was trying to deal with. Ruth's mother liked having children and especially she liked their babyhood and early dependence. She managed the older daughter well and she enjoyed Ruth as a baby right up to the time when she became pregnant with the third child, who turned out also to be a girl. This was in fact a time of worry in the total family

315

situation and Ruth's mother knew that by becoming pregnant she had become involved in a wider set of responsibilities than she could manage. Perhaps for a short while she lost confidence in her husband. The fact that Ruth's mother now had too much to deal with led to her becoming ill during the third pregnancy and Ruth became a casualty, although this was not recognised by either of the two parents at the time when it was happening. Ruth's mother developed rheumatoid arthritis and became a cripple. Towards the end of her pregnancy she also developed acute melancholia. For each of these conditions in turn she was hospitalised, the most serious being after the third child's birth when she needed to spend a few weeks in a mental hospital. She refused physical treatments and returned gradually to resume home life and the satisfactory care of her children. When the baby was a few months old she and her husband began to realise that Ruth had been neglected, although not physically neglected, and it is this period of neglect that showed itself as significant in the therapeutic consultation, a description of which follows.

To complete the picture it is necessary to say that Ruth's mother had a third illness, one which gave her great confidence in doctors and which perhaps carried her through the times of despair. As a child she had had bronchiectasis and she was an early case for surgical removal of the whole of one side of the lungs. The hospital department responsible for this had taken a great interest in her and had made available for her an excellent convalescent home, which indeed she was still able to use almost at a moment's notice when she was a married woman with a family. If she felt unwell she could go and stay there for a fortnight.

When Ruth came to me I had knowledge therefore of these and many other facts concerning the family background. But what I could not tell was whether Ruth would be able to make contact with me in such a way that I could see her childhood through her own eyes. It is hoped that the reader will be able to catch a glimpse from a study of the sequence of events in the therapeutic consultation of the way in which a child can use this specialised situation which we are able to provide. In this particular case it cannot be denied that I used not only my theoretical understanding of the relationship between stealing and deprivation, but also the reinforcement of theory which was provided by what I gathered from Ruth's father as he described the family scene and his own personal problems.

The case has this significance, that Ruth changed towards the end of the consultation, as will be described.

Ruth

I give as little as possible of the history. Ruth was 8 when I saw her. She had a sister of 13 and another sister of 5. Her family was intact. The parents are rather severely interdependent, and this gives the family a feeling of permanence which the children can use.

In my interview with the father I found that the canker worm that was destroying the family and its innate tendency towards self-healing was Ruth's altered character. Ruth had been especially loved and had even been a little spoiled, and then she changed, and now she was stealing. The parents felt very guilty about this because (as they said) they had seen themselves bringing about this change. They could not avoid it, but they saw the change in Ruth happening under their eyes, starting at the beginning of the mother's third pregnancy.

I decided that the first thing to be done in helping this family to rehabilitate was to see Ruth and, if possible, to cure her of her compulsion to steal. To do this I must reach her own version of her deprivation experience. Hence the therapeutic consultation.

There is nothing very unusual about the consultation, except that it marked the end of Ruth's stealing, and also it marked the beginning of a new period of emotional growth, with some improvement educationally. There was a favourable family response to the child's loss of the antisocial compulsion and the parents made good use of their new freedom to get on with their own re-establishment as parents of a family that is very much a going concern.

The Therapeutic Consultation

Ruth was quickly at ease. She told me of her elder sister and of her younger sister who was at school. She said she did not mind much missing school to come to me. If at school she would be doing English. She accepted my suggestion of a game and I made a squiggle

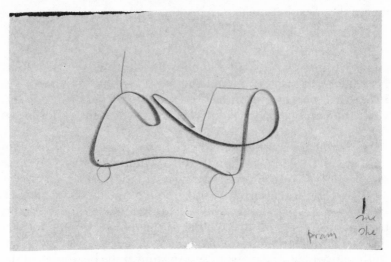

(1) which Ruth quickly turned into a pram, her own pram which she had had for a year. From this I learned that she had three dolls. 'That's all I want,' she said.

(2) Her squiggle which I made into a plant. She called it a geranium.

(3) Her drawing which shows the three dolls which I invited her to draw. She said: 'I'll try to . . .' 'She's not right. . . .'

I said: 'Well, it's not school, it's only that you're showing me what you want to show me.'

She said: 'Rose Mary is the biggest. Judith has curly hair. Poppy has a fringe and a pony tail and bow.'

I asked: 'Would you rather be a father or a mother?' and she quickly opted for being a mother. She said: 'I want as many children as I can get.'

Here was a picture of her own family in terms of dolls. She herself would be represented by Judith. It can be seen in this drawing that her identification with her mother gives her a deformity of a lower limb. Also the hands seem to be missing, which could be a comment on the helplessness of her mother when she was acutely ill.

2
du
nu

Rosemary   Judith   Poppy   3

319

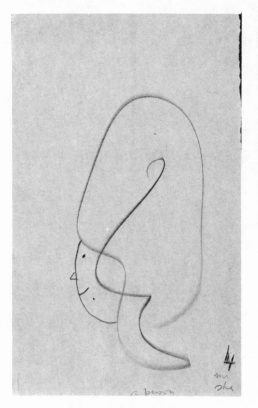

(4) My squiggle which she made into 'a person'.

(5) Her squiggle which made her say: 'Oh! I know!' And she turned her own squiggle into a bow and arrow.

(6) My squiggle which she turned into a butterfly. She spoke here of the way her garden had got messed up by a man putting in a toilet. 'The question is, will it ever recover?'

I suggested: 'Men are clumsy creatures.'

It will be observed that I was not making interpretations. I was simply talking while playing with her.

(7) Her squiggle which I bagged else she would have used it. (In this way I suppose I conveyed to her the idea of my involvement in the game.) I made an aeroplane but she said it was a fly.

6
she
du
butterfly

7
she
me
aeroplane
(she : ap)

(8) My squiggle which she turned into a horse. She was rather pleased with this.

(9) Her squiggle which I turned into an animal which she called a giraffe.

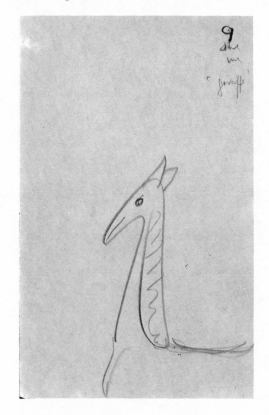

(10) My squiggle: her quick response was: 'Oh, I know!' and while turning it into a harp she talked with me about playing the recorder. A recorder was standing up on a shelf beside her but she did not want to use it.

(11) Her squiggle which I turned into a dancing figure.

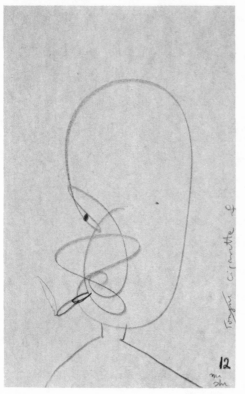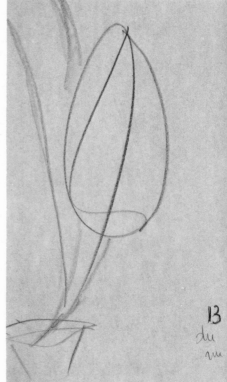

(12) My squiggle which she made into a woman's head. The woman's tongue was out but Ruth changed the tongue into a cigarette, this being more respectable, I suppose.

(13) Her squiggle which I turned into a plant. While I was doing this she offered me a Polo (sweet) which I accepted. I said: 'Are you tired of this game?' and she answered: 'No, I like it.'

This marked the middle phase, which indicates the establishment of confidence, and this can be followed by a readiness to go deeper.

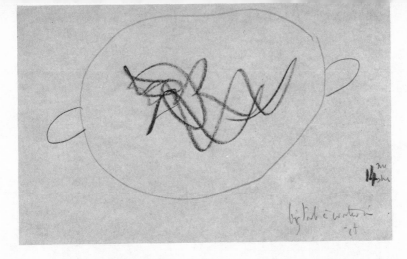

(14) I felt bolder as a result of this and deliberately made a muddle-squiggle. She put a tub round it so that the muddle was water contained in a tub. Here was personal fantasy, and I was now able to approach Ruth's dream world. I asked if when she dreamed she dreamed of things like this. She said she saw something on TV, fish in a tub with a hole in it. I persevered with the idea of dreams and said: 'What about funny dreams or frightening dreams?' Now she switched over to her dream life. 'My dreams are mostly the same. I dream every night.' To illustrate this she took a big sheet of paper.

(In this work this always indicates that something significant is coming up.)

(15) Ships of olden days with water coming in. 'When my little sister was a baby in arms, I was running. It was before mother had bad legs. Water is rushing up. I am bringing things, baby food for the baby. They had got it in because of the baby. The dream ended up nicely. Father came home with the car and went backwards into the garage. He bumped into the ship and smashed it all up and all the water went away. So it ended nicely.'

There had been considerable anxiety in the middle of this description of the dream, before father came and saved the situation.

It will be noted that the mother's mouth is curved, indicating a smile. The child is going towards the mother or is near her. The baby is perhaps unborn, because there is no waist. The mother has useless hands and a deformed lower limb.

This detail from Picture 15 is reproduced in the size to which it was drawn

I did make a comment here, referring to the fact that she ran to her mother full of hope. She felt she could be like mother by helping her with the feeding of the new baby. It had been in fact near the end of the mother's pregnancy that Ruth changed over into an ill child. The first things she had stolen were tins of baby food, and then she had stolen money to buy baby food, to which she had become addicted. In this case I happened to know these background details.

This dream was optimistic and in the end all went well, so there was a pessimistic version of the same dream somewhere. I needed this and so I invited Ruth to draw the very worst.

(16) Ruth's drawing again. This shows the mother with the baby, and *Ruth surprised herself as she drew.* 'Why! it's a little tiny midget!' She said that there was poison in the sea behind her which made the baby shrink up; mother would shrink up too. 'O look, I'm further and further away from mother!'

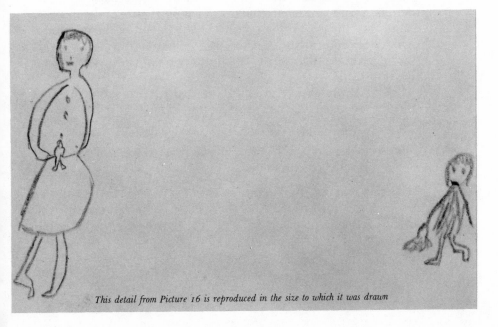

This detail from Picture 16 is reproduced in the size to which it was drawn

This picture gives a direct view of the most severe area of Ruth's separation and the arrival of a sense of hopelessness. In this picture, drawn very quickly and with feeling that had deep roots, she gave the mother a straight mouth (melancholia), and a waist which might indicate that the baby was now born. But the baby was dwindling, because of the poison water (the opposite of the baby food), and while drawing Ruth felt she was getting further and further from her mother.

The drawing of herself was done straight from the shoulder, so that the lines of the mouth went down the arms and became part of the bag that had no baby food in it.

> She said: 'So I had to eat hard. When the poison stopped I got fat again.'

There were further details but these must be omitted here except for the following:

> I deliberately asked Ruth: 'Did you ever pinch things?'
>
> She gave me the answer: 'I did when I was young; I used to steal baby-foods. I just ate the foods. I specially liked the tinned peaches for babies.'
>
> *It was important to get this from Ruth herself.*

Adding up all these details, it seems legitimate for me to claim that this is a true illustration by the child of her deprivation, at the moment of her losing hope of being able to deal with the mother's pregnancy and with the birth of the baby sister by identification with the maternal and feeding figure of the mother. There was already an identification illustrated by the deformity of the doll and of Ruth herself in the dream drawings. But this was identification in terms of illness, not of positive maternal function.

Before Ruth went she and I had two more squiggle-game drawings to bring her to the surface and to make going easy:

(17) Mine, which she made into a fish, and

(18) Hers, which I put on a plate, and it was a dish of food with bread, etc.

In this context my attempt is simply to present this child's drawing in which she caught the feeling of becoming deprived and of feeling hopeless. Having recaptured this experience in full

329

consciousness in the supporting setting of the therapeutic consultation Ruth immediately lost the compulsion to steal, and the lying disappeared along with this. There were also favourable changes in her total personality, as is usual in such cases, and the school quickly forgot that they had been bothered about her and that they had actually asked her to leave.

Summary

In a therapeutic consultation Ruth, aged 8 years, was able to remember and relive the distress that belonged to the time of her becoming a deprived child, and she was able to illustrate this in a drawing. The experience was a therapeutic one for Ruth, and the changes in Ruth benefited the whole family.

FOLLOW-UF

5 years. Satisfactory development, and no stealing. The family has re-established itself.

CASE XVIII 'Mrs. X.' *aet* 30 years
(mother of Anna, *aet* 6 years)

I now wish to include an illustration of an interview with a parent. There is no essential difference between an interview with a parent and an interview with a child except that with adults, as with older adolescents, it is unlikely that an interchange of drawings would be appropriate.

This is a case chosen from my hospital clinic. The daughter had been in our care, transferred by a colleague who is a paediatrician. In the initial interview with the child we discovered that there were features showing us that the mother's attendance with her child at the hospital indicated a need in the mother herself. The mother was unable, however, to think of what she was doing in this way, and she was constantly bringing her daughter for one doctor or another to examine her and to treat her for ailments the severity of which was not as great as the mother's anxiety would seem to indicate. It was necessary in this case for the child psychiatry team to keep in contact with the mother and daughter and to hold the case while waiting for developments. Gradually, after months, the mother lost her suspicion and revealed herself as a person very much in need of personal help.

I was told from the social-work side of the team that the moment had come for me to interview the mother, and I give a description of this interview. The result of this interview was favourable from the point of view of the clinic's efforts to give suitable help to the child since the mother, having communicated about herself, was now able to do a new thing, which was to hand over the management of her daughter to the casework organisation. As a result therefore of the interview we were able to place this girl in a suitable school which in fact carried her through the next few years. Contact between the child and the mother could be maintained because of the school's own special attitude to this matter.

A description of this interview is given not so much as evidence of the cure of the mother, which indeed would require an immense amount of work on the part of someone, as to illustrate the way in which by waiting we arrived at the moment for a communication of a very personal kind. Incidentally, the way the mother gave her history provides a picture of a deprived child as given by that child now become an adult herself with an illegitimate daughter. It is possible to claim in addition that this mother became better able to manage her own affairs following the interview and its sequel: the proper care of the daughter.

> I saw Mrs. X. alone.
>
> I said: 'Hello! You look rather thin.'
>
> She said: 'As a matter of fact I am fat and I can't get my clothes on.'
>
> She was looking serious and worried.
>
> I said: 'Let's talk about Anna—it will break the ice.' (Anna was 6 years old.)
>
> Mrs. X. said: 'She is really good, you know. She does not have a very nice life—I never talk to her, for instance, simply because no-one ever talked to me when I was a child. If I am upset it is then that Anna gets worse, and perhaps really naughty.'

She went on to talk about the handicap she herself had experienced through not having taken the appropriate exams at school, so that she could not be a nurse or other things that she had wanted to be. At 20 she saw a woman doctor at a clinic and was shown the report which said that she was 'amoral, had no background, and was permanently adolescent'; but, as she said, 'It is no good having treatment to let you know what you are like when you know already.' She insisted on her own badness, and in this she persisted to the very end of the consultation.

> 'The trouble is,' she said, 'if I like someone, male or female, for me that is sex. At 19 I had my first hug and kiss and this was the first time anybody was affectionate towards me, so the two came at the same time.'
>
> I said: 'I can't think how you managed.'
>
> She said: 'Well, I masturbated a great deal.'
>
> This was clitoric only. She never knew about deep orgasm until quite recently.
>
> She said: 'The trouble is I ruin everything by becoming possessive. I don't mean to, but I am all "What have you

332

done? where have you been?" as if the man or woman had done everything to hurt me. One of them said: "I can't even go to the lavatory without your being jealous."'

I said: 'Children are often like that—probably Anna has been?'

She said: 'Yes, but isn't it awful when I'm still a child!'

It was here that she started crying.

She said: 'It doesn't matter at all whether it is a man or a woman—if anyone is affectionate then there is a sexual experience for me. I have had two affairs with women, which were perhaps the most satisfactory things that have happened.'

They were both big, plump women—a lot of sex play and breast manipulation and so on.

I said: 'Well, all that is terrible. Something good has happened to you elsewhere but it has got lost. I am sure of that because you can recognise good things in Anna.'

So she went over some of the details of her story again.

She was made a ward of the —— Corporation because her mother was cruel to her. She had her mother until she was 3 or 4 and I said: 'Perhaps mother may have been all right at the beginning from your point of view?'

She said: 'She could not have been if she was so cruel that I had to be taken away from her.'

We talked here about her desperate loneliness, a state which she described both ways: 'I get lonely by being unpopular, but I get terribly jealous of anyone who is popular, especially my girl friend.'

I made a comment here, saying: 'Being alone is safe.'

She said: 'That is what I said to my friend, Daisie, a week or two ago', and she went over again what I had said in her own language.

She went on to talk about Daisie, who is extremely pretty, vivacious, gay and theatrical, 22 years old. She has done everything, she can talk her way into everything, has two bank accounts and plenty of money.

Here and elsewhere it was obvious that she kept her normal

333

self going in the personality of her friends, of whom (in consequence, perhaps) she is inordinately jealous.

> I said to her, because of her description of Daisie: 'Did you have any brothers or sisters?'
>
> She said: 'I remember an orphanage Christmas Party during which someone said: "And this is your sister"; she was very pretty. I never saw her again.'

This led on to her telling me that she was called Polly in the orphanage, but when she saw her birth certificate she found that her father was 'Y.' and her mother 'Z.'. There was no mention of the name she had been called. She found she was born in —— ! She often wonders whether there had been a crime in the family so that the orphanage changed her name to save her from shame. She was in the —— Corporation Society Orphanage, starting off in a big place for 150 small children, and being in smaller homes until eventually going to ——. In one of these there was a Miss ——, a woman from abroad who was the superintendent.

I asked for permission to make enquiries about her childhood and she said she would be glad if I would, but she has always kept away from making enquiries for fear of finding that things are much worse than she thinks. The scanty details she gave me turned out to be correct. All this happened in the thirties.

She went on to describe fits of depression. She has always dealt with these by going to bed early and *day-dreaming*. At these times she always pretends that she is something special and is very good at something or other. Actually she has never been either of these two things. She was a plain, thin child, she said, and for this reason went to hospital. This reminded her of something and made her cry again.[1] She had had one kind person in her life. When 8 or 9 she was in a fever hospital, in a small room, and she had no visitors during the whole of her stay there. One day a woman stopped at her cubicle, opened her bag, and said: 'Choose something.' She chose her mirror. The woman then went and gave it to the nurse, who eventually came to her with it. She says of this that it was 'the only kind thing that ever happened to me in my childhood'. She had no visitors at all during the six

---

[1] My hope is that by now the reader will have got the feeling that, in spite of my freedom in the use of myself, the structuring of the interview truly comes from the patient.

months that she was in the hospital. It must have been six months that she was there because she had both her birthday (summer) and Christmas there. She remembered being wheeled into the ward in black stockings and gradually being persuaded to walk. She does not know what was the illness. She then remembered being taken by a man in blue from the orphanage into the ambulance.

I spoke of the awfulness of being taken from an orphanage, which was different from being taken from one's own home, because of the uncertainty about returning. She went into an isolation ward and remembers Father Christmas, who turned out to be the doctor. I made a remark here about the ward having dealt with her body but seemed to leave out the rest of her. According-ing to her pattern she immediately felt very guilty as she said: 'I feel that people owe me things, but of course it is *me* who is wrong. But because I feel I am owed something I cannot let any-thing go well. If it is going well I destroy it halfway, and so I hurt myself.'

> I said: 'It must be very difficult for you to know what to be angry with, and yet there must be violent anger in you somewhere.'
>
> She said: 'Yes, but it takes an odd form—I feel a shudder going through me. It is a feeling as if *for a split second* (she found it very difficult to describe this) *I might go mad*, but I remember where I am, and it's over.'
>
> I said: 'You mean you *do* go mad, only it is done so quickly that it is all over. Your fear is that you will find you have done something awful while you have been mad.'

She then told me something which she said she had 'never told anyone', and she was very distressed. When she was 14 or 15 she could not be placed out in a factory because it was said that she would be no good, so she was kept to work in the nursery opposite the orphanage where children came from their homes. She had to help with the children or infants and take the place of a teacher who might be absent, and so on. A child was screaming, and it got on her nerves and she nearly strangled it. (This illustrated what I had said perfectly.) She took it by the neck and shook it, but then stopped. On another occasion she would hug children hard in order to get sexual feelings. 'This is horrible and dirty—

do any other women ever do anything like this? Sometimes Anna gets into bed and hugs me and I feel sexy. Has *any* mother *ever* felt this? Of course in the nursery school I was given all the dirty jobs, including cleaning up the babies, but I was never allowed to do anything of the kind that would be important for a baby.'

Those babies in the nursery were all going to be collected by their parents and so I suggested that this could be one reason why she nearly murdered this child, she herself having never had a home to go back to.

She then went on. At 18 she was a maid in somebody's house and she had to get her birth certificate. She repeated herself, telling me that this was very upsetting, for in her day-dreams there were always wonderful things she *might* one day discover about her parents, but when she saw that her name was not the same as the name she knew herself by and that her father was a hawker of no fixed address, she broke down in tears.

So in this house where she was a maid with a wage of 15s. a week, the young mistress had lovely clothes and a beautiful sitting-room, which she was not allowed to use, and the young mistress always carried a lot of money in her bag. Mrs. X. stole a pound to buy herself something pretty, but in spite of having so much money this woman missed the pound and Mrs. X. was sacked.

I went on talking about the anger that must be in her without her knowing where to put it.

> I said: 'God, for instance.'
>
> She said: 'In the orphanage we were taught terrible things about God, and until I was 13 I always slept with my arms crossed in case I died so that I would not go to hell. As soon as I left the orphanage I stopped confession and have had no belief in anything since. Once I wanted to be a nun but that was only so as to look pious. I have wanted a baby terribly since I was 12. Here I am—I've made a mess of my life—how can I recover? Cyril (father of Anna) and his mother did not like me and I am sure it was because of the orphanage. I always blame everything on the orphanage and feel ashamed of it all the time. But some people like Marilyn Munroe make films and let everybody *know* they were in an orphanage, because they have the strength of character which I have not got. We had a lot of beatings Auntie (as she was called) used the wooden spoon on ou

336

hands. I stole a lot of food in the night, biscuits, sugar and cocoa. We never had sweet things except on Sundays when we had a biscuit or a piece of cake.'

She remarked that this craving for sweet things had persisted.

I asked her again about her mother and the question of research into the past, and she said she had not done any lest she got a worse shock which she could not bear.

She said: 'You see, she never came near me all those years from 3 to 16. A friend said to me, though, "you are always searching for something".'

I interpreted here about the link between the compulsive stealing and searching for something, perhaps for a lost bit of good relationship with her mother. She said she does not steal ever now but she still has a terrible urge for sweet things. At any minute she may have a desperate need and have to rush out and buy a cake, even when giving Anna her bath.

I then asked her about dreams and she said: 'Day-dreams?'

I said: 'No, real dreams.' Her real dreams are all frightening, about a mouse or a rat.

She said: 'On the television there was a mouse and I could not sleep at all that night. It is a terrible thing I have about rats and mice. There is a rat in all my nightmares. Even an advertisement about rat poison gives me the shivers. This was a dream I had three times: *I was in a room with someone and an orange. A rat had been eating the orange and there was no food left so that I had the choice of starving or eating the orange which had been bitten by the rat.* I always woke in a terrible state from these dreams and I always keep a light on in any case. I tried to cure myself by going to the zoo with Anna, but the rats and mice there were pretty, and so it was no good. It has always been the same, since I was 18 at any rate.'

'The most awful thing was Emergency Ward 10[1]: a girl had a disease caught from rats and they went to her room and there was a picture of all the rats in her bed. The shock was so bad that I was nearly sick and I couldn't sleep all night.'

[1] TV series.

337

I asked what the trouble was and she said: 'Oh, I think they will eat me.'

I withheld using this dream.

She said: 'There are dreams when you are just falling asleep and wake suddenly—*a line with a train coming and I just wake*—or *I climb a tree and never get to the top*—another, *I run and run and thousands and thousands of little people are running after me. They have little bodies and huge heads.* As a child I used to fall asleep everywhere—at tea, in school, and so on—and I always had a dirty head. The lice in my head would run over the pillows and I felt compelled to touch my head, although it was all terrible. I have always wanted someone to love or cuddle me, but I was never kissed until I was 19. Auntie never kissed any of us good-night. I am all the time ashamed of the orphanage.'

Here she put in an illustration that showed her sense of fun. She said:

'Once on a bus the conductor said to Auntie (who was a nun): 'Are all these your kids?' Auntie was flustered and said: 'Yes, but they have all got different fathers!''

This was like an oasis in the desert. She quickly returned to the desert with:

'This was terrible for me.'

I said: 'It is as if with all these insects you are talking about your own fertility. You longed from the age of 12 to have a baby, which would have been all right, but before then fertility was all mixed up with faeces and dirt and infestation and so on.'

She said: 'I thought having babies must be something awful, my mother would never do that! But then (it must have been Coronation time when I was 10) I read about the princesses, and I saw the queen, and in that way I got away from the horror which came from not being told anything at all about babies. My first period I had in the middle of the night. I was very frightened and woke Auntie ——. She was cross. "Everything you do is different" was all she said. But I had seen blood and I thought I was going to die.'

No-one explained anything at all, but Auntie gave her some

towels, saying 'You must clean these yourself', and this made her feel more ashamed than ever.

I asked her about mixed classes in the orphanage. She said that there were boys, but the boys had bath nights on different nights.

She added, as if remembering something that had been forgotten:

> 'When I was 9 I saw a boy showing himself' (she was confused about details). 'He was asking a girl to kiss him. I remember the words: "Give *it* a kiss", and the children laughed. In walked Auntie and we all got the wooden spoon.'

> She said that Auntie was a woman who was really not suitable for this job. She was eventually dismissed.

> 'As an instance, there was a boy who was liable to wet the bed, and I am upset even now seeing him being sent to sleep 'all curled up' in the cot each time as a punishment. She was naturally unjust. She had a relief twice a week. Some of these were horrible. One was nice, so of course we all took advantage of her; we came home late, ate too much butter and too much jam, and did all our work wrong. You see, she was so sweet that we all went mad. Sometimes she would send the older ones out to get chips and then we would eat them all together! But what I remember about this time was work, work, work.'

> And she gave a vivid description of life in a rush.

> 'We had to do everything, scrub the floors of the school, rush home two miles, get the lunch ready, rush back to school after washing up, rush home to prepare tea, clear up the tea, and then darn socks. We watched the children play, but we had no time for anything.'

Then she remembered a lot of details about brass that had to be cleaned and steps to be whitened. Auntie never talked with the children, and she never remembers having had any toys. I asked her about toys to cuddle. She said that Anna had none and nor did she. She as a child would pull her pillow down and put her head under the sheets so that she could see no light, but she always woke herself at 5 a.m. for two hours of day-dreaming. This day-dreaming involved having her hands between her legs, and she also demonstrated something which was in the pattern of her childhood right through: rocking backward and forward with her thumbs in her armpits. She had had a lot of smacks for this habit.

I made an *interpretation* here. It seemed to me that we had nearly had enough, each of us, and I must do some work. I must act now or not act at all.

> I said: 'You know, it may be that these rats and mice are *in between you and the breast* of the mother that was a good mummy. When you get back to infancy and you think of your mother's breasts the best you can do is rats and mice.'
>
> She seemed shocked, and she shuddered and said: 'How can that be!'

I said dogmatically that the rats represented her own biting, and the breast turning up as a biting object indistinguishable from her own biting. I related this to the fact that her own mother had failed her during the time when she was dealing with the new problem of the urge to bite in her personal development. She accepted this and immediately started looking for something in the relationship to the mother which could be carried over. She said she never had had a nice dream. She may have had a sad one and she said that she always felt she would die unnaturally (not suicide) and that she would never last long enough. Then a significant thing happened. She said that she remembered something—being carried—it had to do with the time before the orphanage. There were two things. One thing had to do with 'pobs', a cereal food in her home county, and so with the period before the orphanage; 'but the other thing is an important memory because I remember going to the orphanage [that is, when she was 4] always trying to think of this rather frightening episode, *because it was the only thing I could carry over from the time before the orphanage*'.

> She tried very hard to get it.
>
> 'There is a voice—feet are running—I know doors are opening—there was a man there—people are shouting and someone has a bag or case.' This was the moment of being taken from home to the orphanage.

This was a memory which was extremely precious to her and which she felt sad to be losing, although it never quite got her back to the early days as the word 'pobs' did.

Mrs. X. had now reached back over the gap, and to some extent had recovered the memory of her own 'good' mummy.

I ended by saying that it would be quite possible for the relationship between her mother and herself to have been good at the start, although from the point of view of people observing, the mother was being cruel to her. We had to leave things in this state. She said, however, that if I really liked she would show me her birth certificate, which she never shows to anyone as she keeps it locked up. Once she could have got married to someone very nice, but at the last minute her birth certificate had to be produced so she ran away from the whole thing.

Although this was an interview with a parent there was the same playful evolution of ideas and feelings as in the interviews with the children. This mother gives quite naturally and in an unsophisticated way the relationship between stealing and both deprivation and hope.

Result

As described in the preamble to the case-presentation, this interview led to a new opportunity for the child to be managed by the clinic team in the way that she really needed and in the way that we had long waited for. The mother had to be given time to gain the confidence in us that was necessary before she could make use of this kind of interview in which it was she herself who was the ill person of the couple. After this interview she stopped using the daughter as ill and in need of medical care. The child went into substitute care, and the good relationship between her and her mother was maintained and enriched. Anna is now almost an adult.

CASE XIX 'Lily' *aet* 5 years

The following brief statement about a girl is inserted to illustrate not so much the interview technique as the way in which the subject of stealing turns up quite naturally in association with transitional phenomena, so that the study of the one involves the study of the other.

Lily was brought to my clinic at the Paddington Green Children's Hospital in 1956.

Family History

    Boy   7 years.
    Lily   5 years.
    Boy   1½ years.

The family was intact although disturbed by the parents' quarrelling, and the two older children were not doing well at school. The mother's mother was a powerful figure in the household, dominating her daughter (the mother of Lily) and now indulging the baby boy.

My first contact was with the brother, but it is the interview with the girl that I wish to describe. The interview was carried out in the presence of two Psychiatric Social Workers and two visitors.

Lily chose to draw and she drew the main figure of her nightmares, a monster. This was a human figure with a lot of hair. I asked her whether any of her actual possessions were like that and she drew her two teddy bears. After this she drew a third one, one which she said had no fur at all. She said her mother was always trying to get her to play with dolls, but she did not want dolls, she wanted her teddies. She liked to call her two teddies mother and father teddies, making it quite clear at the same time that they were not dolls. There was some story about the teddy with no fur having been burned by her mother, who tried to give her a doll instead.

I tried to get at the objective truth of this in conversation with the mother afterwards, and I found that the mother was surprised that the child had remembered an incident which she herself was ashamed of. The mother said that she had given the child a pram, but Lily had deliberately taken the pram and twisted it and ruined it and the mother was very angry at this. She had read in the papers that when a child is destructive you should destroy something belonging to the child, so she took this teddy (the one that Lily had drawn with no fur) and threw it on the fire. Then she realised that this was a terrible thing to do because Lily was devoted to this particular teddy, which in fact had been in evidence since Lily's early infancy. Lily was 4 when the incident took place. Once when looking at photographs of the children Lily had picked out this teddy and said: 'That was mine!'

From this the mother went on quite naturally to talk about the way that Lily had been stealing recently; stealing books, sweets, and a toy watch, for instance; it was as if the mother knew that the stealing was related to Lily's search for the transitional object that the mother had tried to destroy in a moment of anger. In destroying this transitional object the mother had been damaging the mechanism by which the small child related to herself and to her person and to her body and her breasts.

The clinician has opportunity to hear these stories and to believe in them and to recognise the significance of ideas given in sequence by mothers or children when they are at ease and confident and not feeling that they must be on the defensive.

The treatment of this case had to do with bringing the family to recognise that they were in a state of strain and that someone needed a holiday. If the case had been dealt with by my having arranged a treatment for the girl, this would have increased the tendency of the family to disrupt. Dealing with the family and recognising for instance the difficulty the parents had in having the dominating grandmother living with them led to amelioration in terms of the environment and the child was able to make use of this favourable change.

Unfortunately I can look back on a time when as an ardent psycho-analyst, pleased with having learned the technique of the treatment of an individual, I would have referred this child for analytic treatment, and perhaps would have missed the more important thing, which was rehabilitation of the family.

There is no follow-up in this case and the facts as given must be simply taken as illustrative of a point of view.

343

CASE XX 'Jason' *aet* 8 years 9 months

The following case started with a letter from the boy's father. He said that his son had shown signs of emotional stress for some years, currently manifesting itself in a difficulty with arithmetic and in school work generally. The father asked: does he suffer from emotional blockages or from some sort of emotional strain which makes it difficult for him to concentrate? or as a further alternative is it a question of basic intelligence? He asked for guidance and for advice in regard to the detail: would he be better living away from direct competition from his younger brother? There are three sons, aged 8 years 9 months, 7 years, and 3 years 9 months. The father usefully added a list of eight factors 'which may have influenced the boy's development':

(1) Jason was post-mature at birth and apparently born starved.

(2) As he was the first child his parents were inexperienced and anxious, so that his first four months were characterised by colic and crying.

(3) His mother became pregnant when he was 4 months old, so that he had a brother at 13 months. For the birth of this baby the mother had to be absent for five weeks, because of an infection. There was great strain in the home at this time. The father was very busy.

(4) Jason had a hernia operation at 2 years, he had another operation (bad appendicitis) at 4 years, and he had a skull injury after a fall soon afterwards. It was discovered at 6 that he sees with the two eyes in two different planes.

(5) Jason has suffered from repeated bronchitis with some asthma, necessitating absences from school. This feature had nearly cleared.

(6) He is left-handed and also he is not well co-ordinated physically.

(7) In every way he has difficulty in competing with his brother next in age. Head-on clashes with his two parents are regular.

344

In addition, the father claimed to be imperfect as a father because of personal difficulties for which he was having treatment by psycho-analysis. Both the father's illness and his treatment put a severe strain on the boy's mother who was also having psychotherapy.

To this useful enumeration of factors affecting the boy's life the father added the observation that Jason had *started stealing money* from his mother, and that along with this he was taking food without asking, was lying, and was blinking as a signal of distress. The blinking seemed to be linked with his difficulties in arithmetic.

This boy had seen a child psychiatrist half a dozen times with some effect. There was a family doctor who was active and interested. It will be observed that the stealing in this case is only one of a series of troubles and looked at in terms of psychiatric diagnosis it could be said that it was a favourable sign in that there were various defence mechanisms in evidence, and that these were to some extent interchangeable. The case would be easier than would a similar one with no symptom except stealing.

I had explained to the parents that I wished to see the boy alone first before interviewing them. Jason was brought by his father. First I interviewed the two together for five minutes. Jason was lolling back in the chair next to the desk, the chair usually occupied by the parent. The father was rather shyly sitting on the other seat, and he got up when I came in. There was thus a marked contrast between the behaviour of the two. Jason's eyes were twitching all the time and this continued throughout the consultation. This twitching gives the impression, probably correct, that he is all the time seeing with difficulty because of the two planes of vision.

Jason gave me the usual information willingly.

He is 8 (nearly 9).

He has two brothers, one 7 and one 3.

The little one is noisy and a nuisance sometimes because he interrupts what is going on.

His mother is at home; she does the housework and cooking, 'and she is a very good cook', he added.

He then volunteered: 'Something went wrong last Saturday' in the home life. I think this had to do with his father'

345

attendance at a conference which made him late, and probably included his wife's irritation. This mystery was not cleared up.

I asked him what he was going to be and he said: 'Well, I'm thinking about swimming or being the chef on a liner. I can enjoy swimming already, you see.'

Then he broke in with the remark: 'You can't guess how much money I have got in the bank.'

I thought very hard and said: '£13 11 10.'

Then he informed me with the idea of impressing me: 'I've got £100. I got it from my grandfather', and he went on to say how he keeps on getting gifts from his grandparents which he puts straight in the bank. He is saving up and perhaps one day will buy, well, probably a house.

By this time he and I were in communication and I asked the father to go to the waiting-room. I brought forward the small table and I suggested a game, and explained about squiggles.

He said: 'Don't you know a points game?'

He gave the impression that he would not be able to tolerate anything that didn't have winning and losing in it, and I was not hopeful about a productive game based on squiggles.[1] However, I persevered.

(1) Mine, which he turned into a snail.

He gave the impression of feeling that this squiggle game was a very poor sort of occupation and he kept on asking for a points game.

(2) His, which I turned into a worm.

In the course of this I asked him about his home, which has a garden.

(3) Mine, which he turned into an eel or a shark. He took a lot of trouble over this, particularly over the *teeth*, but he continued to say he wanted a game which you can win or lose. In doing the teeth he broke the point of the pencil and apologised. But some viciousness had gone into the drawing of the teeth.

[1] There is an interesting difference between games and playing, the latter being very much nearer (than games are) to creativity and to the unpredictable, and more capable of giving deep satisfaction.

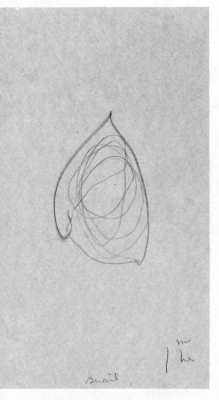

snail

1me he

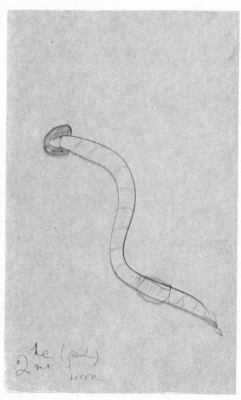

6 2$^{he}_{me}$ (penh) worm

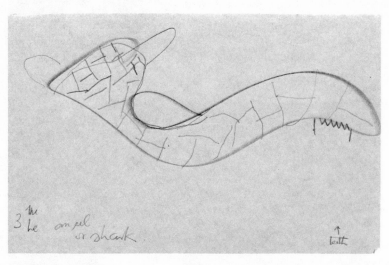

3$^{he}_{he}$ an eel or shark.

teeth

347

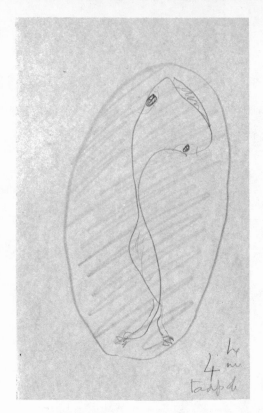

(4) His, which I turned into a tadpole. This was not of much use to him because he did not know about tadpoles. He thought they were fishes and had no idea of their growth into frogs.

(5) Mine, which made him say: 'I'll never . . . I'll have to change it a bit. It will be very hard.' With great effort and concentration he turned it into a beetle with birds and a tree.

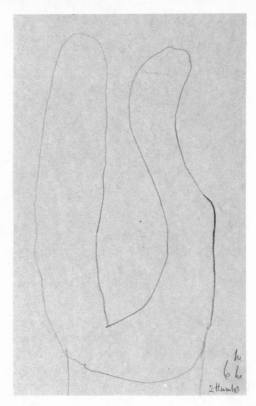

(6) His, which he wanted to turn into something himself. He said: 'I know.' His squiggle was a rather carefully drawn curve. He turned it into 'two thumbs', leaving undecided how two thumbs could come together in this way.

I had my own ideas about the two thumbs, but I did not make any interpretative comment.

(7) His again, which I turned into a dog. He said it ought to have been a duck.

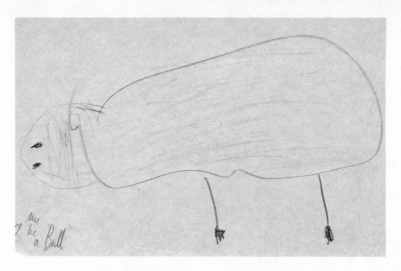

(8) Mine. He said: 'That's rather easy', and quickly made it into what he called a bull.

By ordinary standards this was a very poor representation of a bull for a boy of 8, but I would not let the quality of a drawing influence me too much in the assessment of his intelligence because of its coming in the middle of a game. Indeed we were playing now, and not trying, or acting with deliberation.

(9) His, which I made into a studious type, 'learning Latin from a book'.

(10) There was now a need for me to accept a change of technique to keep things going. He said: '*You* draw', and gave me a large piece of paper.

I drew a picture of him. It is not like him. By drawing him I felt I was not introducing a new idea.

(11) This was all right from his point of view and he responded by drawing *me*. He said he thought his portrait of me 'good except for the face'. As he gradually built up the picture he said he found drawing fun and rather exciting. Then he said he would draw *a picture that he would like to draw.*

(12) He drew a ship on which was a cross captain. Someone has been bombing the ship. All the guns are out. The 'planes are coming over. (Appropriate noises.)

Anxiety showed itself indirectly by his interpolating: 'Where do you think Daddy is?' although he really knew.

I said: 'He's in the waiting-room.'

And he said: 'He may have gone.'

An important idea was introduced in this way, but at the time I was ignorant of what would follow.

'It is an English boat. Then the head aeroplane nearly exploded the ship.' (Realistic noises.)

A shot had fired in the wrong direction from the ship. He traced the bullet and eventually it shot the plane by mistake. There was a big fight in progress. 'I'm going to make lots of 'planes. They really are going to beat the ship. It's the last day of the war. This is the only ship we have left. Here is the head one now. Quick it's dropping, one, two. Blew it up.'

He was getting more and more excited and all the time making noises appropriate to war. 'There are two holes in the boat. Men are going down to mend the holes. Here are the rockets. Very good. They really exploded the boat. Now here is the best from the head 'plane. The ship has no chance. It has put its guns up. It hasn't enough. The rocket blew up two of the 'planes. Knocked bits off them. The head 'plane's going to be blown up. There are only six more 'planes. They are all dumping bombs. The boat will explode.'

Then suddenly with grief he said: 'Poor boat.' The captain is killed.

'They mended the holes and it still can steam ahead. And now the explosion has set fire to all the 'planes and the head one.'

I said something here like: 'It sounds as if you are talking about a family' but it is unlikely that he heard me because of the noises of the war.

'It's blown up now. It's not nice. The ship won. All the crew were killed but one of the crew drove it in, but he was so sad that all the others were killed that he committed suicide and dropped into the water and so the ship drifted in without anybody on board. It just drifted. They baled out the water. It took three weeks to get home. What's the time?'

I said something about: 'Well, you feel a long way away from home.' And I told him the time and how much longer we could be together and I asked him whether he

354

had dreams like this, to which he replied: 'No.' He seemed to be pleased to be diverted from this endless war and he told me his dream.

(The account of the war was not dream, and it could be called 'fantasying'. It belongs to the area exploited in children's comics.)

Dream 'I was running along. I fell in the river. I was going under water.'

I asked him to illustrate the dream, and he drew

(13) 'When I went under water there were all the sea fish. I feel that these fish are eating me up. I got out of the stream and then I fell down an earthquake. I couldn't get up. I stayed there till I died. I just gave up. I killed myself. I jumped 100 feet. I always have this dream ending in killing myself. I'll draw the knife.'

355

Here appeared the 100 of the boast, 'I have £100 in the bank!'

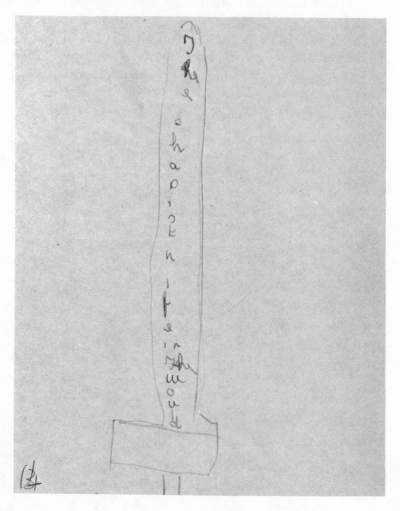

(14) 'Are we wasting your paper? This is the knife I cut my own head off with. It is a sword. There is a message written on it. It says: "The sharpest knife in the world."'

Then he changed his tone of voice for the moment and said: 'Do you know what sort of chopper they had when they chopped off people's heads? You draw one.'

So I drew

(15) and he was very interested in the details of how the head
drops and eventually I drew a fire to illustrate his idea that
it gets burnt up. He said it was probably Cromwell; didn't
he have his head cut off? and I said I had an idea that he
was the one who cut off the king's head, to which he seemed
to agree.

I asked him if he could tell me about himself. I said: 'Now
is your chance to tell me the very worst, the worst that you
can say that is or has ever been in your life; for instance,
where this dream started in which you have no hope and
so you kill yourself.'

He became very serious and real. He said: 'I was 6 when
that dream started; there were two brothers born, one was

357

1 and the other 5. You see, when I was 5 or 4 I went into hospital with appendicitis. It was horrible. They kept coming

(16) and giving me injections into my bottom.' The very thought of this made him get excited. 'That's when I had a frightful dream about the devil who walked right through the houses. You could see his blood veins with the blood all pouring out. He walked through fire. He could walk straight through this house. There was the house and the fire and the devil walking through it.'

I said: 'The devil was the doctor who got right through into you with the injections.' And he continued on with what I had said, saying dramatically: 'And he stuck his knife straight through me.'

He was describing the doctors' lack of respect for defences.

He went on to say: 'You see, Daddy was in the waiting-room and he could come in to me at 9 o'clock; and then he came and it was all right. But the dream was *before he could come*. He was not allowed to come.'

I said: 'Well, I am a doctor and here is Daddy in the waiting-room and just now you wondered if he was still there. So I might be the devil who can do these terrible things to you that you can't stop.'

He seemed to see the sense of this while saying 'No' and then he said: 'Is the devil true?' to which I quickly replied: 'Yes, in dreams, but not when you are awake.' (I find I am definitely pleased with myself for giving this quick answer.)

Anxiety showed by his remark: 'What time do I have to go?' but already the wording indicated that he was *not really wanting to go*.

He now began to show positive feelings and said: 'I suppose someone else is waiting?' The feeling here was that if he had found something good there would certainly be a couple of brothers turning up, as in his experience of family life. He had made it quite clear to me that it was his father and not his mother that he wanted when he was frightened of the devil.

'How many people come to see you—hundreds, I suppose?'

I said: 'About eight a day.'

He said: 'Quite a lot. Why do they come?'

I said: 'Oh, perhaps because they are scared of something like you are.'

He protested: 'I came because I was to find out from you what sort of job I would do one day.'

I said: 'Yes, in a way, that is what you were told, but you really came because you have got terrible fears', to which he replied: 'O.K.'

Then he said: 'Did you know the other doctor I went to? Oh, it was fun when I went to see her'—and he described how he played games with matchsticks and bombs and army tanks and how much he enjoyed it all. He was really now back at the drawing of the war with the ship, and fantasying.

I said: 'Yes, you enjoyed that and you enjoyed the drawing with the ship. But you are not enjoying yourself here. You found here very great fears, terrible dreams, and hopelessness, and killing yourself and the idea that you would be helpless if the devil came while you were awake.'

He said: 'Shall I go and see Daddy?' and I said: 'Yes, but stay a little while', and he said: 'Yes, please.'

I said: 'Well, now *I really want the worst.*'

He said: 'I couldn't get Daddy when I wanted him to drive away the devil in the hospital. *So I killed him off*'—indicating that behind the death of everyone which was sad for the ship (mother), and that led to his own suicide, was anger with the father because he did not come and keep away the frightening idea of the devil when the doctor was giving the injections. Intellectually, of course, he knew, and had already said, that the father was not allowed in until 9 o'clock, so he couldn't help failing his son.

He said: 'I want to go now', and I said: 'Yes. This time there is Daddy waiting, and he will come if you call him'—so he went and called for his father. I said to him: 'I would rather like to have seen Father, but I think you would find it difficult to wait just now', and he said: 'Yes, I would like *to go now with Daddy*'; so I explained to the father how it was, and they both went, with Jason saying: 'Please can I come and see you again? Bye-bye.'

In this case I propose also to give the interview with the parents. The main feature of this interview was that the parents learned to their surprise about the depth of Jason's personality and about the way he had shown himself to have conflicts of an extreme kind in his emotional life of which they were unaware. They came in a sceptical mood and seemed to be somewhat hostile, but when they went they felt that they had a new understanding of their son. This came not from my telling them what to do or from

360

my talking about children in general but from the opportunity that I was able to give them to get into touch with the work of the interview which Jason and I had together. In my opinion, when parents are more or less reliable and not likely to use the material in an irresponsible way in their contact with their child this is the best way to bring about a favourable change in a home situation.

Interview with Parents (Five Weeks after Interview with Boy)

The father and mother of this boy came to discuss Jason's problem, and they did not bring Jason.

We started off with coffee all round. The father gives the impression of being rather nervous, although he does a good job in his profession and obviously is able to cope with the problems of his family. He may not have a very strong personality. The mother gives a somewhat boyish impression. She is slight and lively, and friendly in an active way without being false.

I began by talking about the mother's letter in which she had said that she had hoped by waiting to find some change in Jason which she could report but we agreed that it has to be accepted that he has not changed at all. Replying to my questioning she said that when Jason was born they had a home waiting and they were ready for him. They had a flat then. The mother now realises that she was incredibly lonely at that time. Now they live on the fringe of London and all the neighbours help each other. This provides 'a wonderful life' both for herself and for the three children. They can ride bicycles all day and there is no danger, and they can get muddy, and they live in each other's houses.

We then went into the details of Jason's development. Jason's mother became pregnant when he was 4–5 months old and when he was 13 months old the brother was born. She was glad and she felt that this would give her a second chance as she was dissatisfied with what she had done with Jason, the first-born. The effect on Jason, however, was not good. At 10 months he became more difficult than he had been, because of the mother's pregnancy, presumably. Then to make matters worse at 13 months the mother had to be in hospital for a month because of puerperal fever. He was cared for by her mother, who is a worrier. She took great care when she came back from the hospital, not immediately introducing the new baby boy. She and her husband played with Jason for two hours and then brought the baby in, but it was undoubtedly an awful shock for him.

361

Jason was the kind of baby who instead of crawling sat on a rug and pulled everything towards him as if to say, why bother to move if you want something? At 17 months he walked and he reached developmental stages early. After 13 months his aggressiveness became a marked feature. He would knock the lamp over, pull the books over, and as compared with the other children he was always needing to be watched. He took notice of the new baby but was liable to biff him, and in order to bath the baby the mother had to put Jason securely in the crib. The play-pen in the garden was used for similar purposes (for segregation). It was noticed that when he was 2, boys of 4 were frightened of him! He is always very affectionate with certain people, but this has not included his mother. It could be said that he and his mother have been at cross purposes from about when he was 10–11 months.

At this point the father said: 'Do you remember when he was 3 months old I used to look at his cot and say: "Oh hell, I can understand why people throw children out of the window!"' So it was very early that Jason was dissatisfied, but then he became easy from 4–10 months, until difficulties recommenced, this time with some relationship to the mother's pregnancy.

Jason was fed on the breast on and off for three months. Here the mother described herself as determined to do the right things *including breast-feeding*. She said she knew Spock by heart. She felt that her baby must have the breast because of the antibodies that are in the milk. He undoubtedly suffered from this determination on her part to persevere, and she now feels that it would have been much better if she had given in earlier. She was not helped by the clinic, where the attitude was adopted that mothers *must* feed their babies. She was very disappointed that she could not succeed here and very glad when she managed to feed the second baby for 7 months.

I asked about Jason seeing the baby at the breast and she said that there was no important thing to report about this. She said she knew how children do sometimes throw things at their mothers when they are breast-feeding a baby. She went on to talk about Jason's aggressiveness and his throwing things as soon as he was able to do so and his pushing children, and she always felt if he was in someone else's house that she would come back and find he had done something awful, and he often had.

He was good about giving up the night bottle. In regard to

362

feeding himself this was a bit slow, but he was allowed to make a terrific mess and perhaps in some respects he was normal or even early. The parents' memory was not quite clear, but certainly there was no big delay. The father gave his opinion that on the introduction of solids there was a sunny patch in this child's clinical state. There was a complication somewhere about here in the child's life, a rash on the chin at the messy stage. The mother called it an allergy and she thought it was associated with fish or tomatoes. The father's mother thought it was wool, but this was never proved.

In regard to bowel training the mother was never fussy. The baby would just simply sit on his pot and slide around and just not use it. Then when he was about 2 he got the idea, and in a week this kind of trouble was over. At 2–3 he had to go to hospital because of a hernia. During the five days the mother was with him as much as possible, but not at night, because of her other boy. A girl of 9 in the ward said: 'Your baby does cry a lot', and it appears that he yelled most of the night. The day after the operation he was subdued. The operation was a success. He recovered from the stay in hospital except for a return of messing. After this he went to a small dancing class where he was happy though clumsy. At this time his relationship to other children improved. He was very good at jigsaws and not slow in the activities of the mind. At 1 year he used words. At 1·9 he quite clearly said rain, no rain, flowers. At about 2 he communicated with sentences.

I asked about his preferring mother or father and they said there was nothing special to report here. He may say: 'Isn't it nice when Daddy comes home early', but he has not shown a specific preference. The father brought in here the fact that at the crawling stage Jason did have temper tantrums, banging his head on the floor. He used a low chair with a tray, and if the tray was not in position he would get very angry. On one occasion he threw himself out and hurt his mouth. The parents disagreed over this incident, which the father reported as if it contained a deliberate self-hurting element.

A characteristic of this boy was that he behaved very well in harness or in the pram; for instance he never threw out the shopping on to the ground as other children do, and he could sit for hours watching whatever was going on. Once out of whatever was controlling him, however, he was immediately *a pest*. The mother said she would walk him round the houses for hours in the pram to save the situation; and also she showed him books, pointing things out and always spending a very great deal of time actively concerned with him. This was to prevent his being a pest. A characteristic was the way that he needed the mother to give him time. He learned to tell the time early and he has always been interested in time, which also came out in the interview with me. 'What's the time?' is one of his regular questions.

He has always had something interesting about his face, a look that showed that he might be difficult. There was a deep-set look. The father talked about Jason's use of one of those toys called a posting-box. He didn't catch on to the idea. He gave the impression that he knew exactly what to do but that he was not going to seem to know, as if he was trying to tease his father. The mother said he quite clearly teased her when he was between 6–10 months old. She remembers he was fat and not crawling. He touched her funny-bone and this made her jump, and he went on and on doing it in a teasing way. I asked the mother if she was the sort of person who would tease a child and she thought not.

The parents then described distraction techniques which were evolved for dealing with Jason (preventing him from becoming a pest). They tried him once on slamming the fridge door and they counted fifteen times. He refused to be distracted from this which he was determined to do. The mother said here: 'Of course, I would never slap a child.' She felt that it was against the rules. She said, however, that she did other things when exasperated. For example, when Jason was 1 year or 2 years old she would sit him on a high stool and leave him stranded for a punishment when she was at her wits' end. She very seldom slapped any of the other children. And then she said: 'Of course, when I have lost my temper I have slapped him very hard.' She went on to say that the worst trouble is when she and her husband get across each other and begin to argue. The other children get out of the way but Jason becomes more and more of a fighter, and this has a bad effect. She was implying that he adopts the distracting technique so that she and her husband are unable to get on with their disagreement.

I asked about transitional phenomena.

JASON (8 YEARS 9 MONTHS NOW)

He sucked the back of his hand and then he adopted a bottle

364

which always had to have Rose Hip Syrup in it. This bottle was absolutely necessary for him until he was 2 years and 1 month. He had a teddy in bed but this did not have to be carted around. The bottle addiction ended in the following way. They were staying with the father's parents and he threw the bottle down so that the ring cracked. He kept on saying: 'Broken; broken; broken', and screamed for three-quarters of an hour. This was when he was 25 months old. He never bothered about the bottle again, and this in spite of the fact that he often saw babies with bottles. He would say: 'Baby bottle' and so on, without emotion.

THE SECOND BOY (NOW 7 YEARS 9 MONTHS)

He sucked his right thumb till he was 4. He is one for using fluffy objects. He made special use of the ear of a teddy which eventually came off and had to be sewn on to a ribbon, and the ribbon was pinned to his chair. This was essential for him till he was 4 or 5, that is, after the third baby arrived.

THE THIRD BOY (NOW 4)

He never sucked his thumb or used any object. He loves fluffy things but has never been addicted to them. On the whole the other two boys dislike him. He is a nuisance from their point of view. He teases them and he breaks windows. In this house they have leaded windows with small panes of glass, and he has a way of getting up and bashing the glass out with his foot.

The parents added a detail about Jason. Possibly in relation to the breaking of the bottle Jason has no feeling if he breaks something. It can be seen in everything he does, like the way he throws his bike down. Jason was $3\frac{1}{2}$ when they moved out of London, and it is curious that having once settled in this house with a garden the two elder boys have never tried to get out of the garden gate. The third boy has never accepted this boundary. The two elder boys have accepted the boundary, but within the boundary they do awful things.

At 4 Jason went to a nursery class but almost immediately developed bronchitis, to which he has been liable. He also started blinking, which is still a feature. He became very fond of his school teacher. At 4 years 9 months to 5 years when the new baby was due there was a new complication of serious appendicitis. *He made a very great fuss to do with having injections* (in this way the parents confirmed what had been discovered in my session with him). Later he became fond of the same hospital sister that he had hated because of the injections. He came out after a week but had to go in again. This time he enjoyed hospital on the basis of the whole thing being a dream. He even accepted the injections. After coming home he got back to normal. The new baby did not make any change in his life and in any case the mother by this time did not care so much about every detail. He adopted the technique of playing up the woman help.

I asked the parents about the possibility that at some point they wanted a girl. This meant a lot to them. They wanted a girl for each of the last two, and especially the last. The mother said that she was thrilled when Jason was a boy, especially as she had had a dream that it would be a girl. It was obvious now that I must explore the mother's boyish nature and I asked her about her boy self. This led her to a description of her childhood. As an early adolescent she was a tomboy with an Eton crop, and the best moment was when someone called her Sonnie, when she was 13. She thinks that she was rather a feminine only child when she was small, though as a matter of fact she always played with trains and never with dolls. She then talked about the change in her feelings about her mother. She always thought that she had got on very well with her. They were 'sisters' together and she was never naughty. She complied with her mother and they went for long country walks together, and the question is, where was the hostility? It turned up when the mother behaved in a peculiar way at Jason's birth. Her mother had promised to take time off from work to help, but on the ninth day when the mother was due home from hospital with her tiny baby her mother said: 'Oh, I can't ask the manager for the time off:'; so she failed completely as an old hand backing this young ignorant mother. On the other hand she would come in with gripe water or some useless gimmick. The mother said: 'I can't forgive her for this.' Her mother claimed: 'Oh, I've forgotten about new babies', but the curious thing was, however, that she was marvellous with the new babies of other people.

I said: 'I wonder what your mother wanted, a boy or a girl?' and then she said in a very definite way: 'My mother and father both wanted a boy. They have always been quite clear about this.'

Here then was the clue to the case. Jason's mother has ordinary potential as a woman, but to have a relationship to her parents she has exploited the boy part of her nature. When she had Jason the first test came and she found her mother completely unable to give her a maternal attitude for identification with. On her own, therefore, she had to come around into being a woman, and she did not succeed in this until the second child was born. In talking this over she described other details of significance, one of which was as follows: Jason was post-mature, so that although healthy he was like a Belsen case at birth. She feels she would have managed this except for the fact that the sister in the ward (who was a very good person, and who afterwards became a friend) suddenly said when she saw the baby: 'You have starved him.' This remark roused all her anxiety and went against any tendency that there may have been in her body to produce the milk the child needed. This one remark, although it could be seen to be a joke, uttered at this particular moment and to this particular woman with her specific anxieties, had an effect on the mother's body-functioning and on the whole of this boy's development.

I now discussed the present situation with the parents and I went through the whole of the session showing the drawings. They were astonished to find what had turned up in the hour that Jason had had with me, and on the basis of what they now knew they agreed to let things go for the time being. I would see the boy again (a) should there be any deterioration in the present situation or (b) should he ask to see me.

The father was particularly interested in my answer to the boy's question: 'Is the devil real?' because he felt that he had slipped up here when asked the same question by his son.

I asked for an Intelligence Test to be done.

Following this joint consultation the father and mother wrote a letter which they signed together showing that they greatly valued having had the opportunity to learn about their child in the way we had used. They were able to report the result of an intelligence test:

> 109 on Revised Stanford Binet.
> 121 Verbal Scale.
> 99 Performance.
> 112 Full Scale Wisc.

Two years later I received a new letter from the father. He reported that there had been some improvement in the boy following the interview with me, but that now there was a return of
stealing from the mother. Also the boy had been playing with a
group of boys who were obviously near delinquency although in
fact their escapade had not been discovered. At the same time
there was some recurrence of asthma associated with fears roused
by fireworks on Guy Fawkes' night. Also Jason had been knocked
down by a car and suffered concussion, and there was good evidence that this accident was due to his own action and came from
excited and aggressive behaviour which shows in other ways as
well. The father then enumerated a series of improvements that
he and his wife had noted in the development of the boy's personality, and along with this an increasing ability on the boy's
part to discuss his problems with his parents. He reported also
the arrival of 'another competitor', a sister. There were problems
related to the fact that not only was his rival brother (thirteen
months younger) more clever than he was, but that this brother
had overtaken him at school.

On the basis of this I arranged a second interview with the boy.
Soon after this second interview I was in contact with the father,
who reported that the boy had come through his crisis and that
the stealing had disappeared except for some continued pressure
on his mother as if he needed to force her to give him some special
attention at certain times. Instead of stealing he was now making
demands which she could usually meet, such as: 'Take me to the
swimming pool', etc. The father also said that Jason was no
longer smoking.

Second Interview with Jason, now aet *10 Years · 15 months after
the first*

Jason came with his mother, who knew what was needed of her,
and she went out shopping. Jason felt strange and did not at first
remember coming previously. He knew that something had happened to him earlier and he said that I had had a lot of little men
arranged out on a table. When I helped him he said: 'Yes, that
was when I went to see the other doctor'; and then he was quite
clear that he did not remember coming to me at all.

When we started up the squiggle game this also did not make
him remember, so that when I did

368

(1) mine, he simply did another squiggle over the top of it. I was asking him the odd question and he said he was 10, but he looks forward to being 11. He would leave his present school then for the bigger school. This would be sad because, as he said, he was getting the best teaching at the little school, where he had been for four years, with only small classes.

(2) His; a rather deliberate squiggle in three or four parts. Mine was an encircling squiggle. I copied his idea of one squiggle on another.

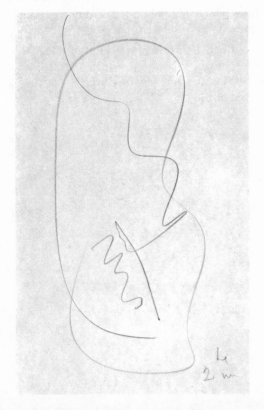

(3) Mine, which he elaborated without making it into any-thing.

(4) His, which I turned into a kind of dog. He said: 'Rather clever.' Even this one in which I made his squiggle into something did not seem to bring back the game that we played in 1965.

(5) Mine. He said: 'Let's see what I can make it into.' And so he was getting towards the game we had had before, but he was copying me and making it into an animal.

(6) His, which I turned into something he called a rabbit.

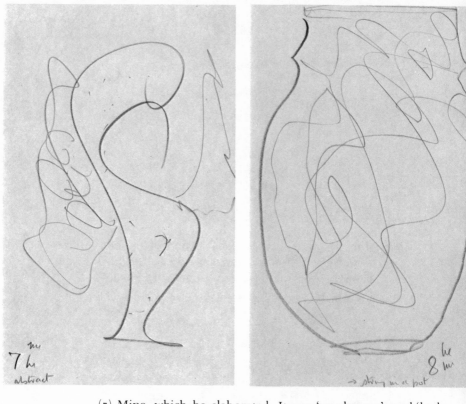

(7) Mine, which he elaborated. It was 'an abstract', and 'had no meaning', as he said.

(8) His. Obviously I could use this in any way I might like as it was a long-continued deliberate use of a line. Eventually I put a pot round it and said it was string ready for use.

(9) Mine. He surprisingly surrounded this with a toothy line and he said it was *a crusher*. It led him immediately to a lovely idea of a mansion full of money, thousands of pounds. The teeth of the crusher had to do with getting through to the inside where the treasures would be.

We made a review at this stage of the drawings from 1–9 and I put in a word about there possibly being dreams in which there was money to be found inside something. He did not get further

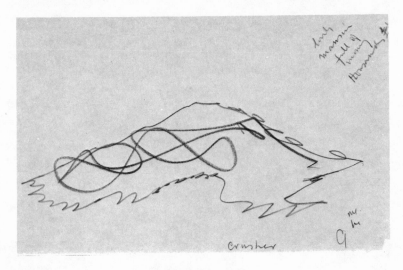

than a simple affirmative here. I knew he was dealing with the dream behind the stealing compulsion.

In the middle of this there was:

(10) His, which was another version of the line as in No. 8. This time, however, he put in an eye. I made this come out of a pot and said it was a genie. *He was very pleased with this.*

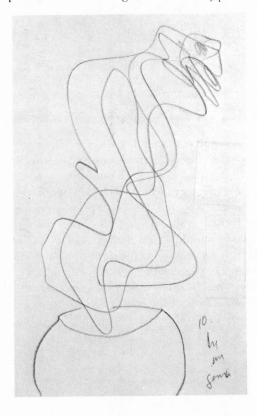

The idea of the dream now took him to his wish to draw
the dream that was most available, so he drew No. 11.

(11) He was glad to have a big sheet of paper to draw this on.
This has to do with himself involved in some terrible earthquake so that he fell. In the drawing he is in the middle of
some of the earth which has spikes out of it. Underneath is
a monster, a robot by shape. It becomes extremely destructive if there is the slightest bit of movement or if water or
anything should cause a short circuit in its mechanism.
There is an animal in the right bottom corner. This is an
automatic swan with special toes and feet. If the swan
presses on the ground with these feet terrible things come
out. By means of the swan he seems to have some kind of
control over otherwise uncontrollable robot mechanism.

374

Outside the earth on the left side of the page is a pre-historic tree.

As soon as he had finished this drawing he wanted me to play a different kind of game with him, quite obviously in an attempt to get away from the anxieties aroused. I played this game without comment for about a quarter of an hour (A.B.C.D.). This had to be gone through with.

When the games came to a natural conclusion I made a remark about the dream, using the material of the forgotten session of two years ago. I remembered about the teeth of the headman, etc.

I said: 'In your dream the terrible thing to me seems to be that you are quite alone. There is no father anywhere unless in the fossil tree, so you have no-one to help you.'

He very quickly responded to this, saying: '*That reminds me*'; and he put in the flying monster at the top. This is a

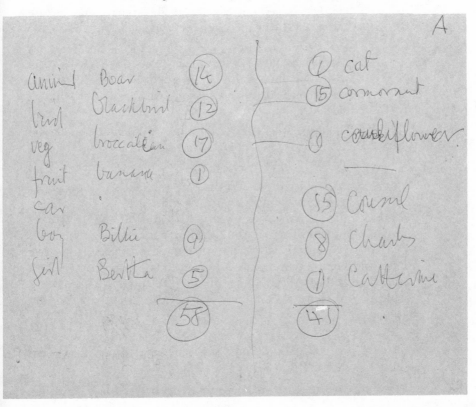

kind of magical and revolting aspect of his father who nevertheless, he said, 'has the power to retract me. He can lift me'—and he went on to talk about the tremendous effect if water should drop on the monster. He seemed to be quite happy about my comment that if father could be relied on to lift him he would not wet the bed.

There was a tremendous potential for fantasying in this drawing of a dream, and it had to do with elaborations around the theme of time bombs and explosions.

He was now back in the drawing and willing to forget all about the distraction of games, and so I pointed out to him that something of the nightmare was already present in No. 9, the crusher.

He said: 'Yes, and in some of the others too.' He picked out my No. 10 and said: *'That was very clever of you seeing that that was a genie. It made it possible for me to get to the dream.'*

He then picked out No. 8 with the string inside the vase and not yet being used, and the string might also be pee.

He referred again two or three times to 'how lucky it was that I had called No. 10 a genie!' He took out No. 3 and said: 'The thing is already there in that pointed bit'—which was of course part of my squiggle, which he had elaborated. He had had no idea at the time that this had any meaning.

Finally we went back to the abstract which he said had no meaning. He picked it out and said: 'Really it's all there in the abstract, but you can't tell it is.'

Here he was able to give up the extreme defence of obscurity hiding clarity. He was now very much calmer and he was able to remember the session of two years ago, and he liked to be reminded of the sad ship that came to land with no-one on board.

I made the central part of the interpretation that it is his love of his mother that dominates the whole scene and makes him want to get rid of everybody, although if he did do so his mother would be sad. This was a hangover from the session of two years ago.

He capped this by saying: 'Often I go to my bedroom and feel exasperated and I say to myself: "If only they would all die!"'

This has to do with his never having been able to have his

376

(B)

animal   ant ⑬
veg   ~~apple~~
car   austin ㉑
bird
fruit   apple ⑯
boy   Andrew ⑬
girl   Ada   Ⓐ
              ‾‾‾‾‾‾‾
              67

dog
potato
Jaguar
Albatross
orange
Italian
Indie

(C)

Animal   ape   ⑯   16
Bird   16
Vegetable   M
                           13
car   apple ⑯   ‾‾‾‾
boy   alan   ⑰   5 b
girl   ann   ⑬
boy
girl

mother to himself. And then he went on to tell me about the new baby, and he proudly enumerated her achievements, the words she could say, etc. He is obviously very fond of her.

He then told me about the car crash, a Jaguar going at 50–60 miles an hour. He went to hospital for three days and was unconscious and he took great trouble to show me the scar above his left knee. He said it was really his own fault, but here I think he was quoting his mother, agreeing with her to a large extent. But it seems quite possible that he did take part in staging this catastrophe which could easily have killed him, and it all fitted in very well with the dominant nightmare.

He elaborated to some extent on the magical powers of this father figure flying in the air in the nightmare. He said that this flying father 'seems to bring "Malta"', which was probably a contraction of 'molten lava'. In the end he was saved, only by now he was out of true dreaming and in the layer of *fantasying*, which carries with it the ability to manipulate ideas. He introduced ray guns and a fantastic shield which protected him even from the rays. He talked about his sister again, how they all say: 'Here comes the wrecker', but he was amused by this; it simply has to do with the fact that a 1-year-old child destroys everything that has been set up in a game when she can get at it.

He ended up by telling me about a family he knows that lives in a small flat and has nine children in it, indicating that there could be something worse than his own condition.

Before we parted we went over the two series of drawings and the comments we had made together. He seemed quite ready to go. The mother was late back, so to kill time I took a photograph of him on the front doorstep, and later on I sent it to him.

Summary

This complex case could be summed up in terms of the boy's relative deprivation in a certain area which could be described as the normal healthy homosexuality of the father–son relationship. This was planted on top of a relative deprivation in infant–mother terms starting from early infancy and including traumatic separations. It would seem that the parents together and the family situation had to some extent 'cured' the boy of the infant–mother deprivation but had left him vulnerable to a repetition in terms of his relationship to his father and the father had found his rôle a difficult one. He could easily manage being the father of his other children, but to be the father of this boy went beyond his understanding and made him confused.

The case was managed on the basis of two interviews with the boy and the interview with the two parents together, and a few telephone conversations spaced over a period of three years. It would seem that the dynamic of the case must be placed in the interview with the two parents, where they were able to see and to learn about the boy as he appeared in his first interview with me alone.

CASE XXI 'George' *aet* 13 years

Finally I wish to describe a case of potential delinquency which can not be dealt with adequately by the kind of work that I am describing in this book. I have tried to illustrate the mechanism of stealing by examining cases in which the rigidity of the defences of the child is not too great so that movement can be detected, and in which an environment that was previously hopeless and helpless now becomes hopeful and effective.

The degree of illness in the following case can be seen in the fact that the details are very much like those of many other cases. It is healthy boys and girls who are entirely individual and unlike each other. Illness patterns have resemblances, and the degree of illness is often measured by the fixity of the illness pattern. Even in this very ill case, however, there was a certain amount of movement following the interview that I had with the boy, and this makes a link with the last case. After my interview with this boy he said to his mother: 'It's funny, the doctor asked me if I ever dreamed about stealing or burglars and I told him that I have never dreamed that kind of dream. But after I saw him I had a dream in which I had stolen a wallet and I went off to the next town where I stole another wallet and then I had to go to another town where I stole another wallet, and so it went on. It's funny I have never dreamed about stealing before.'

If a treatment of this boy were to be undertaken the most hopeful aspect of such a treatment would be to make use of the dreams of this kind, since it is because of the dissociation in his personality which makes his dream world unavailable to him that he needs to keep in touch with dream by compulsive acting-out. Here again, even in this very severe case, the positive element can be seen in that hope is shown so long as a boy or girl is trying to integrate a dissociated personality even when in the attempt anti-social activities appear and give society trouble.

I gave the boy an hour's interview on his own, and later I saw the mother.

Family History

    Sister   17 years.
    Brother 16 years.

George   12 years 11 months.

I.Q. 112 Stanford Binet.
　　　Reading at 10-year level.
　　　'Not functioning at school.'

In a letter which I received before I saw the boy the family doctor wrote that George had been stealing and was generally a problem, and he added that in his opinion the boy's parents had but little insight. He enclosed reports from a previous psychiatric encounter.

There was no difficulty in the management of the interview with the boy alone. He told me about his school which is of a very permissive kind, and where all the arts are treated as of major importance.

I used the squiggle game as an easy way of making contact.

　　　(1) Mine, which he turned into a head.

He was contented with this weird and distorted head and I thought that one could detect that he did not see this as funny. In other words, I quickly became prepared to find that in this case it would not be possible to use the elbow-room which a sense of humour gives and that he and I would probably not find our-selves *playing* together.

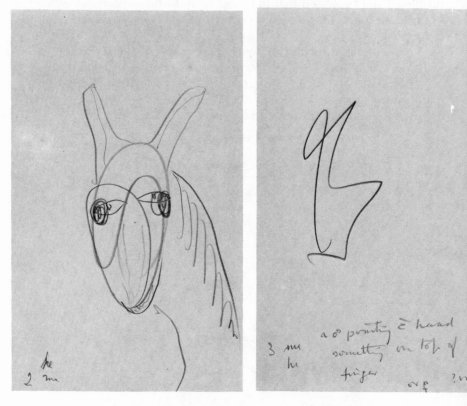

(2) His, which I turned into a horse's head.

(3) Mine, which he said was a man pointing with his hand. There was something on the top of his finger. Or it might be a girl's hand. Perhaps it was a ring on the finger.

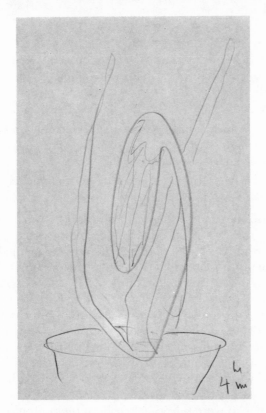

(4) His, which I made into some kind of plant.

(5) Mine, which he turned into a claw of a crab.

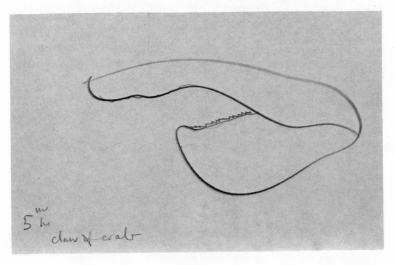

I could not help noting the absence of the man's body in No. 1, the absence of the man or woman altogether in No. 3, and the absence of the crab in No. 5. It was as if we were in a world of part-objects.

(6) His, which I made into a weird creature running in the Olympics. I made a note that we were not getting anywhere, but we went on, and did:

(7) Mine. He turned this into a thing from outer space. Here again was a head and no body.

The lack of play and of sense of humour persisted. I was employing a technique with a boy who looked nice and was nicely dressed and who had good manners and yet who seemed to be in some strange way absent; not absent in a schizoid way so much as absent in a sense of his being uninvolved except politely. He talked about his school and his being glad to have been accepted at the school, and he spoke with a certain amount of boasting rather than pride of the important people connected with the school. He told me his mother's professional name, expecting me to know of her, and there was the germ here of some kind of identification with those who have caught the limelight. He had in fact acted successfully in a play, and apparently he had impressed those who were selecting pupils at the preliminary interview for the school. He told me that his brother was at an ordinary school and from this I gathered that he knew that he was not able to attend an ordinary school, but he did not mind this fact, as far as I could tell.

I began to ask him about dreams at this stage.

olympics

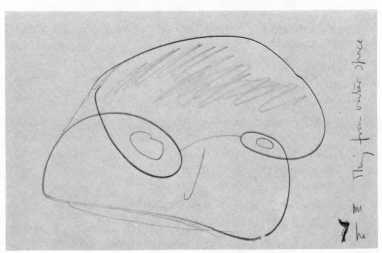

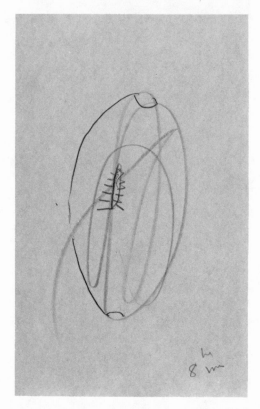

(8) His, which I turned into a football, having nothing else to do.

He quite clearly does not enjoy school games, although he says he may play when it is playtime, and he seems to do well when he does play.

(9) Mine, which he elaborated in a surprisingly rich way. He made it into a head, and here again there was the feature of the absence of the rest of the body. The head could be said to be both weird and ugly, but there was no feeling to be detected in the boy himself.

(10) His, which he himself elaborated.

This was the highest achievement of the consultation. In this and in the previous drawing would lie hidden the clue to his

state. It would seem to me that here he was expressing something very primitive and perhaps something which belongs to the very beginning before environmental adverse factors or deficiencies began to affect his emotional growth as an individual. If one could think of these faces as his visions of the first object, that which is usually called a breast in the jargon of psychoanalysis, and that which is equated with the face, then one can see that he came into a world in which when he went for an object, from his point of view, it was weird and completely lacking in the reassurances which belong to the first experiences of most babies. He called No. 10 a shadow moving fast, and he showed me where the eye and the nose and the mouth could be seen. I felt that he was loosening up after this, and that we were communicating.

(11) His, which I turned into a kind of insect.

(12) Mine, which he elaborated and entitled it 'a nothing'.

From my point of view this was the annihilation of himself. At a significant moment, or in a sequence of such moments, he had reached out and nothing was there for him to find which reflected in any way his basic need, or his creative eagerness. It was as if he was drawing the picture of his own death which came after his birth.

In making this description of him I am using my imagination, deeply affected as it must be by the experience that I was actually having with this boy who seemed to be non-existent. He had everything that could be desired in the way of a false set-up, built on a compliant basis, and he had nothing else. He only knew about part-objects and part-functions, and at the centre was 'a nothing'. Yet he had something in that he could present himself as nothing.

The question as to whether he was glad to be a boy or whether he would ever have liked to be a girl meant nothing to him, as could be predicted. He took himself entirely for granted, built as he was on conformity.

He told me about his father's business and about the extended family. When I asked him directly he told me that he came to me because of stealing, but he had only stolen from his mother. He said: 'I have been stealing since I was 4 years old.' He had been to a Child Guidance Clinic, but he said to his mother: 'I won't tell them anything.' One could almost say that the best part of

him (as he gave himself to me in words during this hour) was that he complained of a headache and of being worried. Also, of course, that he communicated his non-existence. Often he says to his mother: 'I can't help it; I don't want to steal', and he works himself up into a state of remorse; but *at the same time* he is stealing, and no-one believes any longer in his remorse except as another kind of deception. He says: 'I want help', but at the same time he shows signs of that complete hopelessness about getting help which makes an individual avoid looking for it. He did not tell me fully about his stealing, but by seeming to be honest about stealing from his mother he hid from me the major part of his stealing activities.

The worst is that he steals from his grandmother, who lives on her pension and who therefore suffers in a direct way when he takes money that she has set aside for essential bills. He is able to be loving and not furtive at certain times with his mother and he will say to her: 'I love you; I will never steal again.' But this has no relationship whatever to what he has just done and to what he is just going to do. Recently, with other boys, he had dismantled several pianos in this school that gives itself over, among other things, to music and the arts and drama. At this school this was the worst that could be thought of. It seems likely that he was the first to own up, although he may not have actually taken part in the escapade. This would be typical of him, and represents a technique for hiding the persistent lying which is part of his symptomatology in confession of crime he has not committed.

A detail which turned out to be important was that at one stage I asked him if he ever dreamed about stealing. His answer showed that this was out of the question, and in any case dreaming was not something that he knew anything about.

Interview with the Mother

I was naturally interested to get an account of George's early history. A few days after I saw George I was able to see the mother for an hour. Immediately I learned of further delinquencies which George had not told me about, although he had every opportunity to do so. They were in the usual pattern. The mother would go into a room and see smoke coming out of the armchair. He would be quite clear about being completely uninvolved, but when the mother looked she would find burnt matches on the floor by the chair. Nearly all the chairs in the house at some time or other have been set on fire. A typical example of George's behaviour would be that, having a very bad cold, he left the house at the height of a blizzard. He had only been left on his own half an hour and he had seemed quite contented. When the mother came back she found that he had got up from bed and had left without informing his grandmother and leaving no note. He was away from mid-day till nearly midnight. Eventually the police made contact with the family to say that he had been found outside the house of a relative, in a state of cold and hunger, carrying a suitcase. His father fetched him, and he cried and could not explain his action. He said that he would like to spend the night with his relative (uncle) and for many hours he had been riding around and around in the underground, having used his season ticket to get entry. He had had nothing to eat. Eventually he tried to make an explanation, saying: 'You and father are always quarrelling.' The mother said: 'He seemed to mean this, but actually we do not quarrel.' He seems fond of his sister, but he shouts at her when she shows any sign of personal feeling or distress. With his father he is liable to argue without obvious pretext.

In spite of all these things the family seemed to be fond of George, but they are constantly exasperated as when they find the garden shed burning, or the back of the piano showing signs of having been set alight.

EARLY HISTORY

After birth, George cried incessantly from very early times. It could be said that *he always cried all night*. With the other children the mother found that they cry it out, but with George there was no end to the bouts of crying; simply, she said, they ceased and then restarted.

From my point of view it was just here that George was experiencing and re-experiencing being nothing, which is what it feels like for a child when there is a dead imago in the mother's inner psychic reality.

He early developed into a pig, greedy for food and hoarding it; taking it and hiding it and not using it for himself.

His sister very early developed a protective rôle towards him. His brother often tried to get the parents not to make him confess, recognising the futility of this, and of course feeling that for the sake of peace it was better to let George get away with it,

391

whatever had happened. Gradually there developed a regular technique of appeasement and it is in this pattern that the family has managed to survive. This management by appeasement was well organised by the time George was 2 years old.

The story of the early stages contained the following detail. Soon after the mother was married her husband had to be away for some years because of the war. After this they settled down to a hard life and the two older children were born and went through various crises, but the family kept together and the mother was able to do what she felt needed to be done with these two children. Then there was a very bad period in the family history including a near bankruptcy. There was bad luck in all this, so that the parents had to endure seeing their friends who were similarly placed doing well while they were on the rocks. The mother kept things going by fostering some children for payment and she achieved a state of equilibrium on this basis. Then it happened that *she became pregnant and she knew that she would not be able to deal with the position that would arise when the baby was born.* She consulted her doctors in the ordinary way about an abortion and they kept postponing matters so that when a decision was made it had become too late for the abortion. She therefore had to get rid of the foster-children and prepare for a baby that she did not want to have, and she very much resented the way in which no-one had dealt with this matter in a logical way and the decision about the abortion had been allowed to drift.

George therefore had a start which was quite different from that of either his brother or sister. He was not wanted, and indeed from the mother's point of view it would have been her love of children that would have been at the back of her getting an abortion.

The mother fed George at the breast for a month, but the milk was scarce and she could not really make him contented. Then developed this incessant screaming which resulted when he was 2 in the development of the appeasement technique. From 2 years onwards anyone in the family would give George sweets or 6*d.* to get rid of him. In other words, he is alive because he was utterly spoiled, but he was not able to make use of being spoiled.

TRANSITIONAL PHENOMENA

The big girl had a bottle to suck. It had a teat and she used it for going to sleep even although it was empty. Her brother was offered a similar bottle, but his technique for going to sleep was tongue-sucking and he had a peculiar personal method of snuggling into a pillow. In describing these things the mother showed that she knew about the difficulty that all children have in passing from the waking to the sleeping state. George had no object or technique that could be said to be satisfactory to him. Soon he was talking to himself, but there was something abnormal here in his lack of a personal method for dealing with the difficult transition. As soon as he was old enough he began to show a kind of sulking. This did not quite show as a mood. It was more like this, that if he was told off, he would lock himself in the toilet for hours and talk to himself there, sometimes singing or drumming, giving the impression to everyone outside the locked door that he was not bothered. (Clearly, he was beyond hopelessness.)

George acquired a perfect technique for forgetting everything when anyone else would be feeling remorse or guilt. This relates especially to the use of noise. The best of this has been that he has liked being read to by his grandmother. But it was the pianos at school that he dismantled with the gang. At other times he used the alarum-clock or his record-player, and singing and drumming, all of which seemed to be a residue of the incessant screaming of his infancy and early childhood. In the noise lay hidden the last vestiges of hope.

Sometimes with his father he would help at the factory. The father would say that he did the work twice as fast and better, comparing him with the usual workman. This does not mean, however, that he was helping. It is rather similar to the way in which he did much better than was expected when interviewed for the school, but this had no relation to performance in the general course of school routine and in competition with other children. On the positive side the mother reported his recent experience of acting in a play at the school, and his wish for his mother to be there at rehearsals. This goes along with the pride which he is capable of showing in the fact that his mother was once well known on the stage. She herself says that he greatly exaggerated this, but nevertheless it has fact in it. It seems legitimate to work on the idea that when *acting a part* he gets nearer to feeling real than when he is left on his own and is nothing. On his own he seems to have no identity, from his point of view. When he is acting, the fact that he is a false-self person is temporarily less obvious.

393

The mother tried to help me to understand the boy by saying that she herself was not good scholastically, and I had to assume that she herself found an identity through acting, and was aware of the relationship between this and an uncertainty about herself in everyday life.

George has made some improvement since being at this school which he says he loves, except that 'these boys constantly threaten me'. He has even owned up recently to some delinquencies. He is perhaps nearly aware of the madness that there is in the compulsive nature of his anti-social behaviour, and to feel the absence of conscious motive, and to mind about this.

It was here that the mother told me about his report to her of a dream about stealing following the interview with me. While I was interested in this detail which showed that his relationship with me had made some kind of impact I noted that I must not get involved in this case. This detail along with the part-object heads and faces indicated to me that if I saw him two or three times more I would find myself involved in his dreams, and then I would have to take the case over in a big way, and I am not in a position to do this. The treatment of this boy would need close collaboration with a boarding establishment with an informal and specialised attitude, willing to give him full attention, or he would need to be taken over by a team orientated towards the total management of this boy and of others like him. There would be times when the personnel and also the non-human environment would be in danger, physically.

Theoretically it would not be impossible for me to treat this boy. He has an idea that there could be a better life and that he could be a more real person than he is. But he is cut off from being anything and from BEING. In practice the difficulties are immense, and it might be better to be outspoken and to say that the boy cannot be treated.

George told his brother that I was not a psychiatrist but a very nice gentleman. This was in self-defence when the brother unwisely said: 'What did the psychiatrist say?' and: 'What have you been stealing now?'

Among strangers George goes down very well. People could be said to adore him and they say how sweet he is. The mother described his father as being by nature soft, so that she has to be strong and strict whether it suits her nature or not. The grandmother that he loves, the one who reads to him and from whom he steals in a ruthless way, is his mother's mother. It is possible that he is affected by something morbid in her personality. Her depressions give her the idea that the world is just about to end, and she lets people know that she feels like this. Also she uses spiritualism, and she sees faces, which perhaps shows in the squiggle game. All these things lead to arguments with the family, resulting in her going home, and George's mother feels that her mother has a dreadful life. Presumably George thinks so too in so far as he is able to enter with feeling into someone else's life at all. This grandmother's father committed suicide when she was 3 years old, and this undoubtedly had a severe effect on the development of her personality and capacity for happiness.

The mother now found confidence to tell me more about George's heredity. There is a history of suicide and of gross anti-social behaviour on George's father's side, apart altogether from the fact that the father's parents were gassed under Nazi persecution. A good figure in the picture of the whole extended family was the father's mother, whose personality was warm and positive, and who provided somehow an element of hope and some potential for stability in all those who came under her influence.

Added to George's bad heredity and his not having been wanted at the beginning, there were certain unfortunate external factors. For example, when he was 7 he complained that a boy at school had a gun and that he felt he was in danger. The mother pooh-pooh'd the idea of real danger (knowing his tendency to feel persecuted) and went to school with him to investigate. There the boy, who had an airgun, shot George in the head. After this it was no good reassuring him in terms of his delusional systems.

He continues with the tendency that he showed as a toddler to hoard objects and sweets and 'Matchbox' toys, etc. At one time there was a combination of not eating with buying sweets and fearing to get fat.

Recently he brought home an empty wallet; he had found it on the floor of a train. Could he keep it? etc. etc. The mother could see no reason why he should not keep it. Nevertheless the more she thought about it the more likely it seemed to her that there had been money in it, and in any case there was the wallet in the dream that he told her the day after his session with me. No-one can ever know the truth, and by special instances of honesty and confession he hides with success the thefts which are determined by unconscious motive in terms of his own everyday waking self.

395

It is to be noted that he does not play for pleasure, or at any rate, not for long periods, as was shown clearly to me in the interview. He is excessively generous. In competitive play he *must* win. He has no way of protecting his toys, which get broken up one way or another soon after he acquires them. He is always ready with: 'I've got a bigger one', in any contact with boys who boast of anything. The parents have strained their resources to 'buy him off' from early times, but he is a big spender, and this is a permanent problem in the home.

At the end the mother told me that George had a very bad birth. 'It lasted all night. He had his chin up. The doctor wanted to use instruments but I refused to allow this.'

I recommended contact with the Probation Officer, warning him of what may some day come his way, perhaps through the courts. Procedure is under discussion, but I made it clear that I knew that even if I could understand in terms of aetiology I could not alter the basic problem of this family and of George. It surprised me that the mother seemed to be grateful for something, perhaps for having been told what she already knew to be the truth.

Bibliographical Note

By M. Masud R. Khan

In this book, Dr. Winnicott has concentrated almost exclusively on presenting his clinical material with the minimum of theory. This, however, should not misguide the reader into thinking that this clinical work is the result of mere empathy and inspired hunches. There is a very complex and vast theoretical background to it, which Dr. Winnicott has presented in his various articles and books over the past four decades. The material is available in his seven books:

Collected Papers: Through Paediatrics to Psycho-Analysis. 1958. London, Tavistock Publications; New York, Basic Books.

The Maturational Processes and the Facilitating Environment. 1965. London, The Hogarth Press and the Institute of Psycho-Analysis; New York, International Universities Press

Playing and Reality. 1971. London, Tavistock Publications.

The Child and the Family: First Relationships. 1957. London, Tavistock Publications.

The Child and the Outside World: Studies in Developing Relationships. 1957. London, Tavistock Publications.

The Child, the Family, and the Outside World. 1964. London, Penguin Books.

The Family and Individual Development. 1965. London, Tavistock Publications.

It may be useful, however, to single out a few more significant papers from the above books that provide the basic theory for the clinical work reported in this book. These are itemised below under three headings:

A. *Papers on Mother–Child Relationship*

1948 : 'Paediatrics and Psychiatry' in *Collected Papers.*

1948a: 'Reparation in Respect of Mother's Organized Defence against Depression' in *Collected Papers.*

1952 : 'Psychoses and Child Care' in *Collected Papers.*

1956 : 'Primary Maternal Preoccupation' in *Collected Papers.*

1960 : 'The Theory of the Parent–Infant Relationship' in *The Maturational Processes.*

1963 : 'From Dependence towards Independence in the Development of the Individual' in *The Maturational Processes.*

B. *Papers on Early Psychic Development and Ego Pathology*

1935 : 'The Manic Defence' in *Collected Papers.*

1945 : 'Primitive Emotional Development' in *Collected Papers.*

1949 : 'Mind and its Relation to the Psyche-Soma' in *Collected Papers.*

1951 : 'Transitional Objects and Transitional Phenomena' in *Collected Papers.*

1954 : 'The Depressive Position in Normal Emotional Development' in *Collected Papers*.

1956 : 'The Antisocial Tendency' in *Collected Papers*.

1958 : 'Psycho-Analysis and the Sense of Guilt' in *The Maturational Processes*.

1958a: 'The Capacity to be Alone' in *The Maturational Processes*.

1960 : 'Ego Distortion in Terms of True and False Self' in *The Maturational Processes*.

1963 : 'The Development of the Capacity for Concern' in *The Maturational Processes*.

1963a: 'Communicating and Not Communicating Leading to a Study of Certain Opposites' in *The Maturational Processes*.

1967 : 'The Location of Cultural Experience' in *The International Journal of Psycho-Analysis*, Volume 48.

1968 : 'Playing: its Theoretical Status in the Clinical Situation' in *The International Journal of Psycho-Analysis*, Volume 49.

1969 : 'The Use of an Object' in *The International Journal of Psycho-Analysis*, Volume 50.

C. *Papers on Technique*

1947 : 'Hate in the Countertransference' in *Collected Papers*.

1949 : 'Birth Memories, Birth Trauma, and Anxiety' in *Collected Papers*.

1954 : 'Withdrawal and Regression' in *Collected Papers*.

1954a: 'Metapsychological and Clinical Aspects of Regression within the Psycho-Analytical Set-Up' in *Collected Papers*.

1955 : 'Clinical Varieties of Transference' in *Collected Papers*.

1958 : 'Child Analysis in the Latency Period' in *The Maturational Processes*.

1960 : 'Counter-Transference' in *The Maturational Processes*.

1963 : 'Psychotherapy of Character Disorders' in *The Maturational Processes*.

1963a: 'Dependence in Infant-Care, in Child-Care, and in the Psycho-Analytic Setting' in *The Maturational Processes*.

INDEX

Abortion, 392
Acceptance
of interpretation, 10
Acting out (see Re-living)
as recapturing unavailable dreams,
276
of ideas in stealing, 276
Ada (Case XIII), 220
Adaptation, 224
Adolescence,
cure for, 190
Aggression, 48, 62, 175, 194, 249,
251, 296, 362, 368
Albert (Case X), 161
Alfred (Case VII), 110
Ambivalence, 98, 100, 103, 108, 156,
214, 271
Analyst (*see* Therapist)
Anger, 62, 335
reactive, 62
Anna (Case of Mrs. X), 331
Annihilation
of self, 388
Antisocial Tendency, 128, 215, 220,
267, 304, 315, 380
and confusional states, 216
and deprivation, 128, 219, 292, 316
and father-deprivation, 314
and gap in development, 216
and madness, 394
and manic defence, 292
and remorse, 390, 393
as expression of hope, 219, 292,
327
cure of, 217
two types of, 217
Anxiety,
about cure, 2
about retaliation, 77
during consultation, 80, 211, 326,
353, 375
primitive, 70, 77, 83/4, 86, 138
unthinkable, 83, 86
unthinkable and muddle, 138

unthinkable, screened by symbolic
social activities, 120
Appetite,
primitive, 62, 156
Ashton (Case IX), 147
Asikainen, Miss Helka,
as interpreter, 6, 25
Availability
'on demand', 176, 193
'Average Expectable Environment'
therapist's dependence on, 5

Bed-wetting, 61, 141, 143, 217, 220,
300, 339, 376
Belief
in being understood, 5, 7
in God, 209
in reliability, 214
in self, 209
Benign Circle, 8, 194, 265, 330, 341
change from vicious to, by forces of
life and developmental processes,
72 ff.
Bite,
urge to, 340
Blinking, 345
Block,
developmental, removed by interview, 194 ff.
to freedom to regress, 64
Body
as equivalent to mind, 52
functions, 62
Breakdown,
and false self organisation, 87
and trauma, 87
co-existence of, with personality
growth, 301
Breast, 211, 226, 234, 260, 268, 388
attack on, 62, 211, 340
-feeding, 85, 89, 156, 239, 244, 260,
304, 362, 392
Breathing, 110, 121, 130, 157

Candidate,
  ill person made less ill, 1
  selection of, 1
  training of, 1, 2
Cases,
  assessment of, 5
  assessment of environment in
    selection of, 5
  'described' by child, 3
  descriptions of, made enjoyable, 6
  given life by drawings, 3
  reporting on, 3
  selection of, 6, 7, 12, 28
  uniqueness of, 2
  wholly described, 9
Casework, 127
Cathexis,
  withdrawal of, 79, 83
Cecil (Case XIV), 239
Character
  and deprivation, 217
  as organisation of defences, 86
Charles (Case VIII), 129
Child psychiatry
  and psycho-analysis, 1, 214, 218,
    270
Circle (see Benign and vicious circle)
Clue
  to case, 44, 105, 122, 202, 366
Collusive
  defences, 10
Communication
  between child and teacher, 127,
    159, 264
  between child and therapist, 3, 7,
    8, 127, 147, 176, 203, 215, 217,
    270, 346, 388
  between mother and therapist, 331
  between social agencies, 315
  difficulty in mother, 249
  through squiggle game, 13/15, 19,
    84/6, 197
Compliance, 20, 161, 194
  and false self, 388
  and feelings, 67
  and impulse, 67
  and predisposition to perversion,
    194
Compulsions, 226, 292

Confidence,
  and readiness to go deeper, 324
  gained from sense of humour, 32
  in waiting, 228
  of children as sacred, 4
  taking parents into, in squiggle
    game, 3, 4
Conflict,
  between going forward and
    regression, 36, 38, 64, 100, 253,
    260
  emotional, 7
Confusional state, 70, 138, 143, 216,
    229, 236
  and antisocial tendency, 216
Consultation (see Therapeutic
    consultation)
  dream about, 4, 188
Continuity,
  break in, 216, 219
Creativity, 30, 32, 158, 182, 187, 388
  in playing vs. games, 346n
Cure,
  anxiety about, 2, 331
  as threat to individuality, 180
  for adolescence is passage of time,
    190
  of antisocial tendency, 217
  role of developmental process in,
    42
  symptomatic, 8/9, 110, 194, 217,
    317

Day-dreaming, 84, 334, 336
Deadness, 109
Death
  as conception, 157
Deep
  work in first interview, 5, 43
Defences, 60, 210
  against archaic anxiety, 86/7
  collusive, 10
  respect for, 32, 359
  rigidity of, characterising illness,
    32, 60, 380
Dependence, 7, 30, 194, 217, 239,
    251, 267, 302
  defence against, 87
  near absolute, 72, 86

of child on therapist, 5
vs. going forward, 36/8, 64, 253, 260
Delusional system, 395
Depression, 64, 79, 84/5, 90/2, 100, 103, 105, 177, 193, 216, 253, 265, 268, 271, 282, 289, 291, 334, 316
   child's responsibility to, in mother, 100
   effect of, in mother, 84
Deprivation, 61, 63, 144, 217, 234, 236, 263, 267, 327, 379
   and antisocial tendency, 128, 219, 291/2, 316
   and spoiling, 217, 249, 251, 253n, 267, 392
   mother's own, 332
   of father, 144
   of father in antisocial child, 217, 304, 311n, 375
Destructiveness, 217, 335, 343, 365, 379
Detail, importance of understanding, 129
Developmental process,
   role of, in cure, 42
Devil,
   dream of, 358/60
Diagnosis, 298, 345
   change in, 86
   doubt about, 65, 84
   value of, 147
Disability,
   child's awareness of mother's involvement with his, 23/4
   emergence of, in squiggle game, 14 ff.
Disintegration, 87, 216, 289
   and Humpty Dumpty, 68
   and premature ego organisation, 68
   reactivation of, 70
   threat of, 77
Dissociation, 220, 224, 232, 236, 263, 265, 286, 304, 380, 390
   vs. splitting, 304
Distraction
   techniques of parents, 364

Distress,
   and blinking, 345
   distracted by therapist's action, 117/8
   history-taking leads to discovery of, 125
   reliving, of deprivation, 330
Drawings, 3
   indication for significant, using large paper, 54, 78, 204, 325, 351, 374
Dream,
   drawing a, clears up symptoms, 105 ff.
   material, getting into contact with, 32
   of devil, 358/60
   representing deadness, 109
   use of by child in consultation, 62
   use of in therapy, 115
   vs. fantastic, 282
Dreams, 19, 32, 50, 52, 79, 97, 105, 107, 115, 135, 139, 153, 165, 188, 202/3, 208, 228, 257, 262, 266, 276, 288, 325, 337, 355, 372, 380, 384
   about therapist on night before consultation, 4, 188
   and confusional state, 141/3
   and muddle, 139
   as defence, 32
   as indication of child's capacity to deal with material, 115
   of a mother with antisocial tendency, 337/8
   unavailable, recaptured in anti-social acting out, 276
   unremembered, 208

Ease,
   squiggle game reaches to child's, 115
Ego,
   premature reliance on, 68/9
Ego support, 214
   as depicted in squiggle game, 16, 178, 202
Eliza (Case III), 42

Emotional development,
   block in, 5, 147, 158, 194, 214, 216,
      238, 344
   complexity of, 11
   good start to, 216, 388
   theory of, 3, 10/11, 102
Enjoying,
   mutual, in squiggle game, 17, 51
   playing, 60, 360
Environment,
   abnormal, 5
   assessment of, 5, 42, 215, 242, 317
   'average expectable', 5
   facilitating, 216
   illness in, 8, 127
   manipulation of, 2
   reaction to failure in, 70, 72, 77,
      81/2, 86, 216, 219
   relationship of child to, 2, 5, 42,
      101, 159, 194
Environmental factor,
   assessment of, in squiggle game, 3
Envy
   of penis, 185
Erection, 34, 98
Excitement, 65
   and horror, 80
Experience,
   of child in consultation, 3, 69, 81,
      206/7, 211, 214, 216, 229, 238,
      263, 284, 328, 330
   mutual, 3

Face,
   handling of, 34
Faeces, 48, 61, 121, 245, 248, 363
False self
   and compliance, 338
   and part-objects, 388
   organisation and trauma, 87
Family,
   illness in, 8, 127
   normality in, 28, 89, 159, 304
   rehabilitation of, 344
Fantastic
   vs. fantasy and dream, 282
Fantasy, 22, 32, 59, 115, 188, 198,
      230, 274, 276, 282, 284, 291, 325,
      355, 376, 378

   capacity for, 181
   dealing with armchair anxiety, 83
   fear of, 202
   of pre-birth, 22
   of pregnancy, 61/2
   undervaluing of, 276
Father,
   as mother-figure, 246/7, 394
   child's effort to cure, 123/4
   deprivation, 217, 304, 311n, 360,
      375
   -deprivation and antisocial
      tendency, 217
   -deprivation in child of, 144
   instilling moral strength, 293
   's help as corrective of lapse in
      maternal holding, 83
Fears, 135, 206, 299, 359
Feelings,
   and compliance, 67
   at end of dream, 143
Fertility, 235/6, 282
Fierceness, 48, 60, 62
First interview,
   and contraindication of multi-
      plicity of problems, 8
   deep work in, 5
   exploitation of, 1, 4, 7, 63, 159,
      176, 218, 220
   improvement before, 125
Flight from regressive tendency, 267
Found object, 30, 36
Freedom and humour, 32, 267
Friendship, 208, 269, 272, 294
   between son and father, 100
Frustration,
   acceptance of, 278
   reaction to, 271, 291/2

Games, 165, 386, 396
   as flight from anxiety, 375
   vs. playing, 172, 195, 236, 346,
      375
Gap
   and recovery of own 'good'
      mummy, 341
   in development and antisocial
      tendency, 216
George (Case XXI), 380

Gesture,
  importance of, in squiggle game,
    76
God, belief in, and self, 209/10
Good and bad, 161
Good object,
  loss of, 217
Group,
  -situations, 8
  -therapy, 64
Growth, 317
  feeling of natural, 101
  vs. illness breakdowns, 301
Guilt,
  about masturbation, 55
  about sex in mother, 26
  sense of, 26, 156, 265, 271, 295,
    297, 365, 393

Hallucinations
  and music, 154, 159
Hands,
  significance of, 224
Happiness
  and humour, 32
Hate, 26, 108, 161, 174, 250
Help
  and hopelessness, 390
Heredity, 103, 395
Hesta (Case XI), 176
History-taking, 6, 44, 63, 113, 118,
    125, 177, 217, 273, 296, 304
  from child, 44, 220
  vs. collection of facts, 125
Holding, 79, 83
Home,
  use of, as mental hospital, 193, 314
Homosexuality
  as normal, 100, 379
Hope
  and antisocial tendency, 219, 292,
    327
  in therapist, 30
  of being understood, 5, 64, 86, 195,
    216
Hopelessness, 328, 357, 360, 390,
    393
Horrid
  part of self, 52/6, 61

Horror
  and excitement, 80
Humour, 338
  and child's creative imagination, 32
  and rigidity of defence, 32, 60
  as ally of therapist, 32
  sense of, as evidence of freedom, 32
    60, 267, 338, 382, 384
Humpty-Dumpty,
  and idea of integration, 68
Hypnosis, 4

'I am', 38
Id
  and compliance, 67
Idealisation, 85
Identification, 188, 200, 250, 366
  of self, 22
  therapist's capacity for, with child,
    2
  with father, 89, 103, 123, 158
  with God, 210
  with mother, 23, 246, 318, 327,
    367, 376
  with therapist, 24, 72
Identity,
  loss of personal, 2, 157, 175
  through acting, 383/4
Iiro (Case I), 6, 12
Illegitimate child
  and deprivation, 332
Illness,
  child's effort to cure, in father,
    122/4
  finding normality rather than, 102
  in mother, 85
  in parents, affecting child, 64
  in parents and social situation, 8
  reaching to, in consultation, 229
  vs. naughtiness, 314
Imagination, 32, 49, 60, 90, 159, 178,
    182, 222, 226, 255, 280, 388
  creative, and humour, 32
  leading to dream, 159
Imitation,
  warning against, of described
    technique, 9, 11
Impulse, 178, 276
  and compliance, 67

403

Injections,
significance of, 358/9, 365
Instinctual drive
and affectionate relationship, 103
Integration,
capacity for, 281, 289, 291
Intellect
vs. playing, 134, 138
Intelligence, 84, 89, 91, 148, 158/9,
177, 189, 239, 272, 302, 344,
350, 367, 381
Internal conflict,
and professional use of material, 7
brought to first interview, 7, 8, 36,
43, 118, 160
resolution of, 2
Interpretation,
acceptance of as propaganda, 10
as aid to child's own discovery of
self, 62, 69
as collusive defence, 10
child's right to reject, 10, 23
denial of, 9
for benefit of therapist, 10
not main feature, 9, 214, 223
providing bridge into the past, 263
therapist refrains from use of, 15,
43, 49, 57, 69, 72, 157, 180, 182,
188, 207, 223, 226, 230, 232,
284, 286, 320, 338, 349
vs. talking, 69
withdrawal of, 9
Interpreter,
use of, in squiggle game, 12 ff.
Interview (see First interview)
Invulnerability, 87
Isolating
as protection of self, 87
Isolation
as defence against anxiety, 87

Jason (Case XX), 344
Jealousy, 157, 333
of sibling, 90, 98, 174, 250, 253

Keys and fingers, 248
Killing, 108, 157, 166, 175, 230, 360,
376
of self, 177, 357, 360

Knowledge,
dread of therapist's magical, 16
Kuopio (Finland), 12, 15

Language,
distortion of, 70
Lastenlinna (Children's Castle), 12
Learning,
difficulty about, 86, 89, 344
Left-handedness, 114, 344
Lesbian, 176
Life,
use of. towards solution of
problems, 160
Lily (Case XIX), 342
Loneliness, 210, 260, 333, 361
Look,
unwillingness to, 18/19
Love,
capacity to, 282, 292
Lying,
as distress signal, 345

Madness,
feelings of, 220, 335, 394
Magic, 16, 142, 156, 199, 200, 378
dread of therapist's, 16
Management
of case, 5, 9, 28, 193, 239, 267/8,
296, 331, 343, 379, 394, 303/312
Manic, 60n,
-defence, and antisocial tendency,
292
-depressive swing, 177, 191, 193
Mark (Case XV), 270
Masturbation, 55, 84, 140, 224, 226,
230, 251, 332
Maturational processes, 216
Menstruation, 176/7
Milton (Case XII), 194
Mind,
and muddle, 133
and mustnots, 133
as symptom, 129
body-functions as equivalent to,
52
exploitation of, 134, 363
vs. playing, 134

404

Mother,
  and hate of baby, 26
  and need to see child's therapist, 25
  and perception of child's disability
    as punishment, 26
  and use of remedial treatment to
    compensate child, 26
  attack on horrid objects inside, 62
  child's rediscovery of, 218, 234,
    238, 260, 263, 268, 292, 328,
    337, 340/1
  child's responsibility for depression
    in, 100
  conflict in, affecting child, 28, 30,
    64, 240, 263, 268, 271, 315, 331,
    367
  created from own capacity to love,
    292
  depression in, 64, 79, 84/5, 91/2,
    100, 103, 244, 253, 265, 268,
    271, 282, 291, 316
  guilt feelings of, 26, 265
  possessiveness of, 332
  's involvement with child's
    disability, 23/4
  's own boy self, 366
  's use of child's illness, 341
  therapeutic consultation with a,
    332 ff.
  with antisocial tendency, 332 ff.
Mrs. X. (Case XVIII), 331
Muddle, 138/9
  and mind, 138
  and unthinkable anxiety, 138
Music, 6, 160, 244, 299
  as defence against noise, 153, 157,
    393
  displaces hallucinations, 154
Mythology, 120, 260

Need,
  social, and psychoanalysis, 2
  to be loved as born, 25
Neurotic
  organisation against unthinkable
    anxiety, 83
New theme,
  risk of introducing at end of inter-
    view, 24

Nightmares, 52, 54, 160, 358, 378
  about witch, 80/1
Normality
  finding rather than illness, 102
  of child and social setting, 12, 28,
    42, 60, 89, 247
Nuisance value, 215, 363

Objectifying
  the therapist, 88
Objective,
  becoming, 20
Object-relating, 62, 156, 212
  loss of capacity for, 87
  primitive, 62
Oedipus complex, 98, 100, 157, 160,
    360, 376
'On demand' therapy, 176, 193,
    213, 218, 239
Oral sadism, 77, 156, 212, 214, 340
Outcome, 8, 127, 361
  to consultations, 27, 41, 62, 86,
    101, 109, 125, 145, 158, 175,
    192, 212, 238, 264, 292, 312,
    330, 341, 379, 396
Owed something to
  and spoiling, 335

Painting,
  abstract, as hiding place, 154/5
  as escape from hallucinations, 154
Paper, 54, 78, 374
Parents,
  abuse of therapist's confidence in, 4
  and capacity to report objectively, 8
  and confidence in therapist, 7, 8, 42
  as agents of cure, 194, 217, 243,
    263, 265, 267, 296, 304, 379
  attitude of, reflected in dream, 4
  child's responsibility for state of,
    100
  coping with regressive episode,
    296 ff.
  illness in, affecting child, 8, 28, 40,
    64, 123, 127, 240, 263, 268, 271,
    315, 331, 367, 345
  in treatment, 64, 194, 268
  survival of, 217, 392
  taken into confidence of therapist,
    3/4, 7, 28, 42, 158, 212, 360

405

Part-object, 10, 384, 388
Patient,
    capacity to identify with, 2
    's need to control analyst, 158
Penis, 10, 34, 76, 80, 136, 182, 211,
    223
    envy of, 185
Penis envy, 182, 185
Perversion
    and compliance, 194
Peter (Case XVI), 296
Phases in consultation, 55/6, 67, 77,
    202, 230, 324
Phobia, 61, 135, 212, 251
    snake-symbolism in, 10
Playing, 30, 346n
    and not making interpretation, 320
    as sign of normality, 60
    enjoying, 60
    in consultation with an adult
        patient, 341
    loss of capacity for, 245
    of child with therapist, 17, 51, 143,
        178, 181, 187, 214, 301, 320, 350,
        382
    opportunity for, 134
Poem,
    'I have to live', 146
Pre-birth,
    fantasy of, 22
Pregnancy, 26, 223, 392
    child's fantasy of, 61/2, 205
    child's reaction to, 53, 56, 62, 90,
        194, 209, 211, 224, 236, 240,
        243, 272, 317, 327, 361
Premature
    effort and breakdown, 121/4
    reliance on ego, 68/9
Primary defect, 65, 86
Primitive love impulse, 62, 156, 214
Privacy
    facilitates consultation, 7
Problem,
    verbalisation of, enabled by
        squiggle game, 21
Problems,
    multiplicity of, in first interview, 8
Provocation
    and therapeutic retaliation, 2

Pseudologia fantastica, 265, 271, 291,
    345
Psycho-analysis,
    and child psychiatry, 1, 214, 218,
        270
    as treatment, 1, 5, 218
    indication for, 8, 10, 102/3, 147,
        218, 343
    personal, essential for therapist in
        training, 2
    student in training made less ill by,
        1
    unable to meet social need, 2
Psychopathic personality, 298
Psycho-somatic
    functioning vs. thinking, 87

Questions, 301
    leading away from point of conflict,
        63, 208
    provoking symptom, 110

Reaction
    to environmental failure, 70
Real,
    loss of sense of, 87, 393
Reality principle, 188, 190, 292
    and therapeutic 'spoiling', 253n
Regression, 28, 36, 64, 89, 176, 217,
    239, 245, 251, 267, 296, 302
    met by parents, 296 ff
Rejection,
    child's right to, 10
Reliability
    of therapist, 2, 202, 214
Religion, 92, 101
Re-living, 69, 207, 211, 214, 216, 263,
    284, 330
Remembering
    and trauma, 87/8
Remorse
    misinterpreted as deception, 390
Reporting,
    accuracy of, 3, 10
    need for, 8
    over-simplification of, 3
    rewards from, 3
Repression, 232, 271
Resistance, 9/10, 218

406

Restlessness, 196
  and antisocial tendency, 216
  as indication of fear of feelings,
    214, 216
Result,
  warning about symptomatic, 9
Retaliation, 77, 217
  to patient's provocation, 2
Right or wrong
  irrelevant in squiggle game, 18
Robert (Case V) 89
Robin (Case II), 28
Role
  of therapist as subjective object,
    4, 88, 214
  of therapist compared with role of
    parent, 32
Rosemary (Case VI), 105
Ruth (Case XVII), 315

'Sacred moment',
  use of, 4
Sado-masochism, 194, 208, 210
Schizoid personality, 147, 158/9
Schizophrenia,
  infantile, 70, 86, 147
School refusal, 28
Secondary gains, 215, 217
Seduction,
  sexual, 55
Self,
  annihilation of, 388
  belief in, and God, 209/10
  child isolates, as protection of, 87
  child's presentation of, in con-
    sultation, 28 ff.
  horrid part of, 52/6
  love of, 25, 208
  mother's boy self, 366
  patient's need to be loved as, 22
  protected by withdrawn state, 87
  represented by snake, 34/6
  symbol of, in drawings, 10, 22, 38,
    132, 197, 223
  threat to sense of, 180
Separation
  from mother, 85, 289, 291, 327,
    361, 379
Seriousness, 289

Setting,
  child's assessment of, 202
  provision of, 7, 28, 127, 147, 176,
    316
Sexual
  climax, 228
  excitement, 80, 98, 140, 358
  guilt, lack of in mother, 26
  information, 61, 62, 91, 98, 272
  intercourse, 157
  life of mother, 26, 332/3
  seduction, 55
  stimulation, 55, 336
  symbolism, 34, 49, 57, 230
Significant moment
  in Case No. I, 22 (drawing 14)
  in Case No. II, 36 (drawing 13)
  in Case No. III, 43, 48 (drawings 1
    and 11)
  in Case No. IV, 82 (drawing 26)
  in Case No. V, 97 (drawing 7)
  in Case No. VI, 118 (drawing 12)
  in Case No. VII, 133 (drawing 7)
  in Case No. VIII, 139 (drawing 17)
  in Case No. IX, 154 (drawing 13)
  in Case No. X, 162, 174 (drawings 2
    and 17)
  in Case No. XI, 186 (drawing 11)
  in Case No. XII, 204 (drawing 14)
  in Case No. XIII, 229, 232 (drawing
    20)
  in Case No. XIV, 257 (drawing 9)
  in Case No. XV, 286, 289 (drawings
    6 and 10)
  in Case No. XVI, not decisive
  in Case No. XVII, 327 drawing
    16)
  in Case No. XVIII, 340
  in Case No. XIX, 342 (drawing 3)
  in Case No. XX, 358, 374 (drawings
    16 and 11)
  in Case No. XXI, 387 (drawing 10)
Simultaneous
  acceptance and refusal, 154
Sleep,
  and depression, 85
  difficulty about, 90, 176, 241
  in mother as failure of environ-
    ment, 82

Snake
  as symbol of penis and self, 10
  representing self, 34/6
Social agencies, 315
Social need
  and psychoanalysis, 2
Social pressure,
  meeting of, 2, 270
  and therapeutic work, 270
'Spoiling',
  and deprivation, 217, 249, 251,
    253n, 267, 392
  and regression to dependence, 217
  and sense of being owed some-
    thing, 335
  therapeutic, 253n
Spontaneous development, 28, 70, 86,
    230, 352
Squiggle game,
  allows for active participation, 200
  and gesture, 76
  and taking parents into confidence,
    3, 4
  as means of contact with child, 3, 7,
    113
  as road to dream material, 32, 284
  as technique, 3, 177
  creativity in, 30
  child's unawareness of symbolism
    in, 15
  communication through, 13/15,
    19, 84/6, 197
  description of, 12, 110, 196
  humour in, 32
  leading to verbalisation of
    problem, 21
  link with psychotherapeutic
    consultation, 3
  patient surprising himself in, 19,
    23, 38, 97, 226, 284, 327
  reaches to child's ease, 115
Spock, B., 362
Spontaneity, 92, 178, 208, 276
Stammer, 110, 121
Standards
  of parents implanted on child, 92,
    101, 272
Stealing, 215, 220, 224, 236, 252, 262,
    271, 291, 315, 336, 345, 368, 380

and acting out of ideas, 276
and buying, 226, 232, 337
and deprivation, 316/7
and giving presents, 226, 232
and transitional phenomena, 342
Student,
  and the use of these case-descrip-
    tions, 10, 127, 218
  in possession of all known details of
    case, 9, 128, 270
  of psycho-analysis, 1
  selection of, 1/2
  training of, 1
Subjective object,
  and objectifying, 88
  and 'sacred moment', 4
  therapist's role as, 4, 88, 214
Suicide, 360
Super-ego
  and compliance, 161
  and father-deprivation, 217
Surgery,
  orthopaedic: Case I, 12 ff.
Surprise, 1, 4, 13, 18/19, 32, 147, 175,
    276, 342, 360, 367, 372, 386
  of child at own drawings, 18/19,
    23, 38, 97, 100, 226, 284, 327
Survival
  of parents, 217, 392
Symbolism, 10, 34, 49, 57, 182, 185,
    223, 230, 234, 245n, 281
  as defence against unthinkable
    anxiety, 120
  in dreams, 120, 157, 171, 207,
    247/8
Symptoms, 8, 9
  of Ada, 220, 236
  of Albert, 161
  of Alfred, 110, 114, 124
  of Ashton, 148
  of Bob, 64, 84, 86
  of Cecil, 240, 251
  of Charles, 129
  of Eliza, 62
  of George, 380, 388, 390
  of Hesta, 176
  of Iiro, 12
  of Jason, 344, 368
  of Mark, 271

408

of Milton, 194
of Peter, 296
of Robert, 89/90
of Robin, 28
of Rosemary, 105
of Ruth, 315
Syndactyly, 12, 16

Talking
    as facilitating factor, 119
    facilitates consultation, 181/2
    vs. interpretation, 69, 320
Tape-recording, 3
Teaching material,
    case descriptions as, 9, 10, 129
Technique, 1, 6, 127, 214, 220, 384
    flexibility of, 2, 29, 87/8
    imitation of, 9
    of taking cue from child, 44, 217/8
    of squiggle game, 3, 177
    taken for granted, 6
    warning against imitation of, 9
Theory,
    need of, of emotional development,
        2
Therapeutic consultation,
    and squiggle game, 3
    avoidance of, 5
    'benign circle' in, 8
    child's presentation of self in: Case
        II, 28 ff.
    dominated by patient, 10, 29, 334n
    interpretation of the unconscious
        not the main feature, 9
    preparation of child for, 4
    role of privacy in, 7
    role of transitional object in, 102
    training for, in long-term psycho-
        therapy, 270
    with a parent (mother), 332 ff.
Therapist,
    absence of tendency to retaliate
        in, 2
    adaptation of, to need of child, 224
    and contact with parent, 25
    appearing in dream before
        consultation, 4, 188
    as constant factor, 6
    as subjective object, 4

as threat to child's individuality,
    180
capacity of, for identification with
    patient, 2
capacity of, to contain conflicts of
    patient, 2
child's need to objectify, 87, 158
deals with defences as parents do
    not, 32
helps child to assimilate key
    experiences into whole
    personality, 214
humour as ally of, 32, 48
magical knowledge of, 16, 199
patient's need to control, 158
personal analysis of, 2
professional reliability of, 2, 202
's availability on demand, 176
's dependence on 'average
    expectable environment', 5
's playing together with patient,
    187
spontaneity and impulsiveness, 178
use of humour, 138
uniqueness of, 6
Therapy,
    essence of, 62
    how little need be done in, 125
Things,
    horrid, 52/6, 60/2
Thinking
    vs. psycho-somatic functioning, 87
Thought system
    providing easy solution, 2
Thumb-sucking, 84, 95, 245/6, 258,
    299, 365
Tics
    and distress, 345
Training
    by study of total cases, 3
    for psycho-analysis, 1/2
    for therapy, 1/2, 270
Transference, 1, 6, 10, 214, 218
    vs. 'management', 5/6
Transference-neurosis, 214
Transitional objects and phenomena,
    34, 36, 95, 102, 106, 144, 152,
    198, 226, 241, 245, 251, 272,
    299, 305, 339, 342, 364/5, 392

Transitional objects *cont'd*
  and stealing, 342/3
  and waking, 143/4
  role in consultation, 102
Trauma, 87
Triangular situation, 98, 100, 108,
  157, 160, 360, 376
Two-phase squiggle, 182, 186/7, 189,
  190/1

Unconscious,
  approach to through dreams, 120,
  276
  approach to through squiggle
  game, 284, 290
  interpretation of, not main feature
  in therapeutic consultation, 9
  statement of conflict, 36, 42
Understood,
  belief in being, 5
  hope of being, 5

Verbalisation,
  of problem in squiggle game, 21
  relief from, in mother, 26
Vicious circle,
  change from, 42
Violence,
  fear of, 299

Waking, 143, 153, 188
Water,
  fixation on, 270, 272, 278, 281, 291
Weaning, 271, 291
Weird
  vs. humorous, 382
Whole object, 10
  capacity to conceive of, 65
Witch, 79, 83, 116/8, 120, 142/3,
  166, 160/70, 266
Withdrawn
  state as protection of self, 87
Wizard, 170
World Health Organisation, 12n